RESCUING CANADA'S
RIGHT

RESCUING CANADA'S
RIGHT → BLUEPRINT FOR A CONSERVATIVE REVOLUTION

by TASHA KHEIRIDDIN
and ADAM DAIFALLAH

FOREWORD BY MARK STEYN

WILEY

JOHN WILEY & SONS CANADA, LTD.

National Library of Canada Cataloguing in Publication Data
Kheiriddin, Tasha, 1970-
   Rescuing Canada's right : blueprint for a conservative revolution / Tasha Kheiriddin and Adam Daifallah.

Includes index.
ISBN-13 978-0-470-83692-7
ISBN-10 0-470-83692-X

1. Conservatism—Canada.   2. Conservative Party of Canada.
I. Daifallah, Adam, 1979-   II. Title.
JC573.2.C3K45 2005   320.52'0971   C2005-906268-1

Production Credits
Cover design: Mike Chan
Interior text design: Adrian So
Printer: Tri-Graphic Printing Ltd.

John Wiley & Sons Canada, Ltd.
6045 Freemont Blvd.
Mississauga, Ontario
L5R 4J3

Printed in Canada
10 9 8 7 6 5 4 3 2 1

For our parents

CONTENTS

FOREWORD

BY MARK STEYN

Canadian conservatives, don't despair!

Well, okay, that's unreasonable. So at least make sure you're despairing for the right reasons.

After the 2004 election, and the Gomery revelations, and the Belinda Stronach defection, stunned conservatives quite naturally wondered: My God, what do the Liberals have to do to lose? Wrong question. For one thing, they can't. Even when Chretien Liberals and Martin Liberals are locked in some crazed death match like Sherlock Holmes and Moriarty plunging down the Reichenbach Falls, the electors of southern Ontario will in the end haul them out of the drink, dry them off and ship them off to Ottawa for another term.

So, instead of marveling at what Liberals have to do to lose, the question that matters is: What do conservatives have to do to win?

The first thing is to forget about personalities. Conservatives don't lose elections because of Preston Manning's vocal timbre or Stockwell Day's wet suit or whatever it is pollsters claim Canadians find "scary" about Stephen Harper. By definition, any conservative leader—in or out of his wet suit—will be deemed "scary" by the CBC, *The Toronto Star* et al. You could make one of the Teletubbies—let's say the gay one, just for diversity's sake—head of the Conservative Party and within a month

Globe & Mail editorialists would be suggesting he was too "strident" and "out of touch" with "Canadian values".

It's unfair, but in Canada so's the weather. Stockwell Day and Stephen Harper are too scary to be Prime Minister, but a woman who thinks it the height of chic to hang out with leathery old FLQ terrorists is not just ideally suited to be Governor-General but the very "story of Canada". That's just the way it is. The non-scary conservative leader is like the Loch Ness Monster: he may be out there somewhere, a vague blur on the distant horizon, but looking for him's a waste of time. And when you get close up you find he looks a lot like the late Robert Stanfield—ie, a good loser.

So don't bother holding biennial leadership contests. After all, who are the alternatives? When you consider the grim roster of those who've claimed at one time or another to be Canadian conservatives—Joe Clark, Lucien Bouchard, Jean Charest, Scott Brison, Belinda Stronach—you realize that for a couple of generations the Conservative Party has been Bermuda and these empty vessels the Canada Steamship line.

That being so, we might as well also skip the biennial name-that-party contest—unless you're planning to change the title to the Scary Alliance or the Progressive Scary Party, which would be an excellent joke on the Canadian media. For the best part of a decade now, conservatives have focused on process, to the point where they've neglected what it is the process is supposed to be processing to. Conservatism can survive a lack of leaders but it can't survive a lack of conservatism. That's to say, it's a bonus to have a leader who's the life and soul of the party, but first the party has to have a life and soul. A party can embody a movement, but it can't be a substitute for it. That's what this book is about.

You can't have competitive politics without competing visions, and for too long the Liberal Party has been blessed in the faintheartedness of its opponents: a conservative party that isn't conservative, a separatist party that isn't separatist, and a New Democratic Party that hasn't come up with anything new in years. Three out of four parties in the House of Commons are explicitly left-wing: there's a corrupt left, a socialist left and a faux-secessionist left, and a temporarily disenchanted

Liberal elector in Ontario or Quebec is as likely to park his vote with one of the other two as he is to vote Tory. To sell yourself (if that's the phrase) as an ever so slightly right-of-left-of-centre party is to set yourself up not just for defeat in this election but the next one, too.

Oh, to be sure, sometimes even in Trudeaupia the one-party state slips up, and some other fellow finds himself in Sussex Drive. Back in the Eighties, you may recall, when conservative leaders bestrode the world like colossi, Brian Mulroney and Margaret Thatcher were lining up for a group shot of half-a-dozen Commonwealth Prime Ministers from hither and yon. To get a bit of boy-girl-boy balance, the photographer asked Mr. Mulroney to shift positions. He chuckled genially. "It's not often I'm to the right of Margaret."

More's the pity. And that's why, unlike Thatcher and Reagan, Mulroney was not a transformational leader. The Britain and America of the pre-conservative Seventies—ramshackle realms of endless strikes and long national nightmares, of Jimmy Carter's "malaise" and Jim Callaghan's "winter of discontent"—seem like remote planets viewed from their present landscapes. We, alas, still live in Pierre Trudeau's Canada. Mr Mulroney was closer to an Eisenhower or Macmillan—a nominal conservative who accepted the leftist direction of the state as a settled fact and saw his role as being merely to slow the rate of acceleration a little. Canada's last Progressive Conservative government had real accomplishments, but they were self-contained—they didn't strengthen and reinforce each other within any kind of coherent philosophy, and so they were never building blocks in any meaningful conservative realignment.

And Mr Mulroney's greatest achievement—free trade—was with hindsight a huge advantage to the Grits: by limiting the damage the Liberals could inflict on the Canadian economy, it in effect removed the main reservation middle-class voters have about left-of-centre parties—the perception that they'll seriously damage your economic well-being. They still can, but only up to a point. In contrast to, say, Germany's Social Democrats, the Liberals are in the happy position of being able to offer Canadians a unique package—the opportunity to have your cake and eat it: an anti-American polity with privileged access to the American market.

Does this mean Canadian conservatism is doomed forever to be a western protest movement? Not necessarily. It does mean that conservatism-lite—new leader, new name, plus just an eensy-teensy-weensy bit of fiscal conservatism—isn't enough. Ronald Reagan and Margaret Thatcher were both terrific personalities but they had huge intellectual gusts at their back. They led parties with ideas, and they expressed those ideas unashamedly and optimistically. They came up with conservative answers to the great questions facing the nation, at home and abroad. That's what we have to do. We have to build a movement, as the Americans have done—through new magazines, and think-tanks, and talk radio, and Internet sites, and non-party institutions—and we have to launch them in a much more heavy-handed regulatory environment where almost all the props of Trudeaupian orthodoxy are taxpayer-funded.

But it's not a tough choice, is it? Get another new leader with a less scary wet suit and wait for the media to denounce him as a right-wing madman for running well to the left of Tony Blair, or begin the long march of spreading conservative ideas in an ideologically exhausted, globally irrelevant one-party state running on fumes from Expo'67.

When he finally retired in 1984, Pierre Trudeau took his sons on a vacation to Siberia because, he said, that's where "the future is being made". He was about as wrong on that as wrong can be. Is it likely a man who so misread the world got even his own country right? Adam Daifallah and Tasha Kheiriddin's analysis in the pages that follow is bold, provocative and invigorating—and rooted in one great truth: as Mrs Thatcher likes to say, "The facts of life are conservative."

Mark Steyn is Senior Columnist for The Western Standard, *Senior North American Columnist for Britain's Telegraph Group, columnist for* The Atlantic Monthly *and appears in leading newspapers around the world.*

INTRODUCTION

"WE'RE HERE, WE'RE CANADIAN, AND WE'RE CONSERVATIVE"

"If you are trying to change the world, you better be willing to take a few risks."
> —Michael Walker, founder of the Fraser Institute

Proclaiming oneself a conservative in Canada today is (check one):

a) unusual
b) a lonely endeavour
c) political suicide
d) all of the above

Unfortunately, in most parts of the country the answer is "d." North of the forty-ninth parallel, the word "conservative" has become as much of an epithet as "liberal" has in the United States. The latter was no small feat, mind you. It took years of stigmatizing the causes and ideas of the Left by the well-funded American Right, along with the immensely successful presidency and personal popularity of Ronald Reagan, to make liberal a dirty word. In the 2004 election President Bush didn't even need to invent a synonym—he simply called Kerry a "liberal" innumerable times, especially in campaign ads.

In most parts of Canada, it's the reverse. Out yourself as a conservative at many a Toronto cocktail party and you can feel the air suddenly grow thinner, as if you're being sucked into a giant social vacuum tube. Otherwise sensible people will exhibit one of two reactions: either back away and make for the bar, or start berating you for taking bread from the mouths of single mothers. Which is enough to make you need a drink too, or contemplate moving to Calgary. Either way, both temperatures and liquor consumption rise, with the conservative no further ahead in advancing his or her ideas.

Theories abound as to why conservatism has failed to make a significant impact in Canadian federal politics. Some say the general Canadian attitude of mind, as a whole, is not now, and has never been, conservative. Others claim the resources available to conservatives here, in terms of financial and human capital, rank far below those in the United States. Others point to Canadians' obsession with the national unity issue, and the Conservative Party's failure to gain ground in Quebec.

In fact, much of the blame for the state of the right lies on conservatives' own doorsteps. Throughout their history, Canada's federal conservative parties have failed to develop a coherent ideology, to build an infrastructure to support and market that ideology and to provide inspiring leadership. They have also failed at another key task: making conservatism cool. In an article entitled "Conservative Cool," published in June 2005, Rick Petersen, founder of the Vancouver-based Conservative Council, laments that the party "is going nowhere fast, and could remain stuck in a rut leading over a cliff," and that "[i]n our biggest cities, Conservatives have an image problem, especially with women and younger voters."[1]

No kidding, Rick! Since fashion-forward Belinda Stronach swanned across the floor to the Liberals in May 2005, the party's already tepid coolness quotient has plummeted to Hadean depths. Name a cool conservative. We defy you. Peter MacKay briefly flirted with coolness by dating Stronach; Rahim Jaffer, one of the few Tories with any semblance of fashion sense, can be spotted at establishments that pass for cool nightclubs in Ottawa. Sadly, these shining Armani moments are quickly cancelled out by persistent memories of Stephen Harper sporting a too-tight golf shirt and Ken doll haircut, and then defiantly proclaiming that he "doesn't believe in makeovers."[2]

Unfortunately for conservatives, the epitome of political cool in this country remains the late Prime Minister Pierre Elliott Trudeau. Trudeau wore sandals, told the separatists where to shove it, did a pirouette behind the Queen's back and dated Barbra Streisand when she was at the top of her game. Trudeau is etched in an entire generation of Canadians' minds as the ultimate politician, and is the closest thing Canadian public life has ever had to a rock star.

But Trudeau is history, you say? Not so fast. His Trudeauvian coolness has been reincarnated in sons Justin and Alexandre, who have graced innumerable magazine covers despite the fact that by their early 30s their collective works span a couple of films and documentaries, a spread in *Maclean's* and a nice eulogy. As we write this, you can bet the Liberals are preparing to anoint one or the other prime minister in the next decade.

More significantly, the policies put in place by their father continue to shape Canadian society in almost every way. Trudeau's quest to fight Quebec separatism and impose his vision of a "Just Society" produced a country where government is so deeply "embedded" in our lives that, in the words of political scientist Alan Cairns, "Our very identities are transformed ... The public and the private are intertwined."[3] We have gone well beyond the well-worn "the personal is the political" slogan of the feminist movement to a situation where, "Political calculation occupies an ever-increasing significance in the pursuit of individual goals ... Political preference becomes an alternative to market performance in the pursuit of economic survival and profitability."[4]

As a result, Canada's political status quo is not liberal, conservative, right-wing or even classical liberal—it is statist. Statism, as defined by the Acton Institute, is "a program or viewpoint that looks to the state for resolution of social and moral problems, rather than to individual effort. Specifically, a condition where the nongovernmental institutions of a society develop an overextended and unhealthy reliance upon political structures for the solution of problems."[5]

The Perils of Statism

Statism is anathema to conservatism. It leads to citizens placing an increased value on government not only as a means of solving social problems, but as being the preferred means of attaining social status. Think for a moment about the (mostly self-appointed) Canadian elite, particularly its public intellectuals, and you'd be hard-pressed to find a non-statist among them. All the members of the CBC cocktail circuit— Adrienne Clarkson, John Ralston Saul, June Callwood, David Suzuki, Margaret Atwood, etc.—have either been employed by government or advocated intervention of the state to solve our problems.

In the words of Toronto financier Duncan Jackman, "Canada has become a government-sponsored abstraction."[6] It matters less how smart, accomplished, entrepreneurial and able you are, but who you know in Ottawa and whether you qualify as a potential beneficiary of a government grant. This makes for a perversely elitist class distinction which prefers mediocrity to merit and favours opportunists over those who create opportunity.

The ultimate outgrowth of this corrosive attitude is the Liberal sponsorship scandal. Spending $355 million of public money was deemed the solution to solving the separatist problem in Quebec. Only the federal state, it was reasoned, could counter the force of the sovereignty movement. Hundreds of millions of dollars were poured into sponsoring festivals, distributing free flags and even unveiling a plaque in San Martino, Italy (former Public Works Minister Alfonso Gagliano got to personally perform that one). Today, all this money is down the drain, and separatist forces are stronger than they have been in a decade.

Worse yet, as Cairns notes, "[i]t is far from evident that the major beneficiaries of modern state activity are the poor, the downtrodden, the disadvantaged and the helpless": the real winners are people who have political and organizational resources and the money to deploy them.[7] In Canada's case, that makes the Liberal Party the chief beneficiary of the ballooning size of our national government. The losers? Not just conservatives, but everyone who values democracy, freedom and a strong marketplace of ideas. By equating statism with nationalism, Liberals have made the expression of any dissenting view appear un-Canadian. This has not only helped keep them in office, but stifled the national debate on everything from culture to health care. Any voices that call for the removal of state monopolies, an end to corporate subsidies or privatization are seen as heretical, treasonous, or worse yet, pro-American.

Sadly, federal Conservative parties (in their various incarnations) have done little to counter this propaganda. None has fundamentally questioned the role of the state in our lives or attempted to roll it back. The Progressive Conservative Party under Brian Mulroney may have enacted the Free Trade Agreement, repealed the Foreign Investment Review Agency and tinkered around with various government programs, but it also doled out huge corporate subsidies, ran up massive deficits, continued funding a host of left-wing interest groups and failed to limit increases in both taxes and spending. And the new Conservative Party isn't faring any better. As columnist Andrew Coyne lamented after the party's inaugural convention in March 2005: "There is no longer any party at any level of government that has any intention of leading public opinion, or making changes to the status quo—not, that is, in the direction of smaller government or greater personal freedom. The choice, rather, is between parties that are eager to expand the state, and parties that will do so reluctantly."[8]

If conservatives are to ever end the Liberal march toward what Mulroney once called the "Swedenizing" of Canada, they must borrow a page from the gay rights movement, start standing up for themselves and launch their own pride parade. This parade won't march down the Main Streets of Canada's cities, but down the Main Street of public opinion. It is incumbent on conservatives to make their beliefs nonthreatening, welcoming—and even cool. And to do that, they have to invest money, time and energy on a scale not seen before in this country. They have to take a page from the experiences of conservatives in Britain and the United States. The U.S. did not morph overnight into a society prepared to elect an ideological conservative like Ronald Reagan, as it did in November 1980. As we explain later in this book, it took a fifteen-year concerted effort to create the conditions in which a conservative Republican could take the White House.

Moving Forward

So—how do we rescue Canada's right? It's a question we've asked our-selves many times over the past year. Based on exhaustive research, interviews with countless conservatives and an examination of other countries' experiences, we have arrived at what we believe is the an-swer, and laid it out on the following pages.

This book is organized into three parts. The first is an overview of the Conservative Party and its history. Be forewarned: it is a little depressing. Through all its incarnations, splits and revivals, the Conservative elec-toral record at the federal level—and the Tories' performance the few times they have actually held office—has been less-than-inspiring.

If you haven't lost hope after reading Part One, Part Two lays out a plan of action to make things better. First we examine how, in the past forty-odd years, the federal government has promoted and entrenched stat-ism as the dominant ideology in Canada. Much of this has been done without the knowledge of Canadians, and we suspect you'll be as shocked as we were by what we learned. But fear not: we'll also tell you how we can reverse this trend by building a conservative infrastructure encompass-ing all aspects of public life, from the media, to the courts, to academia. We'll explain how conservatives can appeal to New Canadians and to the next generation. Even in Quebec, the least conservative province in Confederation, there is hope to entrench a more conservative culture.

Part Three of the book is devoted to policy. Although policy discus-sion is interspersed through the first two parts of the book, we thought it would be useful to focus on four areas where conservatives could be more innovative: the family, health care, the environment and federal-ism. Going over bread-and-butter conservative positions such as the need for tax cuts, less wasteful spending and a more principled foreign policy is not necessary—that's already the party line. What's needed is a new vision that incorporates those policies but goes further in address-ing other concerns.

Big C v. small c

You will notice that we use the word conservative quite a bit, sometimes with a capital C and other times with a small c. This is not meant to confuse you. It is intentional. We are small-c conservatives, meaning we are believers in the ideology of conservatism. We broadly define conservatism as the belief in smaller government, lower taxes, individual freedom and personal responsibility. We are *not* members of the Conservative Party. In fact, we hold no party memberships. So when we talk about Conservatives with a big C, we are talking about the Conservative Party or its members. When we use the word conservative with a small c, we are referring to the ideology or someone who espouses conservative ideas. The distinction is key. Yes, the Conservative Party has small-c conservatives in it. It also has many people who share some conservative ideals but who call themselves by different names, such as Red Tories, centrists, libertarians, social conservatives, populists and others.

Some people or organizations that we call "conservative" in these pages might not be happy with this label. Many prefer other terms, like classical liberal. Libertarians, for example, hate being lumped in with conservatives. Others aren't fond of political definitions of the liberal-conservative axis at all. Former Reform Party leader Preston Manning, for one, has never liked the terms "left" and "right." But to make narrow ideological distinctions in every case would be confusing and take up much of the book. So for the sake of simplicity, we use "conservative" widely to mean those who are more or less situated on the centre-right of the political spectrum; that is, those people and groups who advocate non state-driven solutions to matters of public policy.

This book has three intended audiences. The first is, of course, conservatives—both big C and small c. We hope they will agree with our findings and adopt the ideas and suggestions presented for bringing the conservative movement forward. The second is corporate Canada and the business world in general. With luck, it is they who will step forward with the financial resources needed to build the infrastructure that will reinvigorate the Canadian political debate. They will be instrumental in developing institutions to challenge statism. And the third audience is regular, non-partisan, civic-minded Canadians. This project is about more than advancing conservatism and its ideas; it is about returning balance to the national dialogue by introducing new ideas that will compete with the platitudes of the past.

With regard to the last group, we need to address the issue of whether Canadians are currently willing to elect truly conservative Conservatives. There are two schools of thought about this. Some believe a mass of small-c conservative voters already exists, just waiting to be tapped into by the right leader and the right set of policies. Others think Canadians, by and large, simply are not conservative and that we are starting from ground zero.

We believe a bit of both. History shows Canadians will vote for a modern conservative party at the provincial level. Witness the two Mike Harris majorities in Ontario and Ralph Klein's victories in Alberta (during the early years, at least). Consider also Sterling Lyon's Conservative government in Manitoba and Bill Bennett's Social Credit government in B.C. For a plethora of reasons—among them weak leadership, poor election campaigns, the theft of some conservative ideas by the Liberals, the inability to penetrate Quebec and just plain bad timing—the national level has seen no such success. While a base of conservative voters exists, more Canadians must be exposed to conservatism and convinced of its merits before we can create an enduring small-c conservative coalition at the federal level.

That's not to say conservatives haven't made progress in the battle of ideas. We've come a long way. Nobody is talking about nationalizing industry anymore. The federal Liberals continue to cut some taxes. Polls show Canadians are more and more open to private health care options. And conservatives have won the argument on monetarism and balanced budgets. Organizations like the Fraser Institute, the National Citizens Coalition, the Canadian Taxpayers Federation, the Atlantic Institute for Market Studies, the Montreal Economic Institute and others do a tremendous job educating and advocating for more freedom and less government in Canadians' lives.

But it's not enough. Too many people still assume that advocating for positive social change means moving Canada to the left. Most Canadians would probably agree with Toronto artist Daniel Borins, who, when confronted by Tasha's self-description of "conservative activist" at one of those deadly cocktail parties, laughed out loud before sheepishly backpedaling, "Well, you don't usually think of activists as 'conservative.'"

If Canada's right is to be rescued, that kind of thinking must change—and soon. We don't want to seem alarmist, but this book is motivated by a certain sense of urgency. The Liberals have now been in power without interruption for nearly thirteen years. As time goes on, the tentacles of socialism and statism will become tougher to dislodge. It is conceivable that at some point it may be too late to reverse the damage.

So the time to get down to work is now. We know Canada can do better. We love this country, and it is heartbreaking to see it not living up to its full potential in a wide range of areas. We are a better country than one whose sole *raison d'être* is to squabble about national unity and stand to the left of the U.S. on social programs.

We realize the changes we propose will not happen overnight. Building institutions, not to mention moving opinion, takes time. But if you're doubtful, remember that in the 1970s some of the world's most respected thinkers believed the Soviet Union would win the Cold War. Things change, and they can change quickly. As columnist David Warren has written, all trends are reversible. Let's get started.

Endnotes

1. Rick Petersen, "Conservative Cool," June 7, 2005.
   www.conservativecouncil.ca

2. Stephen Harper, June 20, 2005, on Vancouver radio station CKNW.

3. Alan Cairns, "The Embedded State: State-Society Relations in Canada," in *State and Society: Canada in Comparative Perspective*, ed. Keith Banting (Toronto: University of Toronto Press, 1986), 75 (hereinafter Cairns).

4. Cairns, 71.

5. Website of The Acton Institute for the Study of Religion and Liberty, www.acton.org/research/dictionary/#socialism

6. Author interview with Duncan Jackman, March 2005.

7. Cairns, 82-83.

8. Andrew Coyne "Amidst the balloons, a white flag," *National Post*, March 23, 2005, A20.

PART one

THE PAST

1 CHAPTER

FROM JOHN A. TO JOE WHO:
How the Conservative Party Failed to Lead Canada

"The number of true believers in the electorate is diminishing. People don't make commitments, they make judgments from time to time on which party, set of policies or person best suits them. So I'm not finding a lot of ideological talk in the [Progressive Conservative] party."
— Rt. Hon. Joe Clark, former PC leader

MANY political movements have the past to look to for inspiration. Not Canadian conservatives. It's not that the federal Conservative Party hasn't made some great contributions to Canada—quite the contrary. It was Conservatives who built the country. Sir John A. Macdonald, working in concert with Sir George-Étienne Cartier and George Brown, the founder of the Toronto *Globe*, formed the Grand Coalition in 1864, which led to Confederation. It was Conservative governments that gave women and native Canadians the right to vote. Prime ministers John Diefenbaker and Brian Mulroney were front-and-centre in fighting South African apartheid. Mulroney also gave us free trade, which despite rancorous debate in the 1988 federal election has recently been confirmed to have boosted Canadian productivity by up to 25 percent since its inception.[1] (We won't say we told you so.)

Sadly, there's little else to highlight. The main reason is that the Conservatives have rarely held the keys to power in Ottawa: for 55 of the 138 years since Confederation, and just over 30 of the past 100 years. And when the Tories have formed the government, they haven't been very illustrious. Just ask Canadian political historians. In a 1997 ranking of "Canada's Great Prime Ministers" by twenty-five scholars, only one Conservative made the top category of "great"—Sir John A. Macdonald. One other, Sir Robert Borden, was deemed "high average." All the rest were lumped in the categories "average," "low average," and "failure." (Four of the five PMs in the failure category were Tories; dead last, no surprise: Kim Campbell.)[2]

Moreover, when the party has been in power, it has rarely done much in the way of implementing *conservative* policies. That's with a small c. To us, small-c conservatism means a political philosophy loosely based on the ideas of *classical liberalism* as outlined in the writings of John Locke, Adam Smith and more modern thinkers such as Friedrich Hayek. It emphasizes free markets, individual rights over collective rights, limited government, private property rights, and personal responsibility. All that freedom stuff. Think Ronald Reagan and Margaret Thatcher, and, on the domestic front, the first terms of provincial leaders like Mike Harris and Ralph Klein.

For most of Canadian history, no mainstream federal political party—including the Conservatives—has advocated small-c conservatism. "At times, classical liberalism has infused people in both parties. On the other hand, you can say that classical liberalism is almost foreign to Canada," says historian Michael Bliss, one of the few academics we know who hasn't spent his career beating conservatives over the head with a cudgel. "Fundamental economic policies pursued by the government of Canada since Confederation have flown in the face of classical liberalism. The policies of both parties were expansionist."[3]

Now, this doesn't mean that Canadian governments didn't exhibit signs of conservatism—or perhaps more accurately, a reluctance to expand the size of the state. In several instances, which we discuss in Chapter 12, Canada was slower in moving toward statist policies than our neighbours to the south. Indeed, one could make the case that

Canada's national government was quite modest—even fiscally conservative—until the era of Diefenbaker and Lester B. Pearson.[4] But overall, federal governments, including Conservative ones, have been pretty dismal from a small-c conservative perspective.

Let's start with Sir John A. Macdonald, one of the Fathers of Confederation and the party's first leader. For all his faults (he was a drunk, corrupt and a patronage king), Macdonald remains the most politically successful federal leader of the Conservatives the country has ever seen, winning six out of seven elections he contested—all majority governments. With the exception of a single term (1874 to 1878) he served as prime minister from Confederation until his death in 1891.

Macdonald's Tories were devoted British sujects, expansionist and non-ideological. (He even used the terms "liberal Conservative" and "progressive conservative" to describe himself.)[5] He exhibited no particular hostility to government spending: Macdonald felt, in Michael Bliss's words, "the more areas of government activity the better ... so long as they seemed to be vaguely useful and the taxpayers did not revolt."[6] He was also a strong centralist, even thinking that eventually provinces would wither away altogether.[7]

Given that he presided over the birth of a country, a strong government hand was necessary. Macdonald brought three new provinces—Manitoba, British Columbia and Prince Edward Island—into Confederation. He created the North-West Mounted Police, which would later become the RCMP. Most famously, he built the transcontinental railway. Unfortunately, Macdonald accepted kickbacks from the man to whom he awarded the contract to build the railway, Sir Hugh Allan of Montreal.[8] The scandal caused him his only electoral loss.

Macdonald's main policy legacy was the protectionist National Policy, which was introduced in 1878. This has led many observers to label Macdonald anti-American and anti-free trade. But according to McGill University economist William Watson, this policy was not Macdonald's preferred route, but a reaction to American protectionism of the day. Macdonald initially attempted to negotiate a free trade deal, but was rebuffed by our southern neighbour.[9]

The National Policy slapped high tariffs on foreign goods in a deliberate attempt to force Canadian trade onto an east–west trade axis.

Some feel this is the source of modern regional alienation, particularly in the West, where it forced farmers to pay more for equipment and closed markets. The National Policy also hurt the Maritimes by taking away their natural trading market in New England.[10] Macdonald used anti-American rhetoric to his political benefit: in his last campaign, in 1891, he cast himself as the great defender of Canada while the Liberals, then led by Quebecer Sir Wilfrid Laurier, would have sold us out to the Americans. He won.

Despite shorts stints in the prime minister's chair by Tories John Abbott, John Thompson, Mackenzie Bowell and Charles Tupper, the Conservative Party's domination of federal politics was over for good with the election of Laurier in 1896. Since that time, the party's story has best been summed up by legendary Liberal cabinet minister Jack Pickersgill: The Tories are the mumps—you get them once in a lifetime.

Sir Robert Borden became Conservative leader in 1901 and headed up her Majesty's loyal Opposition for ten years before actually winning an election. Borden's policies resembled those of Macdonald. He campaigned unsuccessfully in 1904 on "nationalizing part of the CPR's northern Ontario main line, and implementing full government ownership of the whole second transcontinental system."[11] In 1908, Borden lost again essentially campaigning on a "clean government" platform, including merit-based public appointments, stricter rules against bribery and electoral fraud, tightening immigration, Senate reform, a publicly owned utilities commission and nationalized telegraph and telephone services.[12]

Sadly, it was on a resolutely anti-conservative platform, at least by small-c standards, that Borden made his breakthrough in the "reciprocity election" of 1911. Rallying Canadians to the nationalist call for high tariffs, Borden defeated Laurier and his plan for further economic integration with the Americans, thanks to an alliance forged with Henri Bourassa's *Nationalistes* in Quebec. Interestingly, the West voted overwhelmingly for Laurier's pro-free-trade Liberals.

In government, Borden had "no qualms about the vigorous use of power by the state."[13] He extended free rural postal delivery, had government enter the terminal grain elevator business and offered grants to provincial governments to build highways and fund agriculture education.[14] Borden won again in 1917, in the midst of World War I, on a coalition Unionist ticket. He joined forces with pro-conscription English Liberals to win support for the war effort. Borden won that election easily, but with virtually no support in Quebec.

The next Tory leader was Arthur Meighen. Meighen was very smart but fiercely protectionist and another total failure in Quebec. He refused suggestions that the Canadian National Railway be privatized.[15] When Meighen became prime minister after the infamous "King–Byng" affair in 1926, he was only able to hold on to power for three months before losing to Mackenzie King. Foreshadowing a theme that hamstrung the Conservative Party later on, Meighen also had to deal with a Western-based protest party—the Progressives, which had started up after Borden's refusal to reduce tariffs.

R. B. Bennett, the next elected Tory leader, took the Tories back to government in 1930, defeating Mackenzie King. Bennett was another statist, but because he came to power during the Great Depression, we should cut him some slack. As prime minister he created the Bank of Canada, the Canadian Wheat Board and the precursor to the CBC, the Canadian Radio Broadcasting Commission. He also continued the use of tariffs to protect Canadian business.[16] Late in his term he even proposed a package of reforms that he unimaginatively called the "New Deal," just as Franklin D. Roosevelt had in America—things like old-age pensions, unemployment insurance, more regulations on business and a minimum wage. However, it was too late—Bennett was trounced in 1935. Mackenzie King was back and served as prime minister again, uninterrupted until 1948.

In that year, King retired and was replaced as leader by Louis St. Laurent of Quebec, who, in 1949, easily won against George Drew, the former Ontario premier. Drew lost to St. Laurent again in 1953. For twenty-two years the Conservatives roamed the political wilderness. If this sounds eerily familiar, it should. A cynic would say the Tory leaders were the Liberals' best assets, guaranteeing them victory in each election.

It wasn't until 1957 that the Tories got back into power, when John Diefenbaker won a minority government, then a majority in 1958. By now this shouldn't come as any surprise: Dief wasn't a conservative. Indeed, he believed that government was "the great equalizer."[17] If anything, he was an erratic Western populist with demagogic tendencies. While he did bring Canada into the North American Defence Agreement (NORAD) and gave us a Bill of Rights, he swiftly raised the rate of payment for old-age pensions and increased the size of government in general. Under his watch, federal government spending rose 32 percent between 1957 and 1961.[18] "Diefenbaker continued a course the Liberals had set after the war in viewing government grants, handouts and job creation programs not as social welfare but as social justice," Bliss writes.[19] He also increased farm subsidies and established the Royal Commission on Canadian Health Services, which laid the groundwork for our socialized health system. He made a mess of our relations with the Americans, due to his bungling of the Cuban Missile Crisis.

In 1962 the Tories were reduced to a minority government again, which fell in 1963. This time the Liberals formed a minority under Lester B. Pearson. Pearson would call another election in 1965, gaining power again through another minority. It is a true testament to the Liberals' uncanny success in myth-making that Pearson is deified today, despite a failure to win a single majority government in four attempts.

At this time, the Tories were understandably agitating for a new leader. Many thought Diefenbaker was starting to lose his mind and needed to go. But Dief wanted to stay. In 1966 he was forced out in what was Canada's first modern leadership review vote, a crucial event that entrenched the divide between Red and Blue Tories.

Dalton Camp's Red Toryism

The events surrounding Diefenbaker's messy ouster as leader are probably the defining moments of modern conservative history. They have had a profound impact on the nature and development of Canadian conservatism and the party's direction, and it all goes back to one man: the late Dalton Camp.

Camp is the political godfather[20] of modern Red Toryism, the brand of politics that has dominated the federal Conservative Party for four decades. Red Tories are well described by columnist Andrew Coyne:

The Red Tory, as the name implies, does not go in much for logical coherence or philosophical frameworks; indeed he prides himself on it. He is guided, rather, by sentiment, and nostalgia, and an unshakeable conviction that everything can be resolved through "dialogue." ... He has a quite mystic regard for notions like "community," though he does not know what he means by it, or how it conflicts with the "individualism" he despises. He is also against "socialism," though again he can't say why. Above all, he believes in civility—unlike his political opponents, whom he curses in the most strident terms.[21]

Red Toryism is descended from the High Toryism (or so-called "One Nation conservatism") of Great Britain. It fuses the aristocratic concept of *noblesse oblige* (that the rich owe a duty to the poor) with the concept of the modern welfare state. In other words, government takes over where the nobility left off. The redistribution of wealth, not the promotion of individual initiative, becomes the state's main role. Eventually, as in socialist systems, it becomes easier for people to rely on government handouts than to try to earn more money themselves, since most of it is taxed away and redistributed to others. The result is a classist society with limited social mobility, which probably appeals to twenty-first century élitists as much as it did to eighteenth-century dukes.

Camp actually started as an activist in the Liberal Party, but later made the switch to the Progressive Conservatives after attending the London School of Economics, where he was taught by famed Marxist professor Harold Laski. The American-born Camp later protested the Vietnam War, picketing on Parliament Hill with Tommy Douglas and others holding signs adorned with photos of Chinese Communist dictator Mao Tse Tung. According to his biographer, Geoffrey Stevens, Camp "admired Roosevelt and his New Deal. He loathed Richard Nixon and preferred Bill Clinton, with his human faults, to either of the George Bushes, with their lack of humanity."[22]

After working as an advertising director in the New Brunswick Progressive Conservative Party's 1952 election win, Camp told a federal PC campaign committee that the Tories won that election by "consciously not sounding like Conservatives."[23] He took that strategy to Nova Scotia and helped Robert Stanfield become premier of that province in 1956.

Camp was a brilliant public relations man. He formed Camp and Associates in 1959, and among the many Tory-affiliated personalities in his employ at one time or another were Red Tory luminaries Joe Clark, Senator Hugh Segal, Flora MacDonald and Senator Norman Atkins, Camp's brother-in-law and frequent political co-conspirator. Roy McMurtry, now Ontario's chief justice, also inhabited Camp's inner circle. Not many Tories occupy positions of power in this country today, but a good many of those who do can be traced back to Dalton Camp.[24]

As president of the Progressive Conservative Party in the 1960s, Camp masterminded the dumping of Diefenbaker and was the main impetus behind the ascendancy of Stanfield's succession to the leadership in 1967. From that point on, the PC Party was consistently controlled by Camp and the people he mentored. No single person was as influential and as consequential for the Conservative cause—and no person did greater damage to the conservative movement.

In his later years, Camp became a prolific print and radio journalist and spent a lot of time bashing small-c conservatives. In the mid-1990s he used his *Toronto Star* columns to strenuously oppose the Chrétien government's deficit-slashing policies. He talked about the Tories and Liberals being guilty of "abandoning" the poor and attacked modern conservatism as "the enemy of the society those of my generation built over the years since the war."[25] He viciously attacked Mike Harris, Preston Manning and Stockwell Day. He saved his most vituperative words for Conrad Black, deriding the media mogul for his political views and his influence on the Canadian newspaper industry.

Because of his high profile, Camp's views had a wide reach, leading many people to believe Camp's Red Tory brand of crypto-socialism was what conservatism was all about. As *National Post* columnist Lorne Gunter told us, "The CBC et al. love to point to Red Tories who oppose tax cuts, or tough immigration laws, or social conservatism or tougher crime measures and say 'See, even most conservatives are against what so and so is proposing, so why should the rest of us buy it?'"[26]

The strange thing is that Conservatives continued to show defer-ence to Camp—even Brian Mulroney. Mulroney lured Camp away from journalism in 1986 to work as an adviser to the Privy Council, where he championed the creation of the Atlantic Canada Opportunities Agency, and was "the most coherent and persistent advocate of regional de-velopment policy"[27]—aka, subsidies for businesses with government connections. But Camp's greatest period of influence came during Stanfield's tenure as leader, which lasted from 1967 to 1976.

Stanfield kept the Tories ideologically vague. Continuing the general trend that developed after the death of Sir John A., Stanfield was boring and uninspiring. His speaking style was monotonous. A unilingual Anglophone, he had little appeal in Quebec, even though the party had gone to great lengths to woo Quebec support by introducing the *deux na-tions* ("two founding nations") policy. Stanfield was also easy to caricature, given that his family were the makers of the famous underwear.

He lost three straight elections to Pierre Trudeau in 1968, 1972 and 1974. In '68, Stanfield had campaigned on a guaranteed annual in-come—an idea that even the Liberals had rejected proposing because the public didn't want, in their words, "any more of that free stuff."[28] In 1972 he actually promised an income tax cut, along with the removal of capital gains tax on family farms so that farmers could leave their property to their sons. But he also proposed wage and price controls, a scheme which he trumpeted further in the 1974 election and which was later implemented by Trudeau.[29]

In 1976, Stanfield stood down and another Dalton Campite, Joe Clark, took the helm. Clark, then an MP in his first term, was another lacklustre political personality. He came out of nowhere to win the lead-ership contest (hence the moniker "Joe Who?"), surprising just about everyone, including himself. While Clark was a born-and-bred Albertan, he exhibited none of the characteristics usually associated with Western conservatism. A career political hack, Clark was mentored by Camp, worked for Stanfield and married an outspoken feminist lawyer named Maureen McTeer, who might have felt more at home in the New Democratic Party. Some would say Clark might have too. His political ideas—or lack thereof—were close to Stanfield's. A former two-term president of the PC National Student Federation, Clark was totally non-ideological and wedded to the brokerage model of politics.

But by 1979, Trudeau and his policies had become unpopular. The Liberal leader had been in power for more than a decade. Unemployment and deficits were high. The country was ready for a change. Literally anyone but Joe Clark could have won a majority against Trudeau that year. But good old Joe only won a minority. To be fair to Clark, he did run on a platform that was fairly conservative for that time—principally, cutting taxes and reducing the bloated federal budget. The problem was, once in government, Clark did a U-turn and proposed an eighteen-cent per gallon gas tax hike. Clark was defeated on his first budget and called an election for January 1980. Trudeau then won another majority, and would go on in his last term to wreak havoc, implementing the National Energy Program, running up record deficits and repatriating the Constitution without Quebec's signature.

Joe Clark embodies the essence of conservative failure of the past half-century. Sure, he's a nice guy. And sure, he worked hard to learn French and broaden the Progressive Conservative Party's appeal. But he remained totally uncommitted to a coherent ideology or set of ideas. The best he ever came up with was coining the term "community of communities"; thirty years later, Canadians have yet to figure out what it means. He exemplified poor political judgment at every juncture of his career and never appeared to learn from prior mistakes.

With right-of-centre leaders already in power in Great Britain and the United States. Brian Mulroney's landslide majority in 1984 should have been a bright period for Canadian conservatism. But as we will see in the next chapter, it was still fraught with disappointment when it came to implementing many conservative ideas.

Endnotes

1. Rondi Adamson, "Should Canada get out of free trade pacts with the U.S.?", *Toronto Star*, August 28, 2005, A16.

2. Norman Hillmer and J. L Granatstein, "Historians Rank the Best and Worst Prime Ministers," *Maclean's*, April 21, 1997. Posted on the Web at www.ggower.com/dief/text/maclean2.shtml

3. Author interview with Michael Bliss, July 7, 2005.

4. The case for this thesis is made by scholars David Bercuson and Barry Cooper in their book *Derailed: The Betrayal of the National Dream* (Toronto: Key Porter Books, 1994) (hereinafter Bercuson and Cooper).

5. Michael Bliss, *Right Honourable Men: The Descent of Canadian Politics from Macdonald to Mulroney* (Toronto: HarperCollins, 1994), 7 (hereinafter Bliss).

6. Bliss, 18.

7. Bliss, 14.

8. John Duffy, *Fights of Our Lives: Elections, Leadership and the Making of Canada* (Toronto: HarperCollins, 2002), 19.

9. William Watson, *Globalization and the Meaning of Canadian Life* (Toronto: University of Toronto Press, 1998), 95.

10. For an excellent examination of this idea see Fred McMahon's book *Retreat from Growth: Atlantic Canada and the Negative-Sum Economy.* (Halifax: Atlantic Institute for Market Studies, 2001). www.aims.ca/equalization.asp?typeID=1&id=83

11. Bliss, 68.

12. Bliss, 69-70.

13. Bliss, 74.

14. Bliss, 74.

15. Bliss, 103.

16. Bliss, 111.

17. Bercuson and Cooper, 92.

18. Bradley Miller, "What Does It Take for a Tory to Win?" *National Post*, March 23, 2005, A23.

19. Bliss, 192.

20. Its intellectual godfather is unquestionably George Grant, the nationalist Canadian writer who is famous for his book *Lament for a Nation* (1965).

21. Andrew Coyne, "Anatomy of a Red Tory," *National Post*, May 15, 2000, A17.

22. Geoffrey Stevens, *The Player*, (Toronto: Key Porter Books, 2003), 13 (hereinafter Stevens, *The Player*).

23. Stevens, *The Player,* 91.

24. It is interesting to note that many of Camp's people—including Joe Clark and Senators Atkins and Murray—have refused to support the new merged Conservative Party of Canada.

25. Dalton Camp, *Whose Country Is This Anyway?* (Vancouver: Douglas and McIntyre, 1995), 19.

26. Author interview with Lorne Gunter, October 24, 2004.

27. Lowell Murray, introducing Dalton Camp at the Allan J. MacEachen Lecture, at St. Francis Xavier University, February 9, 2000. www.stfx.ca/academic/political-science/Allan%20J.%20MacEachen%20Lecture%20Series/Intro_LM_DC.html

28. Geoffrey Stevens, *Stanfield* (Toronto: McClelland and Stewart, 1976), 217 (hereinafter Stevens, *Stanfield*).

29. Stevens, *Stanfield*, 261.

CHAPTER

IT WAS THE BEST OF TIMES, IT WAS THE WORST OF TIMES:
Mulroney, Manning and Bouchard

"As Leader of the Progressive Conservatives I thought he put
too much stress on the adjective as opposed to the noun."
— Margaret Thatcher on Brian Mulroney

FEBRUARY 18, 1980. Less than a year earlier, Great Britain voted in the staunchly conservative Margaret Thatcher. Nine months later, Americans would elect the staunchly conservative Ronald Reagan. Canada, on the other hand, treated itself to a triumphant-looking Pierre Elliott Trudeau telling supporters "Well, welcome to the 1980s!" after winning his third majority government, taking 147 seats to the Tories' 103—including a staggering 74 of 75 ridings in Quebec.

Trudeau had actually announced his retirement from politics after the Progressive Conservatives' 1979 victory, but Joe Clark's disastrous nine-month interregnum convinced him to stay on. Why did Trudeau win big in 1980? Three main reasons: Clark appeared utterly incompetent after losing the budget vote; the impression of incompetence he created was compounded by the media's portrayal of him as a luggage-losing wimp; and a referendum on sovereignty-association loomed in Quebec. Canadians trusted Trudeau, the canny Quebecer, to keep the country together more than Clark the aloof Albertan.

So while the rest of the Anglosphere rejected the big government consensus of the 1960s and '70s, Canada rehabilitated Trudeau and his so-called Just Society. And in his last term Canadians got the most damaging policies of Trudeau's career: the National Energy Program (which nearly crippled Alberta's economy), the Canada Health Act and the biggest deficits in Canadian history. Trudeau won the referendum, repatriated the Constitution and enshrined the *Charter of Rights and Freedoms*, but more on that later. Welcome to the 1980s, indeed.

After the aforesaid Liberal romp, various factions in the Tory party were itching to get rid of Clark. After receiving a weak 66.1 percent approval rating from delegates to the 1981 PC national convention, he went into the January 1983 party meeting saying he needed to do better. He did, but only marginally so—receiving a feeble 66.9 percent. Clark stepped down and called a leadership race. At the leadership convention that June, Brian Mulroney won on the fourth ballot, defeating Clark, who had decided to run for the job again, as well as John Crosbie and others. It was sweet revenge for Mulroney, as Clark had beaten him for the leadership in 1976. To Mulroney's credit, he would later give Clark senior cabinet posts throughout his tenure as prime minister, adhering to the old political adage "keep your friends close and your enemies closer."

The 1983 leadership change was a watershed for the Progressive Conservative Party. Aside from the fact that both were Roman Catholic, Mulroney was the antithesis of Clark. Whereas Clark was a career politician with little charisma and poor French, Mulroney was an accomplished businessman, charming and perfectly bilingual. More importantly, he was a Quebecer and he could improve Tory fortunes in *la belle province* after the string of Stanfield/Clark failures.

In winning the leadership Mulroney had garnered support from all factions of the party, including from small-c conservatives who thought he could be Canada's answer to Reagan. Among that group were a large number of PC youth who had played a key role in dumping Clark a few months earlier. Finally, many Tories believed, the party had a leader who could bring real small-c conservative change to Canada.

But would he? Mulroney had little in the way of right-wing bona fides. He was not an ideological animal. During the 1983 leadership,

Mulroney had sounded out some conservative ideas, but in '76 he had been considered a Red Tory. According to Mulroney biographer John Sawatsky, Mulroney "had always been instinctively progressive"[1] and when it came to talking issues, he "had no overview, no program, no ideas of his own."[2] The main reason Mulroney ran more to the right in the '83 race, Sawatsky wrote, was because his advisers thought there were more delegate votes to be had there.

Nor was Mulroney the least bit consistent. He had opposed free trade in the leadership, then later embraced it in government. He had lauded the 1981 constitutional repatriation; once elected prime minister, he bashed Trudeau for leaving out Quebec. Mulroney had said he would not "play footsie" with René Lévesque's Parti Québecois, but after winning government said he would deal with the *péquistes* because they were "duly and legitimately elected."[3]

Above all else, Mulroney was a strong, ambitious leader with an engaging personality. Few could match his remarkable networking and negotiating skills. He had spent most of his adult life assembling the team that won him the leadership and 24 Sussex Drive. As an undergraduate at St. Francis Xavier University in Halifax, Mulroney had served as vice chairman of Youth for Diefenbaker in the 1956 PC leadership race, and he later served as national vice president of the Young PCs. From his days at Laval law school onward, he was a key Quebec organizer for the Tories, first for Davie Fulton's 1967 federal leadership bid and then for the man who won that race, Robert Stanfield.

Mulroney assumed the leadership of the party at just the right time. With the country tired of the Liberals, now led by John Turner, Canadians were ready to embrace change. The 1984 Mulroney win was the greatest landslide in the country's history—a 211-seat majority, including 58 of 75 seats in Quebec. It seemed like the beginning of a new era. *Toronto Star* columnist Richard Gwyn, in one of his more imperceptive moments, declared that Mulroney's victory had "almost certainly, made the Conservatives the majority party for the rest of the century."[4]

The real issue in that election was the Trudeau record. Turner had appeared out of touch and rusty after nearly ten years away from politics. Mulroney and the media pilloried the Liberal leader for a series of patronage appointments he had made during his short tenure as prime minister, which were part of a deal Turner had struck with Trudeau. The PCs ran on a platform that included increasing the size of the military by 10 percent, reopening VIA Rail lines scrapped by the Liberals and spending more on social programs. In total, according to a leaked report prepared for then-finance critic John Crosbie, Tory promises topped $20 billion in new spending[5]—an amount that is equivalent to $35 billion in 2005 dollars.

A harbinger of things to come was a comment Mulroney made during the campaign about Canada's bloated social safety net. Deep spending cuts, while bound to be controversial, were sorely needed; the annual deficit when Mulroney took over had reached $38 billion. Yet in a speech Mulroney declared that Canada's social programs were "a sacred trust not to be tampered with," words he would soon regret.

Shortly after the government took office, Michael Wilson, the new finance minister, released a budget statement. The Tories knew they needed to slow spending growth and practise restraint. Wilson spoke of getting the "fiscal house in order" and, while still talking about more social program spending, promised $2.2 billion in spending cuts. The government hinted that it might start means-testing some social programs that at the time were universally accessible.

Then came the government's first budget, in May 1985. Wilson announced some menial reforms, the most controversial of which was that Old Age Security (OAS) and family allowance benefits would no longer be fully indexed to inflation. Instead, benefits would only rise if inflation were higher than 3 percent in a given year. This enraged senior citizens' groups, who took to Parliament Hill in protest. At the demonstration, an elderly woman named Solange Denis was taped on camera calling Mulroney a liar: "You made promises that you wouldn't touch anything.... You lied to us. I was made to vote for you and then it's goodbye Charlie Brown." The opposition couldn't have scripted a worse nightmare for the fledgling government.

The result: a giant Tory U-turn. Days later, Wilson announced that the de-indexing plan was being shelved. (In 1989, the pension was clawed back for seniors who earned over $50,000 a year, meaning they had to pay back fifteen cents of each dollar over that amount.)[6] As David Bercuson and Barry Cooper observed in their book *Derailed*, successful implementation of the de-indexing would have saved the public treasury billions, but as soon as public opposition began to mount the Tories caved. The OAS volte-face set the tone for the next eight years. When Wilson delivered his second budget, in February 1986, "there were no cutbacks in social spending, no de-indexation plans, no attacks on universality."[7] Instead, there were tax hikes and more spending—for example, an additional $375 million over five years for feature film production and subsidies to the book publishing and recording industries.[8]

Another gutless wonder was the government's refusal to reform the overly generous Unemployment Insurance program. Despite the conclusions of several commissions and reports that the program needed an overhaul, the Tories decided to maintain the status quo, which allowed people to work as little as ten weeks a year to get forty-two weeks' worth of benefits. The Tories knew any reform would be politically unpopular, especially in Atlantic Canada where they held 25 out of 32 seats. According to Stephen Harper's biographer William Johnson, this was a defining moment for Harper, who realized that the Mulroney Tories weren't serious about real change. Harper was right. This lack of fiscal fortitude would colour the rest of the Mulroney years. (The UI plan was finally reformed in 1994 under the Liberals by then-Human Resources minister "Pink" Lloyd Axworthy.)

In the 1988 election, with his popularity sagging, Mulroney campaigned almost exclusively on the Canada-U.S. Free Trade Agreement (FTA). He defeated John Turner a second time, scoring the first back-to-back majority Conservative governments since Sir John A. The result was 169 seats for the PCs, far less than in 1988 but still a comfortable majority. This included an astonishing 63 of 75 seats in Quebec, where the Liberals took only 12—thanks in no small measure to Quebec Liberal Premier Robert Bourassa's endorsement of free trade.

The FTA and other bilateral achievements with the U.S. rank as the greatest accomplishments of the Mulroney years. Mulroney's tenure marked a welcome change after the reflexive anti-Americanism of the

Trudeau era. Only weeks after winning the 1984 election, Mulroney travelled to New York to announce that "Canada is open for business again." He subsequently scrapped Trudeau's archaic Foreign Investment Review Agency and collaborated with President Reagan to bring in the Acid Rain Treaty. Under Mulroney's leadership, Canada also contributed 4,500 soldiers to the 1991 Gulf War to liberate Kuwait—a move that was in stark contrast to the Chrétien government's intransigence during the Gulf War sequel in 2003. Canada was a staunch U.S. ally during the Mulroney era, proving the old saying that all foreign affairs are about are personal relationships. The economic benefits reaped from the FTA and the later negotiation of the North American Free Trade Agreement (NAFTA), which Prime Minister Jean Chrétien signed in 1994 despite previously opposing it, are indisputable. As mentioned in Chapter 1, evidence now unequivocally confirms that the free trade deals boosted productivity and strengthened the Canadian economy.

As Professor Kim Nossal noted in an issue of *Policy Options* magazine that assessed prime ministers of the last half century, Mulroney has an underappreciated record in foreign affairs. Like John Diefenbaker, he strenuously opposed Apartheid, imposing economic sanctions on South Africa and working with the Commonwealth to stir up opposition. This put Canada at loggerheads with our allies, especially with Britain, where Thatcher believed sanctions weren't the way to go. Black South Africans "had never seen a white western leader stand up as boldly as Mulroney did," according to political scientist Linda Freeman.[9] Mulroney also signed a deal to replace Canada's decrepit fleet of Sea-King helicopters. Under Chrétien, the Liberals cancelled the deal at a cost of $600 million, only to reorder similar helicopters in 2004. Mulroney was instrumental in establishing *La Francophonie*, the international network of French-speaking countries.

Another of his achievements was to replace the 13.5 percent Manufacturers' Sales Tax with the 7 percent Goods and Services Tax—yet another policy Chrétien repudiated while in opposition but embraced when in office. While the new tax was loathed by the Canadian public, it was actually an improvement on the old one, which was hidden in the price of goods. Mulroney kept interest rates low, deregulated the transportation sector, banks and financial services, reduced the size of the civil service and privatized Crown corporations, including Teleglobe Canada, the Canada Development Corporation, de Havilland Aircraft and Canadair. The privatization of Air Canada began, although not in its entirety and only after much stalling. (Mulroney emerged from a meeting with a Quebec labour leader in January of 1985 saying, "Canada needs a national airline."[10]) Shares of Petro-Canada were sold publicly for the first time, although it also was not fully privatized.

Now for the bad. Mulroney's biggest failures were lack of fiscal restraint, repeated tax hikes and two unsuccessful attempts at constitutional renewal. As Nossal writes, "The Mulroney Conservatives proved no more capable than the Trudeau Liberals at grappling with government expenditures: by 1993, there had been no serious assault on the budget deficit, even though Ottawa was by then operating a surplus— taking in more taxes than it spent on programs."[11]

The national debt more than doubled during Mulroney's tenure: from $206 billion in 1984 to $450 billion for the 1993–1994 fiscal year. When he came to power, the deficit stood at $38 billion; when he left it was $40 billion. There are two ways to interpret this. On a negative note, Mulroney left power running a bigger deficit than when he started. On a positive note, he did actually begin to curtail spending over the course of his nine years, reducing the deficit from 9 percent to 5 percent of GDP. Either way, this is not very inspiring. On taxes, the news wasn't much better. According to one study by economist Patrick Grady of Global Economics Ltd., an Ottawa-based firm, the average Canadian family was paying about $1,900 more in taxes in 1993 than they were in 1984.[12]

Why was this? How could a Conservative government not have done more to reverse the statist trends of the Trudeau years? Part of it was fear of public perception and repercussions, as illustrated previously. Part of it was the fact that so much attention was focused on constitutional reform. But most of it was due to the nature of Mulroney's coalition, which was made up of Western conservatives, Blue and Red Tories from Ontario and Quebec nationalists. The fact that such a broad group of supporters was assembled under one tent is a testament to Mulroney's extraordinary leadership abilities. But keeping this disparate group of supporters happy required making more economic and political compromises than the party, and the nation, could stand. The coalition was so broad that any small crack threatened to turn into a schism.

By 1987, only three years into his first term, the first serious threat appeared. Despite Mulroney's disbanding of the National Energy Program a year earlier, Westerners felt frustrated by the government's perceived indifference to their concerns. They blew a gasket over Mulroney's 1986 decision to award a CF-18 aircraft maintenance contract to Montreal-based Bombardier instead of Winnipeg's Bristol Aerospace. The government chose Bombardier, even though Bristol had put in a cheaper bid. The incident reinforced Westerners' view that the government unfairly favoured Quebec. It stirred up emotions just in time to give a boost to a nascent grassroots-based populist movement, one that wanted to see major change in the way things were being done in Ottawa.

The Rise of Reform

In May 1987, a small meeting of political activists in Vancouver established the Reform Association of Canada, the precursor to the Reform Party. That fall, 300 people attended the Reform Party's founding convention in Winnipeg and chose Preston Manning as their leader. Manning was a lanky, bespectacled policy wonk from Edmonton and the driving force behind the Reform movement. His father, Ernest Manning, had been the immensely popular Social Credit premier of Alberta from 1943 to 1968.

Reform came along at just the right time to capitalize on a wave of discontent. Its slogan, "the West wants in," captured the Zeitgeist west of the Manitoba/Ontario border. Like other Western protest movements before it (the Progressives, Social Credit) Reform was not an orthodox conservative party. It was above all a populist organization. It tapped into the frustration with central Canada common to Westerners from across the political spectrum, not just those on the right. Reform proposed such things as recall initiatives to get rid of unpopular MPs and citizens' rights to initiate referendums.

Manning's party was based on four simple planks: fiscal and social responsibility, democratic accountability (including a Triple-E Senate), equality of citizens and provinces, and rebalancing the federation (which meant a major devolution of powers to the provinces.) The party was also generally socially conservative, but it had room for those who didn't espouse those views. In short, Reform advocated doing some of the things the Tory government should have been doing all along, and some other things unique to Western Canada.

A popular myth is that Manning started Reform solely as a response to Brian Mulroney's unconservative government in Ottawa. In fact, Manning had long contemplated starting a new party; the anger in the West toward the Mulroney government merely gave him the opening he was waiting for. Back in 1967, Ernest C. Manning released a short book entitled *Political Realignment: A Challenge to Thoughtful Canadians*. While its cover bears only the elder Manning's name, young Preston had a large role in researching and writing it.

In the book, the Mannings laid out a set of ideas they called "the social conservative position," which, generally speaking, were the ideas we now describe as modern fiscal and social conservatism. They called for one of the mainline political parties to adopt their ideas, and they favoured the federal Progressive Conservatives. But if no party adopted them, they did not rule out starting a new party to carry the vision forward, which is what happened with the creation of Reform.

Apart from realizing personal political ambitions and giving the West access to the corridors of power, however, Manning claims he had a more important motive in starting the party: saving Canada.

"[The West was] one charismatic leader away from a full-blown separatist movement," Manning told us. "When you have an oil or gas well that's gone out of control and is on fire and is going to blow the country up, you drill a shaft in on the side to take the pressure off. Reform was that shaft that took the pressure off that Western alienation, or channelled it into something more constructive."[13] Ironically, nearly twenty years later, the West is again one charismatic leader away from a full-blown separatist movement—and that leader could appear on the scene at any time.

In the first election Reform fought, in 1988, it made little impact in the seventy-two Western ridings it contested, winning no seats and averaging just over 8 percent of the popular vote. But it sowed the seeds for the future, and given the decreasing popularity of the Tories, the future was looking bright.

The Aftermath of Meech

If the Western end of the tenuous Mulroney coalition was starting to shred in the late '80s, so was its Quebec nationalist wing. Mulroney campaigned in 1984 on a promise to bring Quebec back into the constitution "with honour and enthusiasm." His messaging worked. For one, he was a Quebecer, and the man he faced at the polls—John Turner—was not. Two, Quebecers were still smarting over Trudeau's repatriation of the Constitution without their blessing, and they were looking to punish the Liberals. Three, Quebec nationalists were dispirited after their 1980 referendum loss and sought a way to renew Quebec's place in Confederation. This explains why Mulroney received the quiet support of Quebec Premier René Lévesque and the PQ machine in the 1984 campaign, as part of their *beau risque* strategy. But this alliance was extremely dodgy, for Mulroney was not only bringing nationalists but outright separatists into his inner circle, including Lucien Bouchard, a close friend since their days together at Laval law school.

Mulroney tried valiantly to bring Quebec back into the Constitution with the Meech Lake Accord, which was negotiated in 1987. In order for Meech to pass, it needed to be ratified by all provincial legislatures by 1990. With the clock ticking, it began to look like Meech Lake would fail. Mulroney named young MP Jean Charest to chair a committee designed to assuage the concerns of Newfoundland, Manitoba and New Brunswick—the three provinces that hadn't signed on. When the Charest committee's report came back with a proposal for a companion resolution to the accord, Lucien Bouchard said he couldn't accept it. He delivered a five-page resignation letter to 24 Sussex Drive on May 21, 1990. The next day he quit publicly in the House of Commons to sit as an independent MP, giving a blistering speech in which he accused his government of "making an alliance with those who want Quebec to continue to be humiliated."[14]

When Meech officially died on June 23, 1990, after failing to be approved by the Newfoundland and Manitoba legislatures, other Quebec

MPs followed Bouchard, including Liberal Jean Lapierre, now Paul Martin's Quebec lieutenant and a federal cabinet minister. Bouchard and seven disgruntled Quebec MPs called themselves the Bloc Québecois, and founded the eponymous party of which Bouchard became leader on June 15, 1991. The second fault line in the Mulroney coalition had split wide open.

Mulroney's subsequent attempt to bring Quebec into the constitutional fold failed in an even more spectacular fashion than Meech. On August 28, 1992, Mulroney and the premiers signed off on the Charlottetown Accord, a new constitutional arrangement that included a "social charter," devolution of federal powers to the provinces, stricter controls over federal spending, senate reform (stopping short of a triple-E arrangement) and the recognition of Quebec as a distinct society. This time the agreement would be put to the Canadian people in a national plebiscite.

After receiving initially favourable polling numbers, public support for the agreement began to plummet as Canadians saw it as an untenable string of compromises. When put to a national referendum on October 26 of that year, voters across the country rejected the accord. Fifty-four percent said NO, including a solid 57 percent in Quebec, 60 percent in Alberta and a whopping 68 percent in B.C.

On February 24, 1993, a battered Mulroney announced his resignation as party leader. At the time of his retirement, he was the most unpopular prime minister in history. Most of the cabinet ministers who were expected to try to replace him—Barbara MacDougall, Michael Wilson, Perrin Beatty, Don Mazankowski and others—all declined to run. It became a two-way contest between Justice Minister Kim Campbell and Environment Minister Jean Charest, with the other candidates, Jim Edwards, Patrick Boyer and Garth Turner, traipsing far behind.

Though Meech and Charlottetown had failed, the accords succeeded in casting Charest as the PC's chief cheerleader for national unity. Both attempts at reform provided a platform for the mop-topped Charest to roll up his sleeves and shout himself hoarse in the name of Canada. Nevertheless, this was not enough to beat Campbell, who had more establishment support going into the race. Young, fresh and somewhat cheeky, Campbell was elected leader and became Canada's first female prime minister on June 13, 2003.

When the writ was dropped in September 1993, the Tories were polling ahead of the Liberals, now led by ageing career politician Jean Chrétien. Seen as the new face of the PC Party, Campbell was riding high. She was a relatively unknown quantity, however, and the more voters did get to know her, the worse the Tories' numbers got. After one of most inept campaigns in history (senior Campbell aide David McLaughlin admitted in his book, *Poisoned Chalice*, that the Tories were actually making up policy as the campaign went along), the PCs were reduced to two seats, with Charest hanging on in Quebec and former Saint John mayor Elsie Wayne elected in New Brunswick.

Mulroney's Legacy

The 1993 election results reveal the ultimate legacy of the Mulroney coalition. Reform triumphed in the West, coming out of nowhere to win 52 seats. Her Majesty's Loyal Opposition was formed by a party that wanted to break up Canada—Lucien Bouchard's Bloc Québecois, which took 54 seats in *la belle province*. And the Liberals captured 98 of 99 Ontario ridings, the first of three elections in which they would totally dominate that province, forming the government with a total of 177 seats.

Mulroney, the first Conservative leader to firmly conquer Quebec since Sir John A,[15] saw his coalition spontaneously combust, and with it, though no one knew it at the time, the future of the PC Party in Quebec. The party never recovered nationally either, taking the fewest seats in Parliament in every election after Mulroney's departure until its merger with the Canadian Alliance to form the new Conservative Party in 2003.

Despite his failings, in some ways, Mulroney never got a fair rap. Irrespective of his well-known efforts to woo the parliamentary press gallery, the press repeatedly savaged him on everything from his footwear to his "Irish Eyes Are Smiling" sing-along with Ronald Reagan. After leaving office, few writers made him their subject, and those who did either smeared him or betrayed him. Stevie Cameron's hatchet job *On the Take: Crime, Corruption and Greed in the Mulroney Years*, which tried to link Mulroney to kickbacks from the infamous "Airbus affair," remains one of the best-selling Canadian political books of all time. (It may well be outsold, however, by Peter C. Newman's scurrilous *The Secret Mulroney Tapes: Unguarded Confessions of a Prime Minister*, which is little more than a slapdash compilation of profanity-laced quotes from interviews Mulroney gave Newman.)

As Nossal admitted in his piece: "... [A]ppreciations of [Mulroney's] tenure are made more difficult because of his personal unpopularity; because he has yet to write his memoirs; and because, unlike Trudeau, Mulroney does not have champions in the scribbling classes writing on his years in power, spinning the story of his time in power in particularly favourable ways. On the contrary, books on the Mulroney government's corruption become best-sellers, while in-depth investigations to the charges of corruption levelled against Mulroney himself are not widely read."[16]

What is indisputable is that Mulroney's departure marked the end of an era for the Progressive Conservative Party, and the beginning of a new chapter in Canadian right-wing politics: "Conservatism's Wasted Decade: 1993–2003."

Endnotes

1. John Sawatsky, *The Politics of Ambition* (Toronto: Macfarlane, Walter and Ross, 1991), 400 (hereinafter Sawatsky).

2. Sawatsky, 151.

3. Sawatsky, 545–546.

4. Peter Brimelow, *The Patriot Game* (Toronto: Key Porter Books, 1986), 7.

5. Sawatsky, 548.

6. "Restructuring of the Welfare State: the Mulroney Government," Canadian Public Policy (2002–03), University of Toronto at Erindale. www.erin.utoronto.ca/~w3pol/outlines/K4.htm

7. David J. Bercuson, J. L. Granatstein and W. R. Young, *Sacred Trust: Brian Mulroney and the Conservative Party in Power* (Toronto: Doubleday, 1986), 119 (hereinafter Bercuson et al.).

8. Bercuson et al., 222.

9. Luiza Chwialkowska, "Anti-apartheid Fight Was Mulroney's Finest Hour," *Ottawa Citizen*, September 23, 1998, A1.

10. Bercuson et al., 123.

11. Kim Richard Nossal, "The Mulroney Years: Transformation and Tumult," *Policy Options* 24 (June–July 2003), 78 (hereinafter Nossal).

12. David Bercuson and Barry Cooper, *Derailed* (Toronto: Key Porter Books, 1994), 159.

13. Author interview with Preston Manning, March 31, 2005.

14. David Halton, "Exit Bouchard," CBC News Online archives. http://archives.cbc.ca/IDC-1-73-1180-6494/politics_economy/meech_lake/clip5

15. Many consider Diefenbaker's 1958 achievement to have been a Maurice Duplessis–engineered fluke.

16. Nossal, 78.

3 CHAPTER

MAKING UP IS HARD TO DO:
Conservatism's Wasted Decade. 1993–2003

"The enemy of my enemy is my friend."
— Arab proverb

FEDERAL conservative politics from 1993–2003 can be summed up with an F-word (no, not that one): failure. Or if you want to be more polite, frustration. Canada's divided political right was unable to capitalize on Liberal scandals, even with billions squandered through the failed gun registry and the HRDC boondoggle, chiefly because the Progressive Conservative and Reform/Canadian Alliance wouldn't kiss and make up first. As a result, the Chrétien Liberals had a virtual free ride to three straight majority governments.

While the 1997 and 2000 elections are mercifully a distant memory, it is useful to review them for two reasons. One, they serve as good case studies of the recurring problems plaguing Canadian conservative parties: shoddy campaign strategy, bad communications, negative media, milquetoast platforms, uninspiring leadership—in general, being totally outgunned by the Liberals. Two, it is important to recall how the division on the right hindered the advance of conservatism during the last decade. Because most of the conservatives' energy was devoted to a pointless war of attrition, the uninterrupted rule of the Liberals from 1993 forward made Canada a virtual one-party state.

Let's rewind back to 1997. At that time, the Progressive Conservatives were led by then–Quebec MP, now Quebec Liberal Premier, Jean Charest. Charest, who had served in Brian Mulroney's cabinet, had taken over immediately after Kim Campbell's resignation in 1993 and set out on the unenviable task of rebuilding the party. Touted as the Tories' Great White Hope, he became instead their Great Red Disappointment.

To craft his election platform for the 1997 campaign, Charest hired Ontario Tories Alister Campbell and Leslie Noble, two of the brains behind Mike Harris's Common Sense Revolution. They wrote a manifesto similar to the CSR, although less ambitious. Charest was supposed to run on a 10 percent income-tax cut, reduced Employment Insurance premiums, a lowering of the corporate and business tax rates, spending reductions and getting tough on crime. The platform even spoke of transferring tax points to the provinces, which could have pre-empted the so-called "fiscal imbalance" issue from ever arising between Ottawa and the provincial governments. Most of these policies had been approved at the party's 1996 national convention in Winnipeg, where they had been chiefly championed by the party's youth wing.

But there was a big problem: Charest, a centrist, didn't seem comfortable with the policies he was supposed to advocate. Just before the campaign began, Charest fired Campbell and Noble and abandoned the platform's small-c conservative message. He brought in his old gang of trusted Red Tory advisers, including Jodi White, a Joe Clark crony who had managed Charest's failed 1993 leadership bid. Charest abandoned talk of hope, growth and opportunity and started stumping for his favourite cause, national unity, which wasn't even a campaign issue. Later in the election Charest called Reform Party leader Preston Manning a "bigot" after Reform ran anti-Quebec television ads, thereby writing off any chances the Tories had of winning a seat west of Ontario. Meanwhile, in Atlantic Canada, Tory candidates were running to the left of the Liberals, bashing finance minister Paul Martin's cuts to Employment Insurance.

The result for the Tories on June 2, 1997? Twenty seats: 1 in Ontario, 5 in Quebec and 13 in the Maritimes.

The Reform Party ran on a solid platform of tax and spending cuts in that election, but it went further, proposing to end regional development subsidies, abolish the Office of Official Languages and the CRTC and privatize CBC TV, Via Rail and Canada Post. Also front and centre were Reform's populist bread-and-butter issues of parliamentary reform such as a Triple-E Senate and the ability to recall MPs. Reform captured 60 seats, despite losing their one and only seat in Ontario, and replaced the Bloc Québecois as the Opposition.

In the end, the Liberals continued comfortably on cruise control, winning 155 seats (including 101 of 103 in Ontario) to the divided right's combined 80. The Bloc won 44 and the NDP 21. In a most unrepresentative result, the Liberals formed a majority government with just over 38 percent of the national popular vote.

Manning's United Alternative

After 1997 it was clear, at least to most reasonable people, that neither the PC Party nor Reform could win an election on its own. Reform was stalled at the Ontario/Manitoba border and the PCs were on life support everywhere west of there. Not only were votes being split, but so were other crucial and scarce resources—money, volunteers and candidates. Something had to be done.

Some frustrated conservatives had already talked of "uniting the right" and had made efforts to get the reluctant parties to the altar. In May 1996, conservative writer David Frum organized the *Winds of Change* conference in Calgary, the first formal effort to bring about co-operation. It failed to bring about any changes, but the conference did spawn what is known today as the Civitas society, an organization of conservative-minded intellectuals, journalists and politicians, who meet annually to discuss conservative policy.

In late 1997, Reform leader Preston Manning began talking about bringing together like-minded "anti-Liberal" Canadians to form a United Alternative (UA) to fight the Grits. Though there was some hope the venture would succeed, there was significant suspicion among Progressive Conservatives—principally from Charest and his inner circle—that it was really a veiled takeover bid by Reform.[1]

But in May 1998, Charest exited the federal stage to impose his visionless brand of leadership on the Quebec Liberal Party, thereby removing one of the principal barriers to conservative co-operation. Before his departure Charest had refused to even consider talking with Reform, and it seemed many Tories agreed with him. In his keynote speech to the PC national convention in March 1998, just weeks before he stepped down, Charest received a standing ovation when he thundered "hell hasn't frozen over yet!" in response to Manning's proposal to unite in a common cause.

With Charest gone, hope for reconciliation briefly bloomed. Two Tory leadership contenders, Brian Pallister, now a Conservative MP, and Michael Fortier, a Quebec businessman, were less hostile to Reform. However, other candidates included the Lazarus of PC Party politics, former prime minister Joe Clark, long-time backroom Tory operative and Senator Hugh Segal and anti–free trade crusader David Orchard. In November 1998, Clark won easily, and a whole new round of the right-wing Cold War began.

If Charest had been a barrier to unity on the right, Clark was a mile-wide brick wall. Clark was still gnashing his teeth over the fact that Manning and Reform had dynamited the winning coalition assembled under Mulroney. He also had a long-standing rivalry with Manning. This went back to their youth when they had once been rivals in campus politics and failed in an attempt to merge the Alberta PCs with Alberta Social Credit. Clark held firm to his view that if the PCs were just patient enough, they could outlive Reform. He thought of the party as a tumbleweed that would blow away like other Western protest movements before it.

Despite Clark's strident opposition and veiled threats from senior party officials, some federal PCs did attend Manning's UA convention in February 1999, including long-time Tory fundraiser and Brian Mulroney confidante Peter White, former Ontario lieutenant governor Hal Jackman and then-Ontario Tory MP Jim Jones. The conference was a success, with delegates approving a proposal to create a new political party to take on the Liberals. The Reform Party's members then endorsed the idea in an internal referendum. A second UA convention was planned for January 2000, where the Canadian Alliance was born. The Reform Party membership voted in a second referendum to fold itself into the new party. A leadership race ensued with a vote scheduled for June. Many prophesied it would be a coronation for Manning, godfather of the whole UA exercise. But he was defeated by Stockwell Day on the July 8 second ballot. Day, the former treasurer of Alberta under Ralph Klein, would lead the party into the November 27, 2000 election.

All the while, Joe Clark and the federal PC brain trust tried relentlessly to trip up the UA process. The Tories ostracized members who advocated co-operation, and they endorsed a constitutional amendment at their October 1999 convention mandating PC Party candidates in all 301 ridings. The measure had no purpose other than to prevent non-aggression pacts between the two parties' riding associations. Clark even launched his own pallid attempt to end vote-splitting called the Canadian Alternative. In reality this was just a recruitment exercise for the Tories and, not surprisingly, it went nowhere.

The 2000 election, called by Jean Chrétien only three and a half years into his mandate, proved to be another Liberal romp. Stockwell Day showed promise, but after his wetsuit-wearing shenanigans wore thin he became so demonized by the media that many central Canadian voters were scared away.

When Day first arrived on the scene, he was a welcome new face who was hardly known outside of Alberta. This presented both a huge opportunity and a huge risk. The challenge for Day and his entourage was to brand him in the public eye before the media and the Liberals did it first. Unfortunately, they failed in a most spectacular way.

The press went on the attack almost immediately, reinforcing the idea that the Alliance had a hidden agenda. *Maclean's* magazine put a big photo of Day on its July 10, 2000, cover with the caption "How Scary? Meet Stockwell Day, the mystery man who would be prime minister." The article focused on Day's Christian beliefs, beginning with an interview with a supporter who expressed hope that Day would hold a national referendum on abortion if he formed the government in Ottawa.

But this was just the beginning. During the election things got much worse.

On October 31, *The Globe and Mail* ran a misleading front-page story entitled "Alliance Supports Two-tier Health Care." What Alliance MP Jason Kenney had actually said was that provincial governments should be allowed to use private providers to deliver services, not that a parallel for-profit private system should be established. But the damage was done. The headline was later used by the Liberals in a national scare ad, while Day lamely resorted to holding up a "no two-tier" placard during the televised leaders' debate.

The CBC got onto the Day-bashing bandwagon with a documentary by journalist Paul Hunter, who tried to paint the politician as an extremist by emphasizing his Christian beliefs. Hunter's piece trotted out years-old allegations and conjecture about Day from his days in rural Alberta and highlighted his creationist views. Later on, comedian Rick Mercer made the Alliance leader a laughingstock when he started an online petition to change Day's first name to Doris. Liberal strategist Warren Kinsella pulled out a Barney doll on CTV's *Canada AM* to further mock Day's belief in creationism.[2] Then-minister Elinor Caplan claimed that Alliance supporters were "Holocaust deniers, prominent bigots and racists." By the end of the campaign, Day had been so damaged by the liberal media, their allies and the incompetence of the Alliance campaign, it was a wonder he got any votes at all.

The negative attention paid to Day obscured the fact that the Alliance platform contained many good small-c conservative ideas. The Alliance proposed to revamp the income tax system to move toward two tax rates: 17 percent for all income up to $100,000 a year and 25 percent for incomes above that figure. They also wanted to legislate debt repayment, end corporate welfare, get tough on crime and increase defence spending. But with the weakness of the Alliance campaign (they were seemingly off message more days than they were on), the party's policies barely got out. It also didn't help that Day spent much of the campaign pretending to be something he wasn't: a centrist. As the Montreal *Gazette* editorialized, "Part of the problem is Mr. Day's determined effort in this campaign to move toward the centre. He's been so busy scrubbing away anything from the old Reform agenda that might threaten mainstream voters that Canadians are no longer sure what he stands for."[3]

At the same time, the Joe Clark Tories ran on a lukewarm version of the Alliance platform, with similar but less ambitious plans for tax and spending cuts. They did, however, propose to eliminate personal capital gains taxes.

The result: the so-called scary Alliance won 66 seats—still the best finish by an opposition party since 1988—and the Tories scraped up 12, just enough to hold on to official party status. Interestingly, in May 2004, Sun Media columnist Greg Weston accused senior Tories and Liberals of colluding in the election, specifically to guarantee the victories of Clark and Anne McLellan in Alberta.[4] Even with that, the Tories' 12.2 percent was the worst popular vote total in the party's storied history. Meanwhile, the Liberals roared back to power with their third straight majority, winning 172 seats nationally—and 100 seats of 103 in Ontario. It seemed they were invincible.

The Road to Merger

In the years between the 2000 election and the eventual merger of the PC and Alliance parties in 2004, both parties were as unstable as ever, performing contortions worthy of the Cirque du Soleil as they alternately attempted to kill one another or co-operate. In hindsight, however, the whole exercise looks more like a meaningless sideshow, or freak show, if one is less charitable.

One of the worst episodes was the revolt against Stockwell Day's leadership, which began shortly after the election. By May 2001, eight Alliance caucus members, led by MPs Chuck Strahl and Deborah Grey, had quit the caucus and formed their own dissident group, the Democratic Representative Caucus (DRC). These MPs claimed they were upset about Day's perceived gaffes and poor leadership ability; others said the MPs were just bitter about Preston Manning's loss to Day in the 2000 Alliance leadership race. Whatever their motives, these MPs damaged the Alliance brand badly and fatally wounded Day's leadership. They also threw Joe Clark a lifeline by entering into a formal coalition with him in the House of Commons, following a conference between the DRC and PCs in Mont Tremblant, Quebec, in August 2001.

With the pressure too great for him to continue, Day resigned that December. He later ran to succeed himself. However, he was defeated by Stephen Harper on March 20, 2002. Harper had been a Reform MP from 1993 to 1996 but had resigned from parliament after disagreeing with Preston Manning over the direction of the party. Since that time Harper had headed a fixture of Canada's conservative infrastructure, the National Citizens' Coalition.

For unite-the-right fans, the future looked bleaker than ever, with Clark making noises about staying on for another election and Harper winning the Alliance leadership on a platform of "no truck or trade" with the Tories. But shortly after Harper's victory, he made it known that he was willing to work out some kind of arrangement with the Tories, even if the party was led by Clark.

This was a surprise. Harper had, after all, abandoned the PCs and helped to found Reform precisely because of the indecisive politics for which Clark and company were famous. But in an ironic twist, because he had done so, Harper was perhaps the sole person who could bring the two parties together. If only anti-communist Richard Nixon could go to China, perhaps only right-wing Harper could sell a merger with the Tories to the Alliance grassroots.

Harper and Clark met in April 2002 to talk about the prospects of co-operation. Predictably, nothing happened, probably because Clark was never really serious about collaborating, having termed the Alliance "fundamentally offensive" and "an alliance of people who don't like other people."[5] But Harper got a big boost when six of the seven DRC MPs returned to the Alliance fold, leaving Clark's parliamentary coalition in ruins. Clark announced he was stepping down as leader of the Tories in August 2002. Harper proposed a joint leadership contest between the two parties, but the federal Tory brass rebuffed him.

Peter MacKay won the leadership race to replace Clark in May 2003. MacKay, a second-term MP and the son of Mulroney-era cabinet minister Elmer MacKay, campaigned against inter-party co-operation, but his campaign workers privately said MacKay was open to reconciliation. During the convention, however, Mackay cut a backroom four-point deal with rival David Orchard, who had come second to Joe Clark in the 2000 leadership. The key point: MacKay promised not to make any deals with the Alliance. Orchard's support catapulted MacKay to victory over his closest competitor, Jim Prentice, and left stunned delegates shaking their heads in disbelief.

Happily for the conservative movement, MacKay then proceeded to double-cross Orchard. The new leader started openly talking about working with the Alliance soon after his victory. Why? The PC Party was deep in debt and Bay Street backers were fed up with funding the Tories' losing efforts. Liberal leader-in-waiting Paul Martin seemed poised for another Liberal sweep—a "juggernaut," as *Toronto Star* reporter Susan Delacourt titled her book on the Martin machine. The Alliance was reinvigorated under Stephen Harper's leadership. A fourth straight last-place finish would have been the end of the PC Party, and MacKay knew it. And Tory MPs, fearful of losing their jobs to the Martin-led Liberals, were finally coming around to the idea that something needed to happen.

Out of nowhere and in secret, two negotiating teams were set up to explore a merger, and Belinda Stronach, then the CEO of Magna International, was brought in to referee. Negotiating on the PC side were Don Mazankowski, the former Mulroney finance minister and deputy prime minister, former Ontario premier Bill Davis and Loyola Hearn, then the PC House leader. The Alliance team included former Reform MP Ray Speaker, Senator Gerry St. Germain (a former PC Party of Canada president and MP) and MP Scott Reid.

Despite almost coming unglued a number of times, the negotiations continued through late summer and fall until a deal was announced on October 16, 2003. After all the false starts over the years, the denouement was almost surreal. The Alliance side made most of the concessions to the much weaker Tories, agreeing to adopt their leadership selection system, support official bilingualism and much more.

Both parties' memberships overwhelmingly approved the merger, despite organized opposition in the PC Party by—guess who?—Joe Clark and friends. In the end, 95.9 percent of Alliance members voted to approve the merger, as did 90.4 percent of Progressive Conservatives. In a fit of pique, Clark endorsed the Liberals on television in April, pronouncing "I personally would prefer to go with the devil we know."[6] He went on to campaign for Liberal candidates Anne McLellan and floor-crosser Scott Brison in the 2004 election.

Three candidates aspired to be the first leader of the new Conservative Party of Canada, namely, Belinda Stronach, Tony Clement and Harper.

On March 20, 2004, Harper won with more than 55 percent of the vote on the first ballot.[7] Within three months, he and the Conservatives would face an election. There was no time for a policy convention, and at times it seemed Harper was forced to make up policy on the fly. In a speech in Toronto on May 10, 2004, he even announced a Conservative government would create a national pharmacare plan, effectively outflanking the Liberals on the left on health care.

In the end, the Tory platform was a centrist rehash of old Alliance and PC party planks. Among their proposals were a 25 percent income tax cut for middle-income Canadians and other tax cuts as well as more money for defence and health care. They also advocated cutting corporate welfare, withdrawing the Supreme Court reference on gay marriage, scrapping the gun registry and making various democratic reforms, such as an elected Senate and more free votes for MPs.

Still, the new Tories were better positioned for an election than they had been in a decade. Finally, they were united in one party. They had money and quality candidates coming forward, now that they had a real chance of winning. And the Liberals were facing bad news on a daily basis after Auditor General Sheila Fraser released a report in February shedding light on corruption in the federal sponsorship program. All was looking up when an election was called for June 24, 2004. The Martin juggernaut was falling off the rails—or so it seemed.

The Unravelling of the 2004 Election

Yet again, the same scenario that had played out in every election since 1993 recurred. The Liberals demonized the opposition as anti-gay, anti-abortion, anti-bilingual and even anti-Canada with negative TV ads and clever spin about a supposed "hidden agenda."

The media eagerly played up this fear-mongering. Case in point, *The Globe and Mail*'s front-page sensationalist hit job, "Tory Critic Wants New Abortion Rules," which ran on June 1, 2004. "The Conservative Party's health critic is advocating a dramatic shift in abortion regulations by calling for third-party counselling for women who are considering terminating their pregnancies," read the lead sentence of the story. In an interview, MP Rob Merrifield had stated that counselling for women considering ending a pregnancy may be "valuable"[8]—not regulated, not mandatory, but valuable. What the story also failed to mention was that the day before Liberal leader Paul Martin said he also supported third-party counselling for women seeking abortion.[9]

You can't entirely blame the media, however, when the Tories gave them so much material to work with. Here, from the Election Wall of Shame, a list of the most ill-thought-out remarks and bone-headed screw-ups of the 2004 campaign:

• Scott Reid, the Conservative critic for official languages, went to officially bilingual New Brunswick and told the Moncton *Times & Transcript* that bilingual services should be tailored to demand and that the Tories would not force provinces to offer health and education services for minority groups. Reid later resigned from his post,[10] but the comments proved quite damaging, especially when amplified through the lens of Harper's politically incorrect views on bilingualism from his Reform Party past.

• Ontario MP Cheryl Gallant managed to equate gays with criminals, suggesting that the law protecting homosexuals from hate speech should be repealed because it could protect pedophiles.[11]

• Speaking to a pro-life rally, Gallant drew another bizarre parallel, saying abortion is "absolutely no different" from murder, citing the beheading of Nick Berg, an American contractor who had been killed by terrorists in Iraq.[12] Cue the Liberal women's pro-choice chorus: former Trudeau health minister Monique Begin told the press, "This is a party we do not really know exactly what it's made of and I find that extremely scary."[13]

• As if the federal party couldn't do enough damage, Alberta Premier Ralph Klein glibly announced mid-campaign that he would unveil health reforms that might contravene the Canada Health Act. Even though the Conservatives campaigned on maintaining the public system, Klein's comments gave Paul Martin the opportunity to accuse the Tories of secretly wanting to privatize medicare.

- A week and a half before the vote, Harper publicly mused about a Conservative majority government, counting more unhatched chickens than any politician in recent memory. This repelled queasy voters who weren't necessarily keen on the Tories winning the election but just wanted to punish the Liberals.

- The Tories then spawned a media firestorm with a press release entitled "Paul Martin Supports Child Pornography?" Needless to say, he didn't.

- Days before the vote, a clip from a newly filmed documentary was released showing an eerie-looking Randy White (a retiring MP) saying he would use the Charter of Rights and Freedoms' notwithstanding clause to stop same-sex marriage. Cue: more hidden agenda headlines.

Voters were also confused by the Conservative position on the war in Iraq. Harper was on the record as supporting Canadian involvement; he had even co-written an opinion editorial with Stockwell Day calling Canada's decision to sit out the invasion "a serious mistake." (This appeared in the *Wall Street Journal* in 2003.) But in 2004 he tried to backtrack, claiming that with our depleted military abilities we could not have participated anyway. This weak about-face contributed to the general perception that the Tories were fuzzy on the issues.

The Tories also ran no real attack ads in the last leg of the campaign. While the Conservatives broadcast a humorous ad showing a dump truck shovelling cash into a dumpster while carnival music played in the background, the Liberals showed a woman crunched up in a corner while a voice-over suggested the Tories would limit access to abortion. Apparently the Tories forgot that in this game you have to fight fire with fire.

To cap it all off, in the final days of the campaign, instead of rallying troops in Ontario, where Harper needed votes, he travelled west, where the party was assured of a near-sweep of seats. "We want change and we want in," he told a rally in B.C. The day before the vote, he told an Edmonton crowd: "We're going to bring this part of the country into power in Ottawa."[14] This seemed an odd choice of words for a leader of what was supposedly a national, not a regional, party.

Overall, the campaign's main problem was that it lacked a positive vision—a problem seen many, many times before. The Tories ran mostly *against* the sponsorship scandal, and to a lesser extent in Ontario, *against* a recently announced health care tax by Liberal Premier Dalton McGuinty. Of course the Tories should have run on returning integrity to government and against Liberal corruption. But bashing the governing party cannot sustain a national campaign for four straight weeks. Harper gave few reasons why people should vote *for* him and said little about what he'd do in government. As Liberal strategist John Duffy observed, the Tory campaign had "no second act."

Despite all the mistakes, throughout much of the campaign it looked as though the new Conservative Party might actually win at least a minority government. The sponsorship scandal was hurting the Liberals, voters were restless after a decade of Grit power and Paul Martin looked tired and lacklustre. But as the gaffes piled up, support for the Tories slipped. As they lost momentum, undecided or weary voters moved at the last minute to the Liberal column. In the end, as Joe Clark had exhorted them to do, voters went with the devil they knew.

The result was 99 seats for the Tories—not bad for a party only a few months old, but depressing given how high hopes had risen. The Conservative vote in Ontario was less than the combined totals of the two old parties in the election before. The Bloc Québecois won 54 seats and the NDP 19. The Liberals were forced into a minority with just 135 MPs.

Harper essentially went into hiding for the rest of the 2004 summer. And despite a few media disasters—the infamous proposal to import Belgian-style federalism to Canada comes to mind—the Tories had a relatively uneventful few months before their first national convention in Montreal in March 2005.

Coming Full Circle

Going into the event, the party brass had every reason to be nervous. "Stephen Harper is under pressure to invigorate a party whose cracks are clearly showing," warned John Ivison of the *National Post*.[15] As the first day unfolded, pundits were predicting the fragile new party would split along old Reform and PC lines over issues such as same-sex marriage and

abortion. Then Peter MacKay threw a temper tantrum over a proposed constitutional change; Harper threw a chair upon hearing about MacKay's
behaviour and the media threw themselves into overdrive. For twenty-four
hours, it looked as though the dire predictions of the press might come
true, and the new party would commit hara-kiri on national television.

But by the time the blue, red and white balloons dropped from the
ceiling the next night, Harper finally had a reason to smile. As his children cavorted onstage and pumped-up delegates streamed outside, it
became clear that he had delivered one of the strongest speeches of his
career. Hammering away at the Liberals for the sponsorship scandal
and promising to rebuild the conservative big tent, Harper turned in a
surprisingly passionate performance that night that seemed to unify a
diverse group of delegates.

Despite the previous night's talk of unity, however, cracks still surfaced
the following morning, especially along the social conservative fault line.
After a narrow majority voted not to support any legislation that would
regulate abortion, some social conservatives stormed out of the meeting
room. On the issue of same-sex marriage, Belinda Stronach was resound-
ingly booed when she spoke against a resolution restricting the definition
of marriage to a man and a woman. Despite its desire to project a tolerant
image, it appeared that the party still wasn't ready to tolerate debate on the
more contentious moral issues.

The Conservatives also struggled with their party's style. It seemed
they couldn't decide whether they were populist or conservative. Sitting
in the convention hall, one got the sense that many delegates were still
suspicious of being too "political," as though professionalism and playing by the rules are tantamount to selling out. Delegates affirmed their
populist roots by rejecting the creation of a youth wing, belying their
continued suspicion of intermediary institutions. Yet with the same breath
they voted down grassroots-type resolutions that would have bound MPs
to their constituents' views on moral issues, allowed for MP recall legislation and established a citizens' assembly on Parliamentary reform.

On the fiscal front, the Tories remained similarly confused. In the
words of Gerry Nicholls, vice-president of the National Citizens Coalition,
"they haven't made up their mind if they want to be a pro-free-enterprise

party yet."[16] On the one hand, they endorsed personal income tax cuts, family-friendly income-splitting policies, raising the basic personal exemption and reducing payroll taxes. On the other hand, they voted to continue regional subsidies, corporate welfare and supply management. This contradicted the promise Harper made during the 2004 election that he would lower corporate taxes only if businesses were willing to accept fewer subsidies. Furthermore, the party forsook legislated debt repayment in favour of a proposal to use part of future surpluses to "gradually reduce" outstanding obligations. According to John Williamson, federal director of the Canadian Taxpayers Federation, "the new Conservative policy on this file ... is hardly different than that of the Liberals."[17]

And therein lies the rub. Canadians already have one Liberal party— they don't need two of them. What the Tories finally had a chance to do was position themselves as the party of small, responsible, forward-looking, non-interventionist government, as opposed to the big, wasteful, old-style, expansionist government Canadians currently have. Instead, the result of the convention prompted the *Toronto Star* to crow "Conservatives Shift to the Centre,"[18] a headline that would have Dalton Camp and Robert Stanfield dancing the tango in heaven.

In their quest for that electoral nirvana, the place where the majority of voters are fabled to live, Conservatives chose not to offer Canadians a real alternative but opted instead for "Liberal lite." Instead of challenging the statist status quo, the party veered toward the mushy middle in the hopes that Canadians would eventually just tire of the Liberals and vote for their doppelgangers in blue clothing. Sadly, this is the strategy that has kept the Tories warming the opposition benches for seventy of the last one hundred years.

What the convention did decisively achieve was a consolidation of Stephen Harper's leadership. Harper obtained an approval rating of 84 percent; his candidate for party presidency, Don Plett, was elected, and the youth wing proposal, which was strongly opposed by Harper and his inner circle, was torpedoed *à la* Reform Party by a 51–49 percent vote. Harper was clearly in charge—but in charge of what exactly?

Columnist John Robson summed it up best: a party with "delusions of adequacy."[19] Some opinion makers took an even darker view. Andrew

Coyne astutely remarked that "everything the Tories have just done is to ratify Liberal assumptions and Liberal values."[20] Even CBC hockey commentator Don Cherry waded into the fray, commenting that Harper had "made a definite mistake. ... If the [Conservatives] think they are going to get the left-wingers and Quebec to vote for them, they are nuts. All they have done is alienate people like me."[21]

In short, the dilemma faced by the Conservative Party still boiled down to the same turf war of generations past: a fight between populists and Red Tories, statists and free marketeers, the religious right and libertarians, federalists and decentralists. The problem with marrying the Reform, Alliance and Progressive Conservative parties is that by trying to sew a coat of so many colours you end up with a compromise no one wants to wear. Instead of donning new clothes, the party simply attempted to patch its old ones, and everyone knows what happens to patchworks. They eventually fall apart at the seams, which is what we've been witnessing ever since the convention.

So now matters have come full circle. We are back to the same situation that existed before the Reform Party and the Canadian Alliance came to life: an ideologically rudderless centre-right party obsessed with gaining popularity in central Canada. Sound familiar?

Throughout 2005 Harper and the Tories have tried to be as inoffensive as possible on every policy matter of import while trying to keep the focus on Liberal corruption. About the only issue they've taken a definitive stance on since the last election is gay marriage. For a while it was all they seemed to talk about. The party even promised to revisit the gay marriage law if it ever wins an election. As columnist Don Martin has observed, the Tories should just drop it. Opponents of same-sex marriage are already voting Conservative. Harper's chances of winning new votes only improve if voters can associate something other than being anti-gay marriage with the Tories. Don Martin believes that "[g]etting same-sex marriages out of the Commons at arm's-length from their MPs is the Conservatives' best shot at reversing their poll sliding numbers."[22]

What is most amazing about the last three elections is how often mistakes are repeated. The Tories seem not to have learned that the Liberals will smear each leader and define him before he has the chance to define himself. Nor have Conservatives learned that most of the media are out to get them and will do everything in their power to bring about their defeat. They still don't realize that taking the "high road" in the face of Liberal smears doesn't work, that they have to fight back and that waiting for the Liberals to screw up and fall on their sword is not the path to power.

Unless the Conservatives jettison the losing formula of the past, odds are they will remain an opposition party. And even if they do form government, history suggests that they will fail to advance conservative ideas and rule like a second Liberal party. Either way, small c conservatives and Canadians hungry for real political change—end up the losers.

So how can conservatives bring a truly right-wing government to power in this country? The answer lies not with the Conservative Party but with the conservative movement. As we will see in the next chapter, by focusing on the broader movement, Canadian conservatives can pave the way for a truly small-c conservative party to take office.

Endnotes

1. Criticism of the venture was not limited to the PCs. Some in the Reform Party opposed Manning's initiative, because they saw it as watering down the Reform Party's principles. Others questioned whether Manning was simply trying to preserve his own leadership by creating a new party.

2. For a detailed rundown of how the Liberals branded Day see Warren Kinsella's *Kicking Ass in Canadian Politics* (Toronto: Random House, 2001).

3. "A Foggy Day in Canada," editorial, Montreal *Gazette*, November 8, 2000, B2.

4. Greg Weston, "Clark, McLellan: They had it made," *Toronto Sun*, May 29, 2004. www.canoe.ca/NewsStand/TorontoSun/News/2004/05/29/477687.html

5. Joe Clark to Peter C. Newman, quoted in William Johnson's *Stephen Harper and the Future of Canada* (Toronto: McClelland and Stewart, 2005), 304.

6. "'Devil we know' Martin better than Harper: Clark," *CBC News* Online, April 26, 2004. www.cbc.ca/stories/2004/04/25/canada/clark040425

7. A detailed rundown of all the events leading up to the merger can be found in William Johnson's *Stephen Harper and the Future of Canada* (Toronto: McClelland & Stewart, 2005).

8. Jill Mahoney "Tory Critic Wants New Abortion Rules," *The Globe and Mail*, June 1, 2004. www.theglobeandmail.com/servlet/ArticleNews/freeheadlines/LAC/20040601/ELECABOR01/national/National

9. "The Federal Election: What Really Happened?" *Interim*, October, 2004. www.theinterim.com/2004/oct/04editorial.html

10. "Conservative Party Language Critic Resigns," *CBC News* Online, May 28, 2004. www.cbc.ca/stories/2004/05/27/canada/conservative_bilingual040527

11. "Conservative MP Calls for Repeal of Hate Law," *CBC News* Online, June 6, 2004. www.cbc.ca/stories/2004/06/06/canada/newelxnconshate040606

12. "MP Gallant Compares Abortion to Iraq Beheading," *CTV News* Online, June 7, 2004. www.ctv.ca/servlet/ArticleNews/story/CTVNews/1086654108341_57?hub=Canada

13. "Liberal Women Unite to Denounce Harper on Abortion," *CBC News* Online, June 8, 2004. www.cbc.ca/story/election/national/2004/06/08/elexnlib040608.html

14. Brian Laghi, "Harper Pledges to Give West Clout," *The Globe and Mail*, June 28, 2005. www.theglobeandmail.com/servlet/story/RTGAM.20040628.wxharper28/BNStory/specialDecision2004/

15. John Ivison, "The Tories," *National Post*, Special Section, March 17, 2005.

16. Author interview with Gerry Nicholls, March 20, 2005.

17. Author interview with John Williamson, March 20, 2005.

18. *Toronto Star*, March 20, 2005, A1.

19. Conversation with John Robson, March 20, 2005.

20. Andrew Coyne, "Amidst the ballons, a white flag," *National Post*, March 23, 2005, A20.

21. Don Cherry in an interview with Joe O'Connor, "Beautiful Grapes," *National Post*, April 2, 2005, S3.

22. Don Martin, "Tories missing mark on same-sex debate," *Calgary Herald*, June 22, 2005, A8.

PART two

THE PLAN

4 CHAPTER

THE PATH TO POWER:
Building a Conservative Infrastructure

*"We are different from previous generations of conservatives.
We are no longer working to preserve the status quo. We are
radicals, working to overturn the present power structure of
this country."*

—Paul Weyrich, founder of the Heritage Foundation

IF the Conservative Party is to win elections based on small-c conservative platforms and implement them when in office, small-c conservatives
will have to not only mould the party, but the country and its institutions,
in their image. To accomplish this, they must go far beyond the borders
of partisan politics and organization. Simply padding the Conservative
Party with volunteers, platitudes, star candidates and clever campaign
ads will not fix the problem. What's needed is a genuine movement to
fuel the fire—an organized effort to build a critical mass of conservative counterculture and, in the words of former Mike Harris advisor Tom
Long, "shift the goal posts."

Such a movement would create a vast network of think-tanks, pressure groups and publications to promote conservative ideas. It would train
and place bright young right-wingers in professions which are currently
hostile to the Conservative Party and conservatism, such as the media and
academia. It would establish legal foundations to challenge laws with which

conservatives disagree. It would spread the conservative message to New Canadians and Quebecers, who are currently failing to vote Conservative. It would allow a thousand voices of conservative thought, action and speech to bloom in the desert of Canadian public opinion.

It would require something akin to a revolution.

Conservatives, take heart: lest this sound like an overwhelming task, be aware that it's been done before. In terms of a blueprint for change, the best example lies south of the border. A well-funded conservative infrastructure developed over the past four decades has made conservatism a major force—if not *the* dominant force—in American political life. The result is the Republican Party's present hegemony in U.S. politics.

This did not develop from Ayn Rand's abstractions, however. It only happened because American conservatives were willing to make it happen—and put their money where their minds are. We need something similar to occur here. And it can't happen soon enough.

Now, before you put this book down because you think we're nuts, consider where U.S. conservatives were when they started. American conservatism as we know it today barely existed a half century ago. Much like Canada today, you could fit all the ideological conservatives into a school bus. Frank Chodorov, one of the founders of *National Review* magazine, once joked at a New York meeting of conservatives in 1960 that "if the Commies only knew, they could rub out the entire conservative movement."[1]

According to John Micklethwait and Adrian Wooldridge, authors of *The Right Nation*, a history of the American conservative movement, the term "conservative" was first coined by the Democrats and rarely used other than as an insult.[2] Republicans preferred other labels: President Herbert Hoover called himself a "true liberal," and President Dwight Eisenhower once said cutting federal spending on education would offend "every liberal—including me."[3] Little in the way of conservative infrastructure could be found in the U.S. well into the 1960s. Before conservatives got organized, liberals had eight weekly newsmagazines while conservatives had one—*Human Events*, with a total weekly readership of 127.[4]

After the defeat of Republican presidential candidate Barry Goldwater in 1964, American conservatives realized they were losing the battle and got organized.[5] The issue wasn't just the state of the Republican Party. It was a situation they perceived as a threat to capitalism and democracy as a way of life: the rise of statism in America.

Lewis Powell's Call to Arms

In 1971, this threat—along with ideas on what to do about it—was chronicled by Lewis F. Powell, Jr., an attorney and future U.S. Supreme Court Justice, in a 5,000-word piece entitled "Confidential Memorandum: Attack of American Free Enterprise System." The "Powell Memorandum," as it became known, was distributed by the U.S. Chamber of Commerce to its national membership of leading executives, businesses and trade associations.

Powell wrote of his country's situation as one where the very basics of a functioning capitalist economy—liberty, free enterprise, property rights—were being questioned, and even attacked. But these attacks were not all from the Left.[6] "We are not dealing with sporadic or isolated attacks from a relatively few extremists or even from the minority socialist cadre. ... The most disquieting voices joining the chorus of criticism come from perfectly respectable elements of society: from the college campus, the pulpit, the media, the intellectual and literary journals, the arts and sciences, and from politicians."[7]

Powell went on to chide the business community for its apathy, but at the same time exalted it as holding the key to reversing this trend: "Strength lies in organization, in careful long-range planning and implementation, in consistency of action over an indefinite period of years, in the scale of financing available only through joint effort, and in the political power available only through united action and national organizations."[8]

Powell suggested the U.S. Chamber of Commerce engage in a four-pronged plan of attack, focusing on academia, the media, politics and the courts. The plan would channel money to create a conservative counterweight to the prevailing liberal ethos of the day. It would promote a wide variety of actions, from funding think-tanks and magazines to establishing new media outlets in radio and television, to finding speaking opportunities on college campuses for business leaders. The project would defend the ideals of free enterprise and democracy, while attacking whatever was deemed to undermine these efforts.

The business community's response to the "Powell Memorandum" was immediate and effective. The late beer baron Joseph Coors invested $250,000 to fund the 1971–72 operations of the Analysis and Research Association (ARA), an organization that would became the Heritage Foundation, today the most important conservative think-tank in Washington. Richard Mellon Scaife, of the Mellon bank fortune, chipped in $900,000 to the foundations in 1973. Others, such as the Koch family, the Lynne and Harry Bradley Foundation and the John M. Olin Foundation, soon followed in opening their wallets.[9]

Irving Kristol, grandfather of the neoconservative movement—the group of anti-Communist ex-liberals who converted to conservatism in the 1950s and '60s—published a series of articles in *The Wall Street Journal*. Kristol exhorted "businessmen to use their charitable funds to strengthen the system of private enterprise and limited government."[10] This coincided with the 1978 publication of *A Time for Truth*, written by William Simon, President Ford's treasury secretary. Simon made the point that Americans "who should be on the front lines defending institutions of ordered liberty, i.e., *businessmen*, were the ones underwriting their own destruction—by supporting academics who openly subverted American principles."[11] He called for the creation of a "powerful counter-intelligentsia" that would fight the ever-expanding welfare state.

To give substance to this idea, Simon and Kristol established the Institute for Educational Affairs (IEA). The institute would "seek out promising Ph.D. candidates and undergraduate leaders, help them establish themselves through grants and fellowships and then help them get jobs with activist organizations, research projects, student publications, federal agencies or leading periodicals."[12] The IEA "ended up playing a pivotal role in the rise of conservative college papers founded in the early Eighties."[13]

These new think-tanks and foundations differed from their predecessors. Canadian political science professor Don Abelson, author of *Do Think Tanks Matter?*, affirms that "what distinguished advocacy think tanks from the earlier types of think tanks already established in the United States was not their desire to study public policy issues but their profound determination to market their ideas to various target audiences.

... Ideas in hand, they began to think strategically about how to most effectively influence policymakers, the public and the media."[14]

Over the next twenty-five years, these organizations profoundly altered the American political landscape. They were front-and-centre in the cause of advancing conservative ideas and shoring up support for Ronald Reagan's presidency. The Heritage Foundation played "a critical role" during the Reagan transition of 1980.[15] With generous corporate support, the budgets for the dozens of new think-tanks and organizations that were sprouting up grew rapidly. According to one estimate, the American conservative infrastructure network spent more than U.S. $1 billion in the 1990s.[16]

Today the network helps the Republican Party immeasurably. Washington's roster of conservative think-tanks—the Heritage Foundation (with an annual budget of around U.S. $40 million), the American Enterprise Institute (AEI), the Hudson Institute, the Cato Institute and so on—form the nerve centre of the conservative idea-generating machine. They put out papers, host conferences, help get support for Republican policy initiatives and nominees and endow fellowships for conservative thinkers. It's no wonder the late New York Democratic senator Daniel Patrick Moynihan said the Republicans had displaced the Democrats as "the party of ideas."[17]

A slew of conservative publications—*National Review,* the *Weekly Standard*, the neoconservative *Commentary*, the libertarian *Reason* and many more—all help to promulgate conservative, anti-statist ideas into the public discourse with their print magazines, online editions and weblogs. *The American Spectator*, for example, played a crucial role in the 1990s by exposing titillating details of Bill Clinton's extracurricular activities, which helped lead to his eventual impeachment in the House of Representatives. The growing chorus of conservative media voices was also key in defeating several Clinton administration proposals, such as Hillary Clinton's major government health care reforms.

After George W. Bush's election in 2000, his administration looted these think-tanks and publications to fill various government posts. The list is endless, so we name just a few: Canadian-born David Frum, who was writing for the *Weekly Standard* (among other publications) became a White House speechwriter; John Bolton, the current U.S. Ambassador

to the United Nations, was plucked from AEI to become Undersecretary of State for Arms Control and International Security Affairs; Lawrence Lindsey left his resident scholar post at AEI to become the president's chief economic adviser; and Elaine Chao left her job at the Heritage Foundation to become Secretary of Labor. The constant movement of people between think-tanks, journalism and political jobs in Washington has been described as a "revolving door."

American conservatives have built themselves an ideas factory. Regnery Publishing, a conservative publishing house, consistently churns out one right-wing blockbuster after the next. Pundits such as Ann Coulter have their own fan clubs. Programs on the Fox News channel and right-wing talk radio personalities like Rush Limbaugh and Michael Savage are ratings hits. The Internet is brimming with conservative blogs and chat forums. In an article published in the September–October 2004 issue of *Philanthropy* magazine, James Piereson, executive director of the Olin Foundation, notes that "there is now a robust debate in American intellectual life between conservatives and liberals. The one-sided debate, dominated by the left, is a thing of the past."[18] Indeed, the most interesting debates in America now occur among the various factions of conservatism, not between right and left.[19]

And America isn't the only place to use think-tanks to propel conservatives to office. In Great Britain, think-tanks played a key role in bringing small-c conservatism to 10 Downing Street. Two men, Alfred Sherman and Margaret Thatcher's ideological guru, Sir Keith Joseph, founded the Centre for Policy Studies in 1974. With Thatcher as the institute's vice chairman, CPS developed and, most importantly, marketed the classical liberal economic ideas that later became known as "Thatcherism." Joseph himself said that his aim in setting up the CPS "was to convert the Tory Party."[20] (Sounds like something we could really use on this side of the pond ...)

In the early 1970s, the British Tories were led by the late Edward Heath, who as prime minister between 1970 and 1974 was busy nationalizing the aerospace division of Rolls-Royce, implementing wage controls and forcing Britons into a three-day work week because of a miners' strike. The CPS developed "the drive to expose the follies and self-defeating consequences of government intervention," in Thatcher's own words,[21] and in speeches and papers Joseph criticized the big government inclinations of both the Labour and Conservative parties. The CPS still exists today and continues to promote liberty.

Joseph took his inspiration from another British think-tank, the Institute of Economic Affairs. Established in 1955, the IEA was an early promoter of the works of Friedrich Hayek, whose ideas formed the backbone of Thatcherism, and Milton Friedman. Whereas the CPS was more of a political organization, IEA was more philosophical. Joseph had worked there on and off since the 1960s.[22] The IEA's founder, Sir Antony Fisher, went on to found the Atlas Economic Research Foundation, which provides start-up funds to free-market think-tanks all over the globe, and had a role in establishing the Fraser Institute here. Many other British think-tanks continue to contribute to the British conservative movement, including the Social Affairs Unit, the Adam Smith Institute and the Institute for Fiscal Studies. Britain also has conservative magazines, including the venerable London *Spectator* and the *Salisbury Review*.

To build its own conservative culture, the Canadian conservative movement must replicate these models. Even the U.S. Democrats have realized the necessity of having an extra-party infrastructure. They are starting to get their act together, with new think-tanks such as the Center for American Progress, headed by Bill Clinton's former chief-of-staff, John Podesta, and the Campus Progress National Student Conference, which held its inaugural conference in July 2005, where liberal students gathered to learn how to fight the (now very organized) campus conservative movement.

In an article published last spring in *The New York Times*, former Democratic senator Bill Bradley called on his party to build a "pyramid" based on Powell's blueprint.[23] Bradley describes the pyramid as follows: big donors and foundations form the base. These finance think-tanks, such as Heritage, on the second level of the pyramid. Ideas from those organizations are then "pushed up" to the pyramid's third level, where political strategists use polling and focus groups to tailor messages that make these ideas appealing to the electorate. These messages are then disseminated by the fourth level, conservative-friendly news media. At the top of the pyramid sits the president of the United States. As Bradley succinctly puts it, "Because the pyramid is stable, all you have to do is put a different top on it and it works fine."[24]

Bradley laments that without a proper Democratic infrastructure, the party continues to embrace a platform which he calls "Republican lite." Sound familiar? Put the platforms of the Canadian Conservative Party next to that of the Liberal Party and you will see they are becoming hard to tell apart, to the point where the Tories were dubbed the "Do Anything, Say Anything" Conservative Party by John Williamson, the federal director of the Canadian Taxpayers Federation.[25] In an eponymous article, Williamson lists policies on which the Tories are becoming indistinguishable from the Liberals. These include subsidies to business and respect for federal-provincial state daycare agreements. And Andrew Coyne cynically remarked after the party's 2005 Montreal convention that: "either the Conservatives really mean it when they say they will privatize nothing, deregulate nothing, and make no significant cuts in spending ... [o]r they are simply lying, misrepresenting their true intentions in their lust for power."[26]

When former prime minister Kim Campbell infamously quipped on Day 16 of the 1993 federal election campaign, "This is not the time ... to get involved in a debate on ... serious issues," she got a couple of things wrong. A campaign is no place to *develop your position* on serious issues. Unless you've built the pyramid first, you've got as much chance of establishing a sustained political dynasty as building an igloo in Toronto in July. You might win an election, once in a while, when the voters are really sick of the other guys, but you will be doomed to return to the opposition benches once your time is up. And both the party—and the country—will be no better for your efforts.

The good news is that the seeds of conservative infrastructure have already been planted in Canada. We are several steps head of where American conservatives were in 1964. The Fraser Institute, the National Citizens Coalition, the Canadian Taxpayers Federation, the C. D. Howe Institute, the

Frontier Centre for Public Policy, the Atlantic Institute for Market Studies (AIMS), the Montreal Economic Institute and other organizations are all performing vital work and promoting free-market ideas.

The bad news is that Canadian conservatives are up against some formidable opponents with very deep pockets—and to combat them we need to multiply Canada's conservative infrastructure by a factor of ten or more. Like conservatives in the United States, liberals and leftists in Canada have their pyramid. The difference is that the liberals and leftists are largely funded by the public treasury, not by private institutions or philanthropy. Ironically, it's the Canadian taxpayer who has been the prime contributor to the entrenchment of statism in our nation.

The State of Statism in Canada

According to academic Don Abelson, "in the United States, most free-standing think-tanks are privately funded; in Canada, few think-tanks have the luxury of turning down government money. And that's a huge, huge problem."[27] That it is, especially for conservatives.

Sonia Arrison, a former program director with the Canadian Donner Foundation who now works with the Pacific Research Institute in San Francisco, says "professional Canadians"—her term for government bureaucrats who grant research money—don't want conservatives to go anywhere. She believes, "[they] want to keep Canada in one mode—they love state health care, they speak two languages. There's this idea of what Canada is, and there's this entire apparatus that exists to keep it that way."[28]

This attitude is easily explained when one looks at how Canadian think-tanks got their legs. In the first half of this century, "with few exceptions, the think tank landscape in Canada remained relatively barren."[29] Many of these were also less research institutes than clubs[30] or events where people met to discuss ideas, such as the annual Couchiching Summer Conference on the shores of bucolic Lake Couchiching in Ontario.

Then came the 1960s. While Quebec underwent the Quiet Revolution and Canadians enjoyed the sexual revolution, Ottawa mandarins plotted a statist revolution. The Canadian government got into the think-tank business, establishing a wide network of taxpayer-funded policy research institutes, including the Economic Council of Canada (1963), the Science Council of Canada (1966), the National Council of Welfare (1968), and the Law Reform Commission of Canada (1970).[31] According to authors Abelson and Evert A. Lindquist, these groups "received government funding in amounts that most non-governmental think tanks could only dream about." Although they were in theory independent of government, members were appointed by the prime minister, and the government could make requests for research initiatives to be undertaken.[32]

The exponential growth of the so-called non-governmental sector in Canada—think-tanks, interest groups and foundations—has been extensively documented by Carleton University professor Leslie Pal. Pal found that much of today's "non-governmental" sector was built through what he calls the "Great Ottawa Grant Boom" of the early 1970s and skewed overwhelmingly to the left.[33]

The root of this evil? The Citizenship Branch of the federal office of the Secretary of State (SOS). Yes, the Liberal federal government.

Prior to 1968, Citizenship was a pretty sleepy place. It served a list of voluntary do-gooder organizations, such as churches, women's clubs, Girl Guides and Boy Scouts, service clubs like B'nai B'rith and the Kiwanis Club, boards of trade and the YM/YWCA. But when the separatists began to gain momentum in Quebec, the concept of citizenship became entwined with that of national unity—namely, keeping Quebec in Canada—and Citizenship's role changed forever. In May 1970, the federal cabinet approved five new objectives for the Citizenship Branch: reinforcing Canadian identity and unity; encouraging cultural diversity and bilingualism; preserving human rights and fundamental freedoms; increasing and improving citizenship participation, and developing meaningful symbols of Canadian sovereignty.[34]

Enter Pierre Trudeau's plan to create a "Just Society" for Canada with its promotion of enforced equality, and the rest is unfortunately history.

According to the late journalist Sandra Gwyn, Ottawa bureaucrats Bernard Ostry and Michael McCabe "turned Citizenship into a flamboyant, freespending *animateur sociale* ... massive grants went out to militant native groups, tenants' associations and other putative aliens of the 1970s."[35]

As Ostry himself put it:

The Branch was supposed to develop and strengthen a sense of Canadian citizenship, chiefly through programs that would aid participation and assuage feelings of social injustice. Indian, Métis and Inuit political, social, cultural organizations were established and funded in the teeth of opposition from the Department of Indian Affairs; a women's bureau was set up before the government had commented on the Royal Commission's Report on the Status of Women; Opportunities for Youth, travel and exchange and hostel programs were undertaken without the blessing of Manpower, Welfare or Justice departments, and millions of dollars were made available to the branch to ensure justice and fairness to every ethnic group that wished to preserve and celebrate its cultural heritage.[36]

In 1971, the government upped the ante, declaring Canada officially multicultural, and encouraged the SOS to fund an even wider spectrum of groups.[37] When the Liberals were reduced to a minority in 1972, it put a bit of a crimp into these plans. Also, some in Ottawa were beginning to question the wisdom of funding what could become a "third order" of government. But according to Pal, it was too late to turn back the tide:

Some groups limped and slipped and eventually lost their edge—students and youth, for example—but others, once their fingers and toes gripped the crevices of Ottawa's funding edifice, refused to let go. The programs ... became the foundations upon which key segments of Canadian society defined their identity: women, OLMGs [Official Language Minority Groups], and ethnics. The state, pursuing an eminently statist strategy, had been ensnared by the fruits of its efforts. While the Citizenship Branch thereafter lost some of its élan, and the government as a whole lost interest, the roots of "citizenship participation" among groups and organizations themselves were now firmly established.[38]

From 1971 to 1989 the growth of non-governmental organizations and think-tanks continued to occur mostly on the dole of government. There were some notable exceptions: the C. D. Howe Research Institute was formed in 1973; the Conference Board of Canada increased its presence by moving offices to Ottawa; the Canadian Tax Foundation gained a higher profile thanks to the Royal Commission on Taxation;[39] and the pro-free-market Fraser Institute was founded in 1974. But the bulk of foundations and think-tanks still had links to the state.

Case in point: in 1980 the Canadian Centre for Policy Alternatives (CCPA) was founded "by supporters of social democratic principles to counter the influence of the Fraser Institute."[40] But unlike the privately funded Fraser, which takes no government cash, the CCPA relies heavily on the public purse, even though it has charitable tax-deductible status. In 2003–04 the federal government gave the CCPA $427,000;[41] between 1991 and 2001, B.C.'s then NDP government also handed over $410,231 in public funds.[42] This money supports the CCPA's advocacy of such exotic "alternatives" as higher spending, higher taxes, higher capital gains taxes, a wealth transfer tax and the ending of public-private partnerships.

Special-interest groups also kept getting public money to advance the government's agenda. Just a few examples: Official Language Minority Groups received $76 million between 1970 and 1982; not surprisingly, the number of these groups almost doubled in that time, to 370.[43] The Women's Legal Education and Action Fund (LEAF) received over $1 million in its first three years from the SOS and the Liberal government of Ontario in the early 1980s.[44] The budget for multicultural groups in 1987–88 alone was more than $20 million, with $750,000 funding organizations such as the Canadian Hispanic Congress, the Ukrainian National Committee and the Canadian Arab Federation.[45]

In the 1992 budget, Brian Mulroney's government briefly came to its senses and severed the government's institutional ties with various councils. The Economic Council of Canada, the Science Council of Canada, the Law Reform Commission, the Canadian Institute for International Peace and Security and the Charter Challenges Program were disbanded. (Although we wonder whether these decisions were made because these programs were inherently wrong, or were just about taming the federal deficit.) A year later, the Tories were out of power and the Chrétien Liberals set the gravy train back on its tracks, funnelling money into the Privy Council Office's Policy Research Initiative (PRI).[46] The Law Reform Commission was also re-established in 1997.

The 1990s also saw the creation of the government-funded Policy Research Initiative and Canadian Policy Research Networks. The latter is a quasi-public think-tank with the Trudeauesque mission "to make Canada a more just, prosperous and caring society"; it has received more than $14 million in public money over the past nine years.[47] The PRI was set up to counter the perception that the government was cutting the size and policy-making capacity of the public sector; in 2000, its annual budget was $3 million in public funds.[48] In 2002 and 2001, the Pembina Institute, an Alberta-based organization that has been publicly pushing the Kyoto Accord, received at least $291,371 in funding from the federal government.[49]

Lest the trend be broken, in 2002, the federal government gave a $125-million endowment to found the Trudeau Foundation.[50] Based in Montreal, the foundation's main activity is awarding generous fellowships (worth up to $175,000 over three years) and doctoral scholarships (worth up to $50,000 annually) in the humanities and social sciences. While officially non-partisan, the foundation's work focuses "on four themes that shaped the life and career of Pierre Trudeau," among them "Human Rights and Social Justice" and "Responsible Citizenship."[51] In addition to awarding these taxpayer-funded grants, the foundation has a list of mentors who work with the fellows and scholars. These mentors receive a $20,000 annual honorarium and up to $15,000 in travel expenses. Mentors have included former Supreme Court of Canada justice and current U.N. Human Rights High Commissioner Louise Arbour, former B.C. NDP premier Mike Harcourt, former Saskatchewan NDP premier Allan Blakeney and environmentalist Elizabeth May.[52]

And let's not leave out the taxpayer-funded soapboxes afforded to the Trudeau progeny. Justin currently chairs Katimavik, an organization that sends young Canadians around the country to perform volunteer community work. Meanwhile, Alexandre chairs Canada World Youth, which sends young people to do development work abroad.

Today, the federal government's think-tank army includes a group of fifteen foundations that have received a collective *$9 billion* in federal funding since 1997.[53] Neither the auditor general nor average Canadians can even hold these foundations accountable. They aren't subject to federal Freedom of Information legislation, so it is impossible to know how they're spending taxpayers' money.

In short, Trudeau capitalized on national unity concerns to channel vast amounts of public money and resources into a massive infrastructure of statist organizations that reinforced his vision of Canada. His desire to fracture Canada's English–French axis and to foil Quebec separatists by creating a society of competing interest groups increased the role of the state in every aspect of life. The Liberals succeeded in equating statism with Canadian nationalism, and Canadian nationalism with the big-government policies of the Liberal Party. The Conservative Party failed to challenge these policies—and still fails to challenge them—for fear of being called un-Canadian.

On the Front Lines

Some in the conservative movement have chosen to challenge it, however. The National Citizens Coalition has been indispensable in its fight against the Liberals' attempt to curb third-party election spending, known as the "gag law." The Canadian Taxpayers Federation leads the fight for lower taxes and less waste in government, while its Centre for Aboriginal Policy Change leads the fight for market-based solutions to native issues. The Citizens Centre for Freedom and Democracy, an initiative of Alberta senator-in-waiting Link Byfield, promotes honest, responsible government and renewed federalism.

On the think-tank scene, the Frontier Centre for Public Policy in Winnipeg promotes free-market solutions to problems in the Prairies. The Montreal Economic Institute is a lone voice of classical liberal sanity in Quebec. The Atlantic Institute for Market Studies debunks the notion that regional transfers are a successful way to build an economy and promotes free-market solutions for the East. These think-tanks do good work and punch well above their weight, given that their annual operating budgets are in the range of $1 million or less.

Then there's the granddaddy of Canadian free-market ideas generation—the Fraser Institute. With an annual budget of $7 million, the Fraser Institute has been the lifeblood of free-market thinking in this country since its founding in 1974. And if there's one person Canadians can thank for this, it's executive director Michael Walker.

Walker retired in 2005 after more than thirty years at the Fraser's helm, where he witnessed the rise of the government-funded left. Despite this formidable opposition, Walker thinks free-market ideas have made progress, mainly in what he calls shifting the "centre of opinion": "There's been an enormous change in the substrate of ideas that inform the policy process. The idea of the government nationalizing things, you don't hear that anymore. You don't hear governments bragging about increasing expenditures or how big deficits are. The whole dialogue of policy has changed for the better. Even the radical left is not as radical as it used to be."[54]

The story of the Fraser Institute's founding is a textbook example of how conservative infrastructure can be built. Walker, a bright young scholar who had worked for the Bank of Canada and the federal Department of Finance, was fed up with what he was seeing in Ottawa, especially its penchant for central planning. He wanted out. T. Patrick Boyle, then a vice president at MacMillan Bloedel, wanted to start up a think-tank to counter the socialist initiatives of Dave Barrett's NDP government in B.C. With $175,000 in seed money from seventeen friends of the then chairman of MacMillan Bloedel, Jack Klein, as well as help from Walker, Sally Pipes (now head of the Pacific Research Institute in San Francisco) and others, the Fraser Institute got off the ground and has been growing ever since.

The think-tank the left loves to hate, the Institute has made an immense contribution to the development of conservative public policy in Canada, on matters ranging from productivity to privatization. It is also involved in other non-think-tank-like activities, such as funding a voucher program in Toronto that helps poor families send their children to private schools. The Fraser Institute ranks the performance of high schools and elementary schools in Canada and will soon rank hospitals in the same way. It has helped start up new think-tanks like the Montreal

Economic Institute. And recently it started creating fellowships for retired politicians (among them Preston Manning, Mike Harris and former Reform MP Herb Grubel) so that they may continue to play a role in public life after their departures from the electoral arena.

Walker is a pioneer. And there's no doubt that the think-tank scene is much more promising today than when he began his career. But the question remains: why haven't we seen more growth in the privately funded think-tank sector?

Walker thinks it goes back, even before the Trudeau years, to the country's founding, when the Family Compact and Chateau Clique ruled Upper and Lower Canada, using government as a tool for their own benefit until the 1840s. In his opinion, Canada still isn't a "mature state" like the United States or Great Britain, which have more "effervescent" democracies, to use his term.[55]

According to Walker, in the United States "there is a much stronger base of foundations and private wealth which is aligned with the idea that we have to have an alternative point of view to the government point of view and that we have to fund it. There is this reliance on private money to fund alternative views—what Edmund Burke called the 'little platoons of society.'"[56]

Perhaps there isn't as much private money being offered in Canada because taxes are higher here than in the U.S. Perhaps people have been conditioned to think that "the government should take of these things." Or perhaps they just don't care. Or they just haven't been asked to contribute.

But conservatives *have to ask*. When Walker founded the Fraser Institute and was asking for money, people would often laugh at him. "Their first inclination was to pick up the phone and call up the guys in the white coats," Walker says. But if more people show they're serious about building these institutions, Walker believes the money will follow: "The more of these organizations that there are around, the more resources there will be for new ones to come around. People get more and more familiar with the idea of giving to this kind of activity and they get more and more used to the idea that this kind of work can be effective."[57]

As Walker says, "If you are trying to change the world, you better be willing to take a few risks."[58] If Canada wants to have a bigger and robust conservative movement, and elect a government in its image, conservatives had better start building those little platoons. And for that to happen, Canadian business needs to step up to the philanthropic plate, as we will see in the next chapter.

Endnotes

1. Michael M. Uhlmann, "The Right Stuff: William F. Buckley, Jr., and the American Conservative Movement," *Claremont Review of Books*, Summer 2005. www.claremont.org/writings/crb/summer2005/uhlmann.html

2. John Micklethwait and Adrian Wooldridge, *The Right Nation* (New York: Penguin Books, 2004), 8 (hereinafter Micklethwait and Wooldridge).

3. George F. Will, "Why America Leans Right," *Washington Post*, October 10, 2004. www.washingtonpost.com/wp-dyn/articles/A18879-2004Oct8.html

4. Micklethwait and Wooldridge, p. 43, citing George H. Nash, *The Conservative Intellectual Movement in America Since 1945* (Wilmington, Del.: Intercollegiate Studies Institute, 1998), 317.

5. We must be careful to note, however, that the publication that has, in our opinion, done the most to advance conservatism in America, William F. Buckley, Jr.'s *National Review*, was started in 1955.

6. By "economic system," Powell meant the "free enterprise system," "capitalism" and the "political system of democracy under the rule of law."

7. Lewis F. Powell, Jr., "Confidential Memorandum: Attack of American Free Enterprise System," August 23, 1971, U.S. Chamber of Commerce. http://reclaimdemocracy.org/corporate_accountability/powell_memo_lewis.html (hereinafter Powell).

8. Powell.

9. Micklethwait and Wooldridge, 78-79.

10. James Piereson, "The Next Generation," *Philanthropy* Magazine, September/October 2004. www.philanthropyroundtable.org/magazines/2004/SeptOct/PieresonCommentary.htm (hereinafter Piereson)

11. Bolek Kabala, "The Alternatives," *National Review* Online, January 23, 2003. www.nationalreview.com/comment/comment-kabala012303.asp (hereinafter Kabala).

12. Kabala.

13. Kabala.

14. Don Abelson, *Do Think Tanks Matter?* (Montreal: McGill-Queen's University Press, 2002), 31 (hereinafter Abelson).

15. Abelson, 32.

16. David Callahan, "$1 Billion for Conservative Ideas," *The Nation*, April 26, 1999. www.thenation.com/doc.mhtml%3Fi=19990426&s=callahan

17. Piereson.

18. Piereson.

19. It is important to note how diverse the range of thought in the American conservative movement is. While the left may try to characterize it as a homogenous entity, in fact, there are deep divisions on many issues, especially on matters of foreign policy.

20. Website of the documentary *Commanding Heights: Battle for the World Economy*, PBS. www.pbs.org/wgbh/commandingheights/shared/minitextlo/prof_keithjoseph.html (hereinafter *Commanding Heights*).

21. Margaret Thatcher, *The Path to Power* (New York: HarperCollins, 1995), 253.

22. *Commanding Heights.*

23. Bill Bradley, "A Party Inverted," *The New York Times*, March 30, 2005. www.nytimes.com/2005/03/30/opinion/30bradley.html?ex=1128398400&en=910b78f4360a35fd&ei=5070 (hereinafter Bradley).

24. Bradley.

25. John Williamson, "The 'Do Anything, Say Anything' Conservative Party," June 8, 2005. www.taxpayer.com/main/news.php?news_id=2020

26. Andrew Coyne, "Amidst the balloons, a white flag," *National Post*, March 23, 2005, A20.

27. Author telephone interview with Don Abelson, September 2004.

28. Author telephone interview with Sonia Arrison, September 2004.

29. Abelson, 28.

30. Abelson, 23.

31. Abelson, 30.

32. Donald E. Abelson and Evert A. Lindquist, "Think Tanks Across North America," in R. Kent Weaver and James G. McGann, eds., *Think Tanks and Civil Societies: Catalyst for Ideas and Action.* (Somerset, New Jersey: Transaction Publishers, 2000), 37–66. www.ssc.uwo.ca/polisci/faculty/abelson/

33. Leslie A. Pal, *Interests of State: The Politics of Language, Multiculturalism, and Feminism in Canada* (Montreal: McGill-Queen's University Press, 1993), 47 (hereinafter Pal).

34. Pal, 105.

35. Sandra Gwyn, "The Great Ottawa Grant Boom (and How It Grew)," *Saturday Night*, October 1972, 22.

36. Bernard Ostry, *The Cultural Connection: An Essay on Culture and Government Policy in Canada* (Toronto: McClelland and Stewart, 1978), 115.

37. Pal, 116.

38. Pal, 122–123.

39. Abelson, 34.

40. Abelson, 33.

41. Don Abelson, "Any Ideas? Think Tanks and Policy Analysis in Canada," 10. www.sfu.ca/2/howlett/PA05/abelson.doc

42. Mark Milke, *Tax Me, I'm Canadian* (Calgary: Thomas and Black Publishers, 2002), 160 (hereinafter Milke).

43. Pal, 157.

44. Gregory Hein, "Social Movements and the Expansion of Judicial Power, Feminist and Environmentalists in Canada (1970–1995)," 2nd Dissertation, University of Toronto, 1997, 226.

45. Pal, 200.

46. Abelson, 30–31.

47. Sylvia LeRoy, "The PET Fellowship: Building the Next Government Generation," *Fraser Forum*, May 2002, 5 (hereinafter LeRoy).

48. LeRoy, 5.

49. Milke, 159.

50. LeRoy, 5.

51. Trudeau Foundation website. www.trudeaufoundation.ca/themes_e.asp

52. LeRoy and Trudeau Foundation website. www.trudeaufoundation.ca/mentors_e.asp To be fair, some mentors have had Conservative links such as Yves Fortier, who served as Mulroney's representative to the U.N. and Paul Heinbecker, Mulroney's chief foreign policy adviser. But so far as we can tell none has been a small-c conservative.

53. "Auditor General Questions Foundation Funding," *CBC News*, February 15, 2005. www.cbc.ca/story/canada/national/2005/02/15/foundations-auditor-report 050215.html

54. Author interview with Michael Walker, July 5, 2005 (hereinafter Walker).

55. Walker.

56. Walker.

57. Walker.

58. Walker.

5 CHAPTER

INVESTING IN IDEAS:
Donors Wanted!

"Money is like manure; it's not worth a thing unless it's spread around encouraging young things to grow."

— Thornton Wilder

IF a conservative revolution is going to happen, it's going to take a lot of cash, sweat, dedication—and even more cash. Don Abelson, an expert on think-tanks, puts it bluntly: "You need a philanthropic revolution, institutions prepared to bankroll it, and a stronger entrepreneurial spirit; [you need] people who are prepared to step up to the plate, are passionate about policy issues and are prepared to support them."[1]

This needs to be done with the long term in mind. There is no point in setting up foundations without vision and stable funding, or seed groups that are experimental and may disappear. Canada has seen its share of conservative initiatives that didn't last, such as the Northern Foundation. Established in the late 1980s in the hopes of emulating the conservative think-tank movement in America and Great Britain, it hosted a few conferences and published a few newsletters, before in-fighting among board members led to its demise.[2] If conservatives are going to see these sorts of organizations flourish, they must commit both time and resources in a serious fashion.

↓   ↓   ↓

To date, unlike their American counterparts, Canadian entrepreneurs who have profited from the free-market system have not actively sponsored policy research and pressure groups supportive of capitalism and limited government. "You could list on one hand the number of philanthropic foundations in Canada that support or bankroll the efforts of Canadian think-tanks," says Abelson. "For the conservative movement, if they could somehow tap into some success stories in the United States, they could really have an impact, and what it might come down to is drawing on conservative foundations in the United States and elsewhere to support the policy initiatives they want to advocate."[3] Sure, some major Canadian corporations donate money to the Fraser Institute, the Atlantic Institute for Market Studies and other think-tanks. These organizations would not exist without their support. But they don't do nearly enough, especially when competing against the deep pockets of the government-funded left. Why is this the case—and how can this be changed? Some observers, such as Ken Azzopardi, CEO of the Canadian Taxpayers Federation, point to Canada's lack of charitable tradition. "There is a much higher expectation in Canada that the government and tax dollars will provide the support," he says. "This is really obvious in artistic and sport endeavours in this country. A plethora of grants are available; in Canada they are government grants; in the U.S.A. they tend to be foundation and corporate grants."[4]

Sheer numbers would appear to bear this out. In 2003, Canada had approximately 2,290 active grant-making foundations, which controlled assets of $12 billion. Total assets held by U.S. foundations? Over $400 billion.[5] Even factoring in that America's population is ten times the size of Canada's, think-tanks south of the border have disproportionately more resources to draw on.

Canada is also burdened by antiquated charities laws that prevent registered charities from engaging in "political" action. (Note to the federal Conservative Party: reforming these laws must be near the top of the agenda whenever you win an election.) The Canadian Revenue Agency (CRA) mandates that charitable activities must either promote:

- the relief of poverty;
- the advancement of education;
- the advancement of religion; or
- other purposes beneficial to the community in a way the law regards as charitable.[6]

Furthermore, the CRA stipulates that "under the *Income Tax Act*, a registered charity can be involved in non-partisan political activities as long as it devotes substantially all of its resources to charitable activities. Any political activities have to help accomplish the charity's purposes and remain incidental in scope."[7]

The result is that to get and maintain tax-exempt status, think-tanks such as the Fraser Institute and the CD Howe Institute must focus on the "charitable" activities of education and policy research but are essentially barred from political advocacy. Groups that engage in advocacy, such as the Canadian Taxpayers Federation and the National Citizens Coalition, cannot obtain charitable status, which hampers their fundraising efforts, as they cannot issue tax receipts or receive substantial donations from foundations.[8] This is different from the United States, where section 501(c)3 of the Tax Code allows think-tanks and similar organizations to have charitable status and engage in advocacy as long as they do not directly try to lobby for or against a particular piece of legislation.

Furthermore, the term "political advocacy" is defined subjectively by the CRA. Former Fraser Institute executive director Michael Walker recounts a story from one of several audits, when he was forced to meet face to face with CRA officials:

> They said the [Fraser Institute's] work was too much of a political nature. They were interpreting "political" as presenting a particular point of view. ... [T]he guy said. 'You've got to show both sides of things; you can't just show one side of things. [T]he assistant deputy minister was sitting at the table with us, and I knew that he had been at the Department of Finance and, in fact, had been in charge of getting the GST adopted. When the

GST came out, we strongly supported it. We felt it was a much better tax than the Manufacturers Sales Tax, which it was going to replace, that it would be better from a technical economic point of view. So I said to the guy, "Okay, here's the policy [on] the GST. Do you think that the Fraser Institute should have been out saying that on the one hand the GST is a good thing, but on the other it's a bad thing? Or should we have used whatever power we had to create a sensible analysis of what the GST would likely produce?" And literally about two minutes later the ADM said, "I think we should close the file now."[9]

Finally, as Walker suggested in the previous chapter, the elite Canadian business class and politicians have enjoyed a cosy, non-adversarial relationship with government since the days of the nineteenth century and the Family Compact. This has resulted in a greater reliance on government to generate public policy ideas as opposed to the private sector, and may account for the business elite's unwillingness to upset the apple cart by funding non-governmental advocacy organizations.

Many big businesses in Canada profit directly from government subsidies, to the tune of $4 billion a year.[10] These include Bombardier Inc., the greatest beneficiary of government largesse, which at last count has reaped $1.12 billion in taxpayer dollars since 1982.[11] This does not take into account any loans or financing guarantees provided over the years to its clients through Export Development Canada, which, as of December 31, 2003, had $6.5-billion in outstanding loans to the aerospace industry. Of that, 85 percent is reported to have gone to Bombardier's customers.[12] Bombardier returned the favour by pouring $952,844.64 into Liberal coffers from 1993 to 2003.[13]

And Bombardier is hardly alone at the government trough. According to Mark Milke, the author of *Tax Me, I'm Canadian*, between 1982 and 1997, Industry Canada gave businesses $11.3 billion. Over half of this money was in the form of grants or other non-repayable contributions; in other words, taxpayers will never see it again. About $2.1 billion went to five companies: Pratt and Whitney, De Havilland, Bombardier/Candour, El Groupie MIL Inc. and Air Ontario.[14] Other recipients included General

Motors of Canada Ltd., Noranda Inc., Cornerbrook Pulp and Paper Ltd., Dominion Textile, Magna International Inc. and even Rolls-Royce (Canada) Ltd.[15] Apparently in our country even the luxury car sector needs government help.

But this situation isn't an excuse for business' failure to fund conservative think-tanks and intellectual infrastructure. The United States has a long and depressing tradition of business subsidies as well, one that continues today; yet entrepreneurs there mobilized in the 1970s to shore up conservatism. Neither is the fact that many contributions are not tax-deductible under current charities laws an excuse not to give. If a cause is important enough, men and women of conviction will rise to the occasion and overcome the obstacles in their way.

We refuse to believe that conservative principles are only the preserve of policy wonks labouring away in dusty libraries. There are many Canadian business leaders who share a desire to improve society and to create a culture of opportunity. But they need to be approached in a professional, organized way. They need to be informed of the urgency of the situation, the danger that continued one-party statist rule poses for Canada, and the benefits that a small-c conservative culture would provide. They need a latter-day "Powell Memorandum" to make the case for rescuing Canada's right, right now.

Preston Manning's Mission

One man making that case is former Reform Party leader Preston Manning. Manning buys into Senator Bill Bradley's aforementioned political pyramid scheme; in fact, he's drawn up his own diagram, with investors at the bottom, think-tanks, advocacy groups and the media in the middle and the Conservative Party at the top. Since leaving politics, he's been toting this drawing to meetings with businesspeople, great and small, trying to sell the conservative community on the need to invest in an ideological infrastructure. Manning laments, "There's a number of think-tanks that have bigger research departments than the entire Official Opposition in Ottawa, by far, so you need think-tanks and links with academia that can do idea generation, policy analysis."[16]

The result of his efforts is the recently established non-profit corporation, the Manning Centre for Building Democracy. Why that name? Because in Manning's view, this project is greater than simply building a conservative movement: "This is essential to democracy—if you don't have a competitive political marketplace, then you threaten democracy itself. Call it more 'building democratic infrastructure.' I'm coming to it from a conservative angle. If you want to come at it from a socialist angle or somebody else's angle, that's fine. But I think every party ought to have this."[17]

A grand notion, but a true one. Canada's marketplace of ideas today resembles a Soviet-era department store: plenty of shoes, but only the left ones are available. There is not enough variety of voices; the weeds of statist conformity choke the roses of right-wing dissent. If we are to cultivate a thousand conservative flowers, they need an intellectual hothouse in which to bloom.

Manning proposes to build that hothouse one windowpane at a time. His Centre is endowing conservative research and advocacy groups in areas where none exist today, in fields such as culture, science and the environment. The Centre will also keep track of what is being funded and where, to ensure that the need for conservative activism is met equally in all sectors of society.

This project isn't an overnight affair: Manning estimates it will take *up to ten years* to build a serious conservative infrastructure. Nor is this type of pyramid-building an exercise reserved for big business: small business and individual conservatives are key as well. To date most of the money for the Centre has been raised from a large number of small donors.

And the timing is right for these types of organizations to be built. Ironically, the recently enacted Liberal campaign finance laws present a huge opportunity for conservatives, as they limit the amount of money corporations can donate to political parties. As of January 1, 2004, corporate and union fundraising is now essentially banned. Companies and unions can only donate up to $1,000 a year to each party and its riding associations or candidates. Individuals may donate up to $5,000 a year.

As a result, business and businesspeople may well seek another "political" outlet for their money. So might the aging baby boomer generation as it aspires to leave a legacy for future generations. "Canada will undergo a $1-trillion intergenerational wealth transfer over the next decade," according to Sylvia LeRoy, a policy analyst for the Fraser Institute. Non-profit groups will have access to a whole new market of potential donors. "This is a huge opportunity for conservatives—as long as the message gets out and they take up the challenge."[18]

Businesses, large and small, can get in on the action. So-called community foundations allow multiple donors to pool donor-directed funds of as little as $25,000 each for a common cause. Since a typical foundation requires a minimum investment of about $1 million, which most individual contributors don't have, the community model allows smaller donors to get in on the action and have a say in how their money is spent. Last year, Canadians put a record $210 million into these types of organizations.[19] The money is out there: all you have to do is ask for it.

Encouragingly, when asked to gauge the level of support for the Fraser Institute, where he is a senior fellow, former Ontario premier Mike Harris said: "I found quite a willingness amongst the business community in Toronto and in Ontario to step up to the plate and to assist. ... Once you get to explain the message and talk to them, they are supportive."[20]

Conservatives do face some hurdles, however, when pitching to corporate Canada. Not the least is the perception that the Liberal Party is just as good for business as the Conservative Party would be. To be fair, the Liberals under Jean Chrétien did implement many business-friendly, small-c conservative policies. They balanced the budget, lowered personal and corporate taxes and extended free trade throughout North America.

Business should remember, however, that the Liberals did not implement these policies out of conviction, but out of necessity. Does anyone recall the infamous Liberal *Red Book* of the 1993 federal election? In this aptly coloured manifesto, the Liberals promised to expand the state, including everything from housing and infrastructure programs, to national daycare, to stable funding for the CBC. They also pledged to end child poverty and to replace the GST with a fairer tax.

The only relief taxpayers got from this was that MP Sheila Copps mercifully disappeared for a while, after being forced to resign her seat over the broken GST promise.

Indeed, shortly after taking office, the *Red Book* went straight into the shredder. Quite simply, the Canadian economy was a mess: "By 1995, the federal government had been spending more than it collected in revenues for 25 consecutive years. The deficit ... was $37.5 billion on a public accounts basis ... Canada's total debt load ... had grown from $20 billion in 1971 to over $545 billion in 1995. By 1994/95, covering the interest costs alone was costing Canadians $42 billion—more than the annual deficit and some 26% of the entire federal budget."[21]

And critics were calling for change. The International Monetary Fund was "pressing the federal government to impose draconian spending cuts that would take billions of dollars a year more out of the pockets of the unemployed, the elderly, the sick, and even war veterans."[22] In an editorial that appeared on January 12, 1995, the venerable *Wall Street Journal* referred to Canada as "an honorary member of the Third World."

At the same time, Canadian voices on the political right, particularly in the West, were loudly calling for balanced budgets, tax cuts and debt reduction. According to Preston Manning, as the Opposition, the Reform Party pushed the Liberals to act like conservatives and moved the centre of political gravity to the right. In the 1993 election Reform had advocated balancing the budget over three years, a measure termed impossible by the Liberals at the time. Yet in the 1995 budget, surprise, surprise, Martin began reducing provincial transfer payments, delayed the cutting of EI premiums and started reining in the deficit, eventually balancing the books in the 1997–1998 fiscal year.

An observer may well shrug and say some international arm-twisting and a healthy right-wing Opposition are all you need to keep the Liberals on a small-c conservative track in this country. They would be mistaken. In the long term, such a conservative shift is unsustainable because statism is embedded in Liberal thinking and in the current system of government. The Liberals' entrenchment of big government produces a constant leftward drift, because calls for redistribution of wealth (which are funded by the state itself, as we have seen) will always be louder than calls for the creation of wealth. And as we have shown previously, the Conservative Party is hardly a reliable watchdog, having itself wandered to the left of the Liberal Party on more than one occasion.

For a true small-c conservative government to take power, the groundwork must first be laid outside the party—and it is in business's interest to do so. Shaping a less statist culture and philosophy is a wise investment, one that will pay dividends for years down the road. Building a nation that values hard work and advancement based on merit and not enforced equality will inevitably lead to a more robust business climate and a stronger, more market-driven economy.

The Funding Challenge

The benefits to business of small-c conservatism and its market-driven principles are not hard to grasp. A smaller government extracts fewer taxes; this frees up more capital for companies to invest. It leads to improved productivity as resources are not wasted on bloated governments. It means more privatization, opening new opportunities for businesses to sell services. It creates a more entrepreneurial climate that encourages talent to stay in Canada, stemming the "brain drain" and developing domestic industry.

For example, consider the opportunities for Canadian business if the government were to allow the development of a private parallel health care system alongside a universal public system. Apart from the benefits to citizens—shorter waiting times, more choice of services, better quality care—the benefits to the economy would be enormous. The Canadian Independent Medical Clinics Association estimates a domestic private health care industry could be worth $10 to $40 billion in additional private investment per year, generating thousands of jobs and markets for products and services. American health care consumers might well come north of the border to take advantage of the exchange rate.

Today, faced with a Liberal minority government that has sold its soul to the NDP, corporate Canada can see what the Liberals are really about: power at any cost, regardless of the consequences. And business leaders are becoming alarmed.

In June 2005, the Canadian Council of Chief Executives, a national pro-business lobby, released a stinging report describing Canada as "adrift" and warning that years of progress were being "frittered away" by the actions of the minority Liberal government. The document was signed by six corporate titans: Gwyn Morgan of EnCana Corporation, Dominic D'Alessandro of Manulife Financial, Gordon Nixon of the Royal Bank, Paul Desmarais, Jr., of Power Corporation, Rick George of Suncor Energy and Jacques Lamarre of SNC-Lavalin.

Their report said: "In the political arena, the very idea of strategic policy-making is drowning in the swirling search for momentary tactical advantage. What is painfully absent today is any ambitious vision of what Canada could achieve over the next five to 10 years and any coherent strategy for realizing this vision in ways that could mobilize support across Canadian society." They called on the federal government to focus on six principles, including public sector reform, more public–private partnerships, lower taxes, boosting productivity and attracting higher-skilled immigrants.[23]

Yet, the very men who signed this document represent companies that are some of the country's biggest Liberal backers. Between 1993 and 2003, Power Corporation gave a total of $528,402.32 to the Liberal Party of Canada, not including donations from the company's subsidiaries or the individual donations from owners and senior executives. (Those were also numerous—André Desmarais, Paul Jr.'s brother and another company exec, is married to Jean Chrétien's daughter, France.) To be fair, Power did give $453,021.70 to the old PC and Reform/Alliance parties in the same period.[24]

SNC Lavalin gave $471,885.91 to the Liberals between 1993 and 2003, and a paltry $68,583.41 to the PC and Reform and Alliance parties over the same period. EnCana gave $316,911.04 to the Liberals from 1993 to 2003 and $246,931.01 to the old Tories and Reform/Alliance.[25] (It is interesting that an Alberta-based energy company so willingly filled the coffers of the party that brought us the National Energy Program.) Suncor gave $91,380.46 to the Liberals and $88,094.21 to the centre-right parties, while Manulife gave $149,430.15 to the Liberals and $129,650.25 to the two conservative parties. The Royal Bank was the only company to give more to the Reform/Alliance and Tories: a grand total of $701,029.01 from 1993 to 2003 to the right and $576,304.83 to the Liberals.[26]

So even though the Liberal Party has instilled statism as the national virtue, business has continued to pour money into Grit coffers—so much so that the party has been virtually beholden to Big Business in the last decade for its survival.

Why? Most businesspeople are not ideological. They are pragmatic. They don't want to rock the boat. They have no use for the opposition, really, because only the government can create or change laws that will benefit or hurt them. And because so many Canadian industries are highly regulated (the media being one of the most regulated, as we will see in the next chapter), business can't afford to offend the governing party.

This explains why, for example, the country's big banks load up their government affairs departments with people with connections to the Grits and praise the Liberals' budgets. As the *National Post*'s John Turley-Ewart explained, the head of government relations at the Royal Bank, Charles Coffey, is a partisan Liberal and has for the past two years "been promoting the Liberals' national daycare program" while the bank's economics department "has been cheering big-spending Liberal budgets."[27] The head of Scotiabank's government relations operations, Kaz Flynn, is a former John Turner hack who worked for one-time Nova Scotia Liberal premier John Savage. The bank of Montreal's Paul Deegan has Liberal connections and Gregory Tsang of CIBC worked in the finance department under Paul Martin. Turley-Ewart says the government relations departments "find themselves supporting Liberal social programs that call for even more spending" because they want bank mergers, "yet the banks never get their payback and unwittingly support the clientism Grits have successfully used to co-opt business in Canada."[28]

But as the business community filled Liberal coffers, they got virtually nothing in return. Not only are banks still waiting for the go-ahead on mergers, a September 2005 study from the C.D. Howe Institute reported that at 39 percent, Canada's marginal effective tax rate on business capital was the second highest of 36 industrialized and leading developing countries.[29]

To be fair, business also never had a good reason to give more to the conservatives in the 1990s because they were split in two parties. Most people, business elites included, realized that conservatives could never form the government as long as they remained divided. If conservatives couldn't even get their own internal affairs in order, what right did they have to run the country?

In the Liberal decade from 1993 to 2003, Canada's business community gave $91,436,281 to the Liberals, $39,253,276 to the old PC Party and $18,089,629 to the Reform/Alliance. Take a look at the years 2001 to 2003 alone:

Business/corporate federal giving from 2001–2003

Year	Canadian Alliance	Progressive Conservative Party of Canada	Combined totals for "conservative" parties	Liberal Party of Canada
2003	$1.3 million	$1.2 million	$2.5 million	$10.8 million
2002	$1.1 million	$1 million	$2.2 million	$5.1 million
2001	$860,000	$1.5 million	$2.4 million	$6.5 million

Source: Elections Canada, statements of contributions received.[30]

And the Conservatives are derided as the party of Big Business? Think again.

In each of these years, the Liberals received more than twice as much money as the combined conservative parties, and in 2003—the last year in which business could give big bucks to the parties—the Grits astonishingly raked in more than four times as much.

With the new fundraising rules, however, corporate Canada cannot continue to fill the Liberal financial belly. Indeed, the Chrétien legislation banning corporate donations is severely hamstringing Grit fundraising efforts. In 2004, without the help of their corporate pals, the Liberals took in $5.2 million in private donations while the Tories took in $10.9 million.[31] In the first quarter of 2005, the Conservatives raised $2.6 million, compared with $2.2 million for the Liberals.[32] Obviously the Conservatives have more individual donors on their side.

These donors now need to turn their attention to where it matters: to the building of a conservative infrastructure. This applies to money old and new. Hal Jackman, Hugh Mackenzie, Michael Sabia, James Kinnear, Bob King, Jim Pattison, Jim Ross, Harry Steele and countless other conservative benefactors of means great and small—the conservative movement needs you! Canada needs you! If you truly believe in this country and want to make it a better place, you can make a lasting difference by funding the initiatives that will help move our nation forward with confidence into the twenty-first century.

And there is no end of work to be done. As the following chapters will show, from the classroom to the courtroom, there are plenty of liberal fields where a thousand conservative flowers need to bloom. All they need is the funding to start growing.

Endnotes

1. Author interview with Don Abelson, September 2004 (hereinafter Abelson).

2. Abelson.

3. E-mail interview with Link Byfield, July 25, 2005. What was left of the Northern Foundation was later taken over by extreme rightists who allegedly had links to racist groups like the Heritage Front.

4. Author interview with Ken Azzopardi, July 26, 2005.

5. A. Abigail Payne, "Firm Foundations: Putting Private and Public Foundations on Level Ground," C. D. Howe Institute Backgrounder, No. 88 (February 2005), 1 (hereinafter Payne).

6. Canadian Revenue Association, Summary Policy CSP-C01, October 25, 2002. www.cra-arc.gc.ca/tax/charities/policy/csp/csp-c01-e.html

7. CRA's website. www.cra-arc.gc.ca/tax/charities/policy/csp/csp-p02-e.html

8. Payne, 4: "In general, foundations are designed to collect and then distribute at least 50% of their income to registered charitable organizations."

9. Payne, 4.

10. Canadian Taxpayers Federation,"Up, Up and Away: Corporate Welfare Takes Off," News Release, May 13, 2005. www.taxpayer.com/main/news.php?news_id=2007 (hereinafter Canadian Taxpayers Federation).

11. Canadian Taxpayers Federation.

12. Canadian Taxpayers Federation.

13. Unofficial Canadian Political Contributions Search Tool, Bound by Gravity. www.boundbygravity.com/SEC/ECSearch.aspx (hereinafter Bound by Gravity).

14. Mark Milke, *Tax Me, I'm Canadian* (Calgary: Thomas and Black Publishers, 2002), 118 (hereinafter Milke).

15. Milke, 119–123.

16. Author interview with Preston Manning, March 31, 2005 (hereinafter Manning).

17. Manning.

18. Author interview with Sylvia LeRoy, September 2004.

19. Oliver Moore, "Charitable Foundations Reaping the Benefits of Canadians' Largesse," *The Globe and Mail*, April 21, 2005, A5.

20. Author interview with Mike Harris, July 5, 2005.

21. "The Federal Debt," Statistics Canada website. http://72.14.207.104/search?q=cache:ewq0vjVd6R4J:142.206.72.67/03/03a/03a_005d_e.htm+canada+deficit+debt+1995&hl=en

22. "IMF pressing Ottawa to Slash Billions More in Deficit Fight," *Southam News*, December 10, 1995, citing the International Monetary Fund, "Consultation with Canada, Statement of the Fund Mission," Ottawa, December 7, 1995.

23. Paul Vieira, "Canada 'adrift': CEOs: Political 'Vacuum' Threatens Nation's Standard of Living," *National Post*, June 28, 2005.

24. Bound by Gravity.

25. EnCana was created by the merger between the Alberta Energy Corporation and the PanCanadian Energy Corporation in 2002. These figures include the pre-merger donations of the separate entities.

26. This includes only donations made under the name "Royal Bank" and does not include money from affiliates such as RBC Dominion Securities.

27. John Turley-Ewart, "The Problem with Merger Hype," *Financial Post*, July 26, 2005, 19 (hereinafter Turley-Ewart).

28. Turley-Ewart.

29. Jacqueline Thorpe, "Taxes caging 'tiger': Canada's business taxes 2nd highest behind China's," *National Post*, September 21, 2005.

30. The figures for these donations can be found at www.elections.ca/scripts/ecfiscals2/Default.asp?L=E&Page=ChooseElection These include monetary and non-monetary donations.

31. "Liberals Struggle to Raise Money in New Era of Party Financing," *Canadian Press*, July 17, 2005. http://news.yahoo.com/s/cpress/20050717/ca_pr_on_na/liberal_party_finances

32. Paco Francoli, "Conservatives Out-fundraised Liberals in First Three Months," *Hill Times*, June 6, 2005. www.thehilltimes.ca/html/index.php?display=story&full_path=/2005/june/6/conslibs/&c=1

6 CHAPTER

REBALANCING THE MEDIA:
Image Is (Almost) Everything

"Most Canadians feel safe and comfortable with Liberal/liberal
values. Get over it"
— Antonia Zerbisias, *Toronto Star* media columnist

Conservatives should never underestimate the power of the press. The media are the filter through which Canadians receive their news and views of this country and the world. In Canada as elsewhere, journalists have the power to make or break public figures. If they're on your side, you have it made; if they're not, you're roadkill.

Case in point: former PM Jean Chrétien's testimony before the Gomery Sponsorship Inquiry in February 2005. After Justice John Gomery had derisively labelled Chrétien's taxpayer-funded, self-promoting golf balls "small-town cheap," the former PM produced a handful of similar balls, each bearing the name of a political leader, including that of former U.S. president Bill Clinton. Never mind that $355 million in public money had vanished into the coffers of Quebec ad firms: the media swooned like a giggly White House intern. "Le P'tit Gars de Shawinigan Is Back," trumpeted *The Globe and Mail*; "Chrétien's Revenge against the Westmount Snobs," snickered CTV's online news service.

Like most Liberals, Chrétien knows how to wow the press. He left the wetsuit in the closet, because he knew that humiliating someone else is much more fun than humiliating yourself. This is a lesson that many conservatives have yet to learn. Think of Stephen Harper sporting a clinging gold golf shirt while extolling the virtues of Belgium as a model of federalism or bashing gay marriage. Conservatives consistently play into the stereotypes that journalists have created of them—that is, they are bigoted, bumbling white men with bad fashion sense who would happily send women to the kitchen, gays to jail and journalists to the gulag.

Media Bias 101

Conservatives can never forget a basic fact: most of the media are out to get them. That's partly because most members of the media assume conservatives are out to get *them*. One might ask how CBC reporters can objectively cover the antics of the Conservative Party when, at various times, it or its predecessor parties directly threatened their jobs and livelihood. In light of the 2005 CBC lockout, Conservative Heritage Critic Bev Oda (quite sensibly) called for Parliament to debate the broadcaster's future. In 2002, MP Jim Abbott, then Conservative Party Heritage critic, told the *National Post*, "Why do we need [the CBC]? Why should we have it?"[1] A decade earlier, delegates to the 1991 Progressive Conservative Convention in Toronto had endorsed a resolution to privatize the CBC, which was quickly rejected by then-minister of Communications and future CBC president Perrin Beatty. Such a resolution would never have seen the light of day at a Liberal Party convention. *Au contraire*, big government—aka the Liberal government—pledges to continue to support the CBC, the arts, culture, the Canadian star system, and so on.

So despite cutbacks to the Mother Corp. during the Chrétien years, the Tories still pose a greater threat to its survival and that of the self-appointed cultural community at large. A Conservative government, it is feared, would padlock the CBC, kill all arts funding, let the Americans buy up our publishing industry and wipe out all upstart lefty magazines. As in any business, the lifeblood of the media is money, and unfortunately in Canada that often means taxpayer money. Whether it's direct funding for the CBC, documentary grants from Telefilm Canada or the National Film Board, or cash from various outfits like the Canada Council, it's our tax dollars that keep many Canadian journalists out of the unemployment line. So the media will scrutinize conservatives more closely than the Left, thus holding them to a double standard. It's been this way for decades. There are so many examples of this phenomenon that we could fill this entire book just citing them. Former Tory leader Robert Stanfield put it best, once observing that if he walked on water, the next day's headline would read "Stanfield Can't Swim."

After doing in Preston Manning and Stockwell Day, the media set its sights on Stephen Harper. One of the chief offenders in this regard is Canada's self-proclaimed "National Newspaper," *The Globe and Mail.* Much like the late Dalton Camp, *The Globe* is often erroneously described as "conservative." While it does espouse some small-c conservative views on its editorial pages, such as support for free market principles in the areas of trade and health care, it maintains a raging hate-on for the big-c Conservative Party and its leader.

For example, on May 14, 2005, the paper ran a piece by reporter Gloria Galloway, entitled: "Is Tory Leader Justifiably Hot at Liberals, or Just Too Angry?" If readers missed that, *The Globe* published not one but two op-eds on Harper that day: Jeffrey Simpson's "Come on Stephen, Will It Hurt You to Smile?" and Margaret Wente's "Mr. Harper and the Not Nice Politics of Rage." These articles appeared at the same time that some of the juiciest testimony at the Gomery Inquiry was playing out—yet dwelling on Harper's anger management skills was deemed more important.

The paper also ran a front-page story on May 2, 2005, titled "Tory MPs Question Need for Snap Vote," trying to show the Tory caucus was getting cold feet about forcing a spring 2005 election. The problem is, the article only cited one MP questioning the vote—Bruce-Grey-Owen Sound member Larry Miller. And when *The Globe* called Miller for a quote, guess what he was doing? Riding an ATV across the countryside! (What else do good ol' boy conservatives do for fun on the weekend?) Said the story: "Reached yesterday while riding his all-terrain vehicle, Mr. Miller struck a note more in tune with his party, insisting that the Liberals have lost the right to govern and must go. But he continued to suggest there's no rush. 'I think we should wait a little bit here,' Mr. Miller said."

Then there was the front-page headline story *The Globe* ran on May 27, 2005: "Christian Activists Capturing Tory Races: Some in the Party Worry New Riding Nominees Will Reinforce Notion of 'Hidden Agenda'." It was as if holding religious beliefs and running for office were a crime. Imagine a story where the word "Christian" was replaced with "black," "Jewish" or "Muslim." In addition, the story was pure hyperbole: only four of the Tories' 308 candidates were so-called Christian activists, hardly constituting a *coup d'état* of the party's agenda. But it certainly bolsters the Liberals' fear-mongering campaign against the Tory party.

There are some conservatives in Canadian print media. The *National Post*, while more centrist today under CanWest Global than it was under the ownership of Conrad Black from 1998 to 2001, is still supportive of many conservative views. The *Sun* chain of newspapers has a conservative editorial bent. Under the new leadership of *National Post* founding editor Ken Whyte, *Maclean's* has adopted a more balanced tone since its Day-bashing era. The magazine now features positive stories about conservatives and it questions the motives of unions. But the vast majority of print and TV media is still liberal.

And it's not just the journalists themselves who take sides. In January 2005, blogger and conservative pundit Stephen Taylor analyzed political party donations made by the CBC's board of directors. He found that 82 percent of their donations went to the Liberal Party of Canada, 15 percent to the Bloc Quebecois, and a measly 3 percent to the Conservative Party.[2] And in May 2005, the prime minister named Rai Sahi, chief executive of Morguard REIT, to the CBC board. According to John Spence of the online media watchdog www.cbcwatch.ca, Sahi is a personal friend of Prime Minister Martin's, a former business associate of Canada Steamship Lines and a donor to the Liberal Party. One of his companies, Morguard Corp., also happens to own the building the CBC leases as its head office in Ottawa.[3] (And lest we forget, the president of the CBC is directly appointed by the prime minister himself.)

There have been many academic studies of Canadian media bias too. Recently the Fraser Institute published a study of CBC's news coverage of the United States in the period between the terrorist attacks of September 11, 2001, and the March 2003 invasion of Iraq. Not surprisingly, media scholars Barry Cooper and Lydia Miljan found that negative comments about America outnumbered positive comments by more than two to one. Miljan and Cooper have found evidence of systemic left-wing bias in other Canadian media as well. Studies done by the Fraser Institute's now-defunct National Media Archive (NMA, which Miljan led) have shown that members of the Canadian media are more likely to be fans of big government and state intervention than the average Canadian.[4] The NMA analyzed the content of media coverage of more than eighty different political and economic issues in the 1990s. According to Miljan and Cooper, "one of the consistent findings has been that, on major issues, media coverage is not balanced and that the imbalance tends to favour the same position. Similar to [a study of] the US media, Canadian journalists have tended to support left-of-centre positions."[5]

Perhaps most alarmingly for conservatives, the NMA's research found that: "almost without exception, the media advocated increased government spending and regulation as the solution to the ills of society ... This pattern of reporting ... points to advocacy of an expanded state."[6]

Looking in the Mirror

Ironically, this reinforces statism under the guise of counterculture. It is assumed, often by journalists themselves, that they are a somewhat radical group, that they challenge the establishment, seek out the truth and expose injustices. Yet by advocating for more government intervention, journalists are not challenging anything at all: they are merely reinforcing the statist status quo. To act in a truly countercultural fashion, journalists today would have to demand less state intervention, not more, and more freedom, not less. But as writer and broadcaster Michael Coren succinctly puts it, "It's chic and fashionable to question conservatism."[7] Andrew Coyne has a more cynical view: "The ordinary journalist is too lazy and ill-read to have formed anything so coherent as an ideology. His attachment is not to right- or left-wing, but to convention; he seeks not to change society, but to be thought clever by his fellows."[8]

The problem with discussing media bias is that bias is in the eye of the beholder. The offending party members—media lefties—will never admit that they report with a certain slant. That's because they genuinely believe that their views are objective and impartial. They think the left-wing view is the one held by sensible people. It would never even occur to them that there are people who might question the fundamental premise of a given story or an assertion that they present as fact.

When Miljan and Cooper analyzed journalists' views about political, economic and social views, the results confirm what most conservatives already suspected: in many respects, the media leans toward statist, "progressive" and left-wing views more than the general population, and state-owned media even more so. In 1997 the scholars interviewed two sample groups, 804 ordinary Canadians and 270 journalists, through COMPAS public opinion research. They found that 36 percent of French-Canadian journalists described themselves as moderately left wing, vs. 19 percent of the general French-Canadian population. In the 1997 election, 20 percent of anglophone journalists voted NDP compared with 8 percent of the general anglophone population; 6 percent of francophone journalists supported the NDP, vs. 1 percent of the general francophone population. CBC English radio journalists were more likely to have voted NDP than English private-sector journalists: 40 percent vs. 14 percent. Fifty percent of English-speaking journalists and 44 percent of French-speaking journalists thought that communism in the former Soviet Union "may have been a good idea, but was wrecked by bad leadership" vs. 25 percent of the general anglophone population and 17 percent of the general francophone population.[9]

These kinds of views mirror American findings about the U.S. media. A study done by researchers Tim Groseclose of UCLA and Jeff Milyo of the University of Chicago found that 7 percent of journalists voted for George Bush in 1992 vs. 37 percent of the voting public.[10] A 2004 study by the Pew Research Center found that 34 percent of national journalists in the United States and 23 percent of local journalists describe themselves as liberals, compared with 19 percent of the public, while 7 percent of national news people and 12 percent of local journalists describe themselves as conservatives, compared with a third of all Americans.[11]

Unlike conservative Canadians, though, conservative Americans have their own news outlets to turn to for information—specific television networks such as the Fox News Channel, all manner of talk radio, and, increasingly, the Internet. In fact, another Pew study found that only 15 percent or fewer of Republican voters watch the evening news on ABC, CBS or NBC, compared with 34 percent of all Americans.[12] Fox, whose motto is "We report. You decide," has become the most successful cable news network in the country, consistently beating CNN in viewer rankings. So while left-wing bias exists, right-wing Americans can tune it out and get the information they want from a perspective that appeals to them.

Changing the Broadcasting Act

This is not the case in Canada—but it's something a Conservative government could someday remedy by amending certain sections of the Broadcasting Act. Section (i) (iv) of our Act mandates that broadcasters must "provide a reasonable opportunity for the public to be exposed to the expression of differing views on matters of public concern." Paradoxically, it is this very requirement of balance that makes it impossible for conservatives to establish conservative media outlets. Recently, writer Linda Frum wanted to set up a conservative radio station; friends in the industry told her "not to even bother" because she would never get CRTC approval for a "one-sided" station.[13] While Canadian talk radio has some right-of-centre voices—Charles Adler in Winnipeg, Lowell Green in Ottawa and Dave Rutherford in Alberta—these stations are required to give equal time to opposing views in the name of balance. A home-grown version of Fox News would never get a licence here, because it would be deemed to have a right-wing bias. (The CRTC only allowed the real Fox News to be broadcast in Canada in late 2004, and only after it had approved the anti-American, anti-Semitic Al-Jazeera Arab network). Yet as we have seen, the CBC and other broadcasters routinely express a left-wing bias, and they are still on the air.

How can this happen? Because this left-wing bias is written into our laws. It is actually prescribed by the content regulations of the Broadcasting Act. Section 3(1)(d) states that:

(d) the Canadian broadcasting system should
  (i)   serve to safeguard, enrich and strengthen the cultural, politi-
        cal, social and economic fabric of Canada...
  (iii) through its programming and the employment opportunities
        arising out of its operations, serve the needs and interests,
        and reflect the circumstances and aspirations, of Canadian
        men, women and children, including equal rights, the lin-
        guistic duality and multicultural and multiracial nature of
        Canadian society and the special place of aboriginal peoples
        within that society ...

This section of the Act not only prescribes that broadcasters strengthen and
safeguard our social "fabric," *it defines what that fabric is made of.*
Questioning the values enumerated in Section 3 would be "un-Canadian."
A network that made it its sole business to question policies of enforced
equality, of state-funded multiculturalism and of the need for aboriginal
self-government would not be fulfilling the criteria set out in the Act. It
would not be granted a license. Never mind that there are hundreds of
voices out there expressing the opposite point of view, such as ethnic specialty channels and the Aboriginal People's Television Network. Those
stations are within the law. They are not required to balance their views because their views are assumed to be correct in law. The result is that those
voices grow louder and louder, entrenching the state's Trudeauesque vision
of the Canadian identity and drowning out any dissenting voices.

    Yet there are many Canadians who disagree. No one would deny that
Canada is a multicultural, multiracial country with a significant aboriginal population. No one would deny the Charter of Rights protects our
right to equality. But many people question the wisdom of the policies
the federal government has implemented in relation to these realities.
They would argue that the government has played politics of division,
encouraging Canadian society to coalesce into myriad interest groups
whose only common element is that they depend on the government for
their survival and privileged status. Where is the overarching Canadian
identity in that? And why shouldn't conservatives be allowed to present
the other side?

Until 1987, the United States had a similar "fairness" doctrine in its broadcast regulations. The Federal Communications Commission (its version of the CRTC) had issued this policy in 1949, encouraging radio stations to air editorial opinion while requiring them to seek opposing viewpoints for rebuttal. However, "[d]espite its apparent intent of bringing more political diversity and debate to broadcasting, the Fairness Doctrine seemed to have the opposite effect. Many station owners simply avoided taking controversial positions on the air, thus relieving themselves of any obligation to seek out political opponents for the purpose of giving them free airtime."[14] The policy was repeatedly challenged as a violation of First Amendment rights and it is no longer enforced as a consequence of a commission proceeding and a federal court's decision in the case of *Syracuse Peace Council v. FCC*, 867 F. 2d 654 (D.C. Cir., 1989).[15] The result was the proliferation of conservative radio and television news outlets in the 1990s.

Broadcasting content should not be regulated by anything but the public taste and laws prohibiting obscenity and the incitement of hatred. Even *The Globe*, to its credit, called for the abolition of the CRTC in an editorial on June 17, 2005 arguing that "[w]ith cable TV, satellite TV and now satellite radio, viewers and listeners can choose from hundreds of options at the click of a remote. To have a group of federal officials deciding which of those options Canadians should and should not be allowed to see is like having a special tribunal deciding which kinds of mustard or soup supermarkets can put on their shelves."

Another argument for getting rid of the CRTC has to do with its June 2004 decision not to renew the broadcasting licence of the popular Quebec City radio station CHOI-FM. The CRTC said the station had been "the subject of numerous complaints with respect to the conduct of the hosts and the spoken word content that is aired, including offensive comments, personal attacks and harassment." Apparently the CRTC found it offensive that "the station's hosts were relentless in their use of the public airwaves to insult and ridicule people." And, shock and surprise, the CRTC claimed in its decision that CHOI was not meeting "the objectives of the broadcasting policy for Canada set out in the *Broadcasting Act*."[16] The CRTC chided CHOI for what it called "remarks that could expose individuals or groups to hatred or contempt," thus creating "harm" that "undermines the cultural, political and social fabric of Canada. ..."[17]

Thank you, taste police. Obviously, the citizens of Quebec City must have a different standard of programming, because CHOI was the most popular radio station in town. It was also unapologetically right wing and anti-establishment. Residents were outraged at the decision—so much so that tens of thousands of Quebecers took to the streets in protest. Five thousand or so even made their way to Parliament Hill in Ottawa to show their disgust.[18] The station appealed the CRTC's decision in federal court, and it is now on its way to the Supreme Court of Canada.

Championing CHOI's cause would have been a great way for the federal Tories to make some political hay in Quebec. Unfortunately, they were asleep at the dial, showing their usual reluctance to get out in front of issues. While Mario Dumont's Action Democratique du Québec rode the pro-CHOI wave to a September 2004 provincial by-election victory, the Conservatives failed to substantively weigh in on the debate until the story was off the front pages.

Ultimately, however, the CRTC is not the main issue—the Broadcasting Act is. Unless the law is changed, abolishing the CRTC will not change the underlying requirements for broadcasts in Canada. But removing or reforming the CRTC is important for another reason. In an age of media convergence, media owners become beholden to the commission for more than just a TV licence. Companies like CanWest Global, which owns television, radio and print outlets, and Rogers Communications, which also sells cable TV, cellular, telephone and Internet services, depend on the CRTC to license most of those outlets and services. This dependency has the potential to impact editorial decisions in their media outlets, including whether to challenge the dominant statist ideology—or even the party in power. The *Western Standard*'s publisher, Ezra Levant, says it creates "a type of libel chill. If you go too far you may find restrictions on your TV or radio licence."[19]

If conservatism is to succeed in Canada, conservatives must inject some semblance of ideological balance into the media. They should make the point that increased deregulation of the broadcasting industry will not benefit them only, but all Canadians, by allowing the establishment of an unfettered marketplace of ideas. Canadian identity should not be dictated by bureaucrats in Ottawa or self-appointed elites in ivory towers. It should not be an identity of enforced equality, where the CBC is an entity more equal than others. It should be determined by Canadian viewers through the expression of their choices as to what programs they want to consume.

More than anything, the CBC should reflect this, since it is directly funded by taxpayers. This is where conservatives should advocate another type of reform. Short of privatizing the CBC (which in a 400-channel universe is having more and more trouble justifying its existence), the network should at least have to raise its own funds directly from the viewing public. This process could be facilitated by simply having members of the public check a box on their income tax forms; or the CBC could conduct its own pledge drives, like PBS in the U.S. If Canadians really want the CBC, let them make it in their own image: a station of the people, for the people. If it cannot survive, then arguably it shouldn't be getting public funding in the first place.

Unfortunately, conservatives cannot change the Broadcasting Act, the CRTC or the CBC until they send a conservative government to Ottawa. So in the meantime, what should they do to rebalance the media and get their message out?

Playing the Game

First, until there are more right-wingers on the media's front lines, conservatives have to play by its current rules. Like any other institution, the press operates by its particular code of ethics, behaviour and routines. These are often either misunderstood or ignored by conservatives, in particular the Conservative Party, at their peril.

Two cases in point: first, when erstwhile Alliance leader Stockwell Day decided to hold daily press briefings in the Charles Lynch Media Theatre in the Centre Block of the House of Commons, instead of holding the customary scrum in the foyer after Question Period, this meant Parliamentary reporters had to scramble from the foyer (where every other politician was) down the stairs to the Theatre just to get Day's sound bite. Second, at the Conservative Party convention in Montreal in 2005, journalists covering the event were refused a lowly box lunch, and had to literally scrounge among the leftovers after delegates had been fed. Small details, perhaps, but these unnecessary irritants only predisposed the press to hating the Conservatives all the more.

It would behoove all conservative candidates and politicos to shadow a member of the press to better understand how the media does its job. The time limits of the news cycle, camera shortages, and even lack of coffee can turn the most professional reporter into a pit bull looking to exercise its jaws. While no one says the media should be coddled, a healthy appreciation for the challenges of the job is essential.

Conservatives, both big and small-c, should remember that what all journalists most value is respect. Despite our culture's obsession with media and with the personalities that populate it, there are still many sectors of society, especially professionals and businesspersons, who harbour a disdain for the scurrilous minions of the press. Conservatives can be disproportionately found in these groups, and shoot themselves in the foot when they let their contempt show through. It is perhaps no wonder that the Canadian leaders most beloved by modern media (Pierre Trudeau, René Lévesque) had been journalists themselves, while some of the most despised and ridiculed (Brian Mulroney, John Turner) were businessmen and lawyers. They don't realize that the Respect Factor is huge, and that like common courtesy, it can take you very far in your dealings with the media.

Conservatives should also realize that what the press wants are sto- ries—and what they love are narrative stories about political leaders. Once they latch on to one, they rarely change the script. Trudeau was the sexy debonair intellectual. Jean Chrétien was the "little guy from Shawinigan." But Brian Mulroney was an arrogant Montreal lawyer who wore Gucci shoes, and Preston Manning, Stockwell Day and Stephen Harper are all angry Albertans whose views are out-of-touch with real Canadians. The media is constantly hammering home their pre-conceived storylines about political players, which fit into news consumers' predispositions. Conservatives have to work on spinning the narrative in a way that is positive for them.

And how should a conservative cope when faced with a journalist who is asking disrespectful questions? Answer: Fake it. Never ever let them see you sweat. Charm is the best offensive. Frustrating, yes, but there is nothing more confusing to a journalist out to skewer a victim than a polite victim, especially one who confounds preconceived notions of what conservatives should be (i.e., smug, disrespectful, eats widows and orphans for breakfast).

The moral of the story is simple. If they like you, it will be harder for them to kill you. And since you are a conservative, they won't expect to like you, which will leave them somewhat defenceless and confused. An important truth to remember is that some of the nicest people are lefties. They're not bad people, they're just misguided. So until the world is populated with right-wing journalists, conservatives should kill the others with kindness, whenever possible.

Changing the Rules

In the long term, the rules must be changed, or else conservatives, no matter how well-behaved, will too often continue to be lambs to the media slaughter. This means becoming the people who call the shots, not just those who answer the questions. If the medium is the message, then the medium needs to be more conservative.

Where should conservatives start? Simple—on the Internet.

Charlotte Bell, the vice-president of Regulatory Affairs at Global Television and a previous policy adviser to former CRTC chairman Keith Spicer, told us: "If I wanted to do single-issue programming, I wouldn't bother with conventional broadcasting mediums. I'd go to the Internet."[20] In May 1999, the CRTC decided to leave the Internet out of its regulatory grasp. As a result, the Net is still the Wild West of media.

New weblogs are springing up daily—and many of them are conservative. Initiatives such as the "Blogging Tories" (www.bloggingtories.ca) help coordinate conservative-minded bloggers across the country. Conservative journalists like the *National Post*'s Colby Cosh and Lorne Gunter, as well as the *Calgary Herald*'s Danielle Smith, are now blogging. www.freedominion.ca is a popular online conservative message board.

News portals such as Neale News (www.nealenews.com), which is similar to the U.S.-based Drudge Report, have the ability to quickly draw attention to a breaking news story.

The Web (and blogs in particular) is conservatism's best hope. The Internet is free and uncensored. There are no filters. There are no middlemen—just the broadcaster, writer and reader. Like Ronald Reagan in his radio commentaries, conservatives do best when they talk directly to the people. And as more and more people get their news online, grassroots influences will continue to grow. Because of that, the possibilities are limitless.

Second, conservatives must know the enemy and publicize their activities. They should establish a conservative media monitoring centre, similar to such U.S. groups as the Media Research Centre (MRC) and Accuracy in Media (AIM). AIM and the MRC monitor left-wing bias in the press, draw attention to the media's liberal spin and refute their false claims. Conservatives need a giant bias detector working around the clock. A Canadian version would not only track bias in the news, but could aim to help reverse it. It could sensitize the public, conduct educational programs, make complaints to the CRTC and lobby to change laws that limit free speech. Since the Fraser Institute no longer maintains its National Media Archive, conservative philanthropists should step in and found such an organization.

Third, conservatives must promote the education of more conservative-minded journalists. They must encourage them to be not only opinion writers but to go into hard reporting jobs at mainstream news outlets. Also, since journalism is not a lucrative profession in Canada, monetary incentives must be created. These include the establishment of fellowships and scholarships to facilitate study, reward excellence and develop talent. The Atkinson Fellowship at the *Toronto Star* is one of the most coveted in the country—it provides left-wing journalists with a wonderful year-long research sabbatical and a stipend, as well as the subsequent publication of a series of articles based on their work. Conservative philanthropists should establish a similar program for right-leaning journalists.

Fourth, conservatives must establish more print media. It is fine to criticize national newspapers for bias. Keep in mind, however, that in

Canada, most voters don't read them. The paper with the biggest circulation is the *Toronto Star*. Most people read only their local paper. This is where the action is—and the action needs to be more conservative. In addition, the local weekly frequently sits around the house like a coffee table magazine, and it is picked up and read repeatedly by both household visitors and neighbours.

And what of conservative magazines? The left has its standard-bearers: *Adbusters, This* magazine and the *Walrus*, to name just three. The latter, which did not even exist two years ago, was started by left-wing Toronto philanthropist Ken Alexander, and it has gone on to win a slew of journalism awards. Meanwhile, the right has the *Fraser Forum*, which hardly qualifies as a popular read, and the *Western Standard*. The publisher of the latter is breathing fresh life into the conservative literary scene, a scene that has seen other publications come and go.[21] But these publications cannot do it alone. Conservatives must create a dozen *Western Standard*s east of the Manitoba–Ontario border—the area where conservatism needs the most help.

Finally, not all journalism happens in papers, magazines, radio and TV. The right-wing printed word also gets short shrift from Canadian book publishers. As conservative authors, including yours truly, can attest, getting a book with a conservative slant published in Canada is like pulling teeth. (Perhaps this has something to do with the government grants Canadian publishers receive?)

To rescue the right, conservatives must stop hating the media—and become the media. They must get to the other side of the keyboard, Internet portal and camera lens, or they will always be on the outside looking in.

Endnotes

1. Jane Taber, "'Elites' should pay for CBC, Liberal MP says: 'Chemical traces' of a television audience," *National Post*, February 5, 2002, A1. Abbott believes the CBC English-language service should be scrapped and some of its news gathering functions transferred to CBC Newsworld.

2. Blog of Stephen Taylor. www.stephentaylor.ca/archives/000179.html

3. Blog of cbc.watch. http://72.14.207.104/search?q=cache:XcEGJerZTNMJ:www.cbcwatch.ca/%3Fq%3Dnode/view/1111+sahi+cbc+morguard&hl=en

4. Founded in 1987, the NMA was created to "acquire, preserve and make available a complete resource of news coverage in Canada," assess said news coverage in terms of how issues are represented, and encourage other researchers to "research the public information function performed by the national media." Lydia Miljan and Barry Cooper, *Hidden Agendas: How Journalists Influence the News* (Vancouver: UBC Press, 2003), 42 (hereinafter Miljan and Cooper).

5. Miljan and Cooper, 42.

6. Miljan and Cooper, 48.

7. Michael Coren, "The Liberal Media Bias," *The Toronto Sun*, September 25, 2004.

8. Andrew Coyne, "Readers less gullible than institute thinks," *Financial Post*, August 9, 1989, 11.

9. Miljan and Cooper, 67–94.

10. Bruce Bartlett, "The Economics of Media Bias," *National Review* Online, June 23, 2004. www.nationalreview.com/nrof_bartlett/bartlett200406230852.asp (hereinafter Bartlett).

11. Pew Research Center, "Bottom-Line Pressure Now Hurting Coverage, Say Journalists: Press Going Too Easy on Bush," May 23, 2004, Section IV, "Values and the Press." http://people-press.org/reports/display.php3?ReportID=214

12. Pew Research Center, "News Audiences Increasingly Politicized," June 8, 2004. http://people-press.org/reports/display.php3?ReportID=215

13. Author interview with Linda Frum, March 22, 2005.

14. "Broadcasting, Radio and Television," Encyclopedia article, Microsoft Encarta. http://encarta.msn.com/encyclopedia_761566157_4/Broadcasting.html

15. Federal Communications Commission FactSheet. www.fcc.gov/mb/facts/program.html

16. CRTC press release, "The CRTC Decides Not to Renew the Licence of CHOI-FM Québec," July 13, 2004. www.crtc.gc.ca/eng/NEWS/RELEASES/2004/r040713.htm

17. Broadcasting Decision, CRTC 2004-271, Ottawa, July 13, 2004, par. 61. www.crtc.gc.ca/archive/ENG/Decisions/2004/db2004-271.htm

18. "CHOI-FM Fans Rally to Protest Station Shutdown," *CTV News*, August 11, 2004. www.ctv.ca/servlet/ArticleNews/story/CTVNews/1092138768829_82/?hub=TopStories

19. Author interview with Ezra Levant, May 27, 2005.

20. Author interview with Charlotte Bell, June 9, 2005.

21. Examples include Michael Taube's *From the Right*, the *Idler*, the *Northern Institute Quarterly*, *Gravitas*, Peter Worthington's *Influence Magazine*, and *Alberta Report* in its many incarnations.

7 CHAPTER

CALL IN THE LAWYERS!:
Can Conservatives Make Friends with the Charter?

"Bad laws are the worst sort of tyranny."
— Edmund Burke

The cornerstone of any free and democratic society is a fair and accessible legal system. "The law is reason free of passion," said Aristotle, meaning that law should not be influenced by the whims of emotion and extraneous considerations. To the extent that modern legal concepts have strayed from that notion of black-letter law, one often wonders if law is not often devoid of reason as well.

The Canadian legal system is unusual, in that it incorporates two legal traditions, civil and common law, the legacy of the French and English founders of our country.[1] But this dualism is hardly the main factor that defines our legal landscape today. It is in the area of rights-based law that the greatest changes have and continue to take place, thanks to the 1981 patriation of our Constitution and the attendant adoption of the Charter of Rights and Freedoms.

The Charter has fundamentally changed the way the law and public policy evolve in Canada. Designed to protect minorities from Alexis de Tocqueville's infamous "tyranny of the majority," it instead imposed a new tyranny: that of interest groups on the legal system. For conservatives, it's been the judicial equivalent of the Siege of Leningrad, as court case after court case battered right-wing views on nearly every social and fiscal issue.

Charter Fallout

The notion of a constitutionally entrenched charter was conceived in the fertile brain of the late Prime Minister Pierre Trudeau. It was not foreseen as a means of protecting a wide spectrum of rights, but as a way to embed the country's two solitudes. According to Osgoode Hall Law professor Michael Mandel, "Trudeau saw the entrenchment of a general Bill of Rights, that is one not restricted to language rights, as an *expedient*, as a means to break the logjam of constitutional reform, which was itself just an expedient to his goal of entrenched bilingualism."[2]

Trudeau's Charter entrenchment project, which he began fomenting as minister of justice under Pearson in 1967, accelerated dramatically after the election of the Parti Québécois in Quebec in 1976 and the subsequent referendum on sovereignty-association. In his famous federalist plea made at the Paul Sauvé Arena in Montreal, on May 14, 1980, Trudeau gave a "solemn commitment" to "renew the Constitution." Immediately after the referendum, he announced that he had only two pre-conditions for this renewal exercise: a strong federal government and a charter with language rights.[3] He went so far as to say that "we consider everything else to be negotiable."[4]

Instead of a negotiation, it turned into more of a capitulation, as far as conservatives were concerned. A parade of left-wing lobby groups appeared at the hearings on the proposed charter. Most of them were the same groups created by the government through Secretary of State funding during the previous decade (discussed in detail in Chapter 4).[5] Feminist organizations were highly prominent. Representatives from the National Action Committee on the Status of Women (NAC) "successfully urged the rewording of their favorite Charter provision—section 15 [on equality rights]—and succeeded in inserting s. 28, which exempts the principle of equality of the sexes from the notwithstanding clause."[6] Together with the Canadian Civil Liberties Association, "feminists heavily influenced the wording of key Charter sections" including the original version of section 1, which women's groups demanded put a stronger onus on the government to justify laws that infringed Charter rights.[7]

From the start, it was clear that the left intended to use the Charter to advance its view of equality (read: the state enforced kind.) A long list of interest groups, including the Charter Committee on Poverty Issues, Equality for Gays and Lesbians Everywhere (EGALE), the Canadian Prisoners' Rights Network, the Canadian Committee on Refugees and the Equality Rights Committee of the Canadian Ethnocultural Council, sprang up and began litigating test cases. Between 1988 and 1998 organizations presented 819 claims and intervened in 30 percent of cases heard by the Federal and Supreme Courts.[8] Two decades later, "interest group litigation is now an established form of collective action."[9]

Since conservatives have been an oppressed minority in so many elections, you would think they would have invoked that status somewhere along the line. Maybe they just couldn't find the right lawyer. By contrast, the feminist movement found a whole battalion of them. In 1984, the Canadian Advisory Council on the Status of Women published a paper calling for the creation of a unified national "legal action fund" to coordinate and fund the systematic litigation of strategic test cases.[10] Though technically women are a majority at 51 percent of the population, this led to the founding of LEAF, a women's Legal Education and Action Fund, in 1985. LEAF has since become the most frequent interest group intervenor at the Supreme Court.[11] Its goal is "to advance the equality of women in Canada through litigation, law reform, and public education using the *Canadian Charter of Rights and Freedoms*."[12]

LEAF decided to attack any law that discriminated against a woman's right to what it deemed "substantive equality."[13] Substantive equality is the Orwellian concept that in order to be equal, different groups must not be treated the same—they must be treated differently. In simpler terms, it's like handicapping a golf game. Because you did badly in the last round, you get to start a few strokes ahead of the pack in the next. As head golf pro, the state becomes a massive social engineer, constantly "correcting" whatever inequalities are identified, even in situations where those inequalities have a rational basis or could be overcome by means other than state intervention.

LEAF was instrumental in entrenching this concept in law through its advocacy in the case of *Andrews v. Law Society of British Columbia*.[14] Ironically, the plaintiff was a British white male lawyer, who argued that the B.C. Law Society's refusal to admit him because he wasn't a Canadian citizen was discriminatory. Not exactly your classic victim, but LEAF went to bat for him anyway because the case had the potential to advance the "substantive equality" doctrine. And so it did. The Court's decision in favour of Andrews laid the foundation for more successful challenges down the road involving freedom of speech, abortion, gay rights and pornography.[15]

Andrews also advanced what is known as the "political disadvantage theory." Politically disadvantaged groups are those whose interests are excluded from, or do not dominate, other branches of government, such as the executive or the legislature.[16] They resort to the courts to attain the objectives they cannot achieve in the democratic arena. The concept is actually drawn from a footnote in the 1938 American Supreme Court case of *United States v. Carolene Products Co.*[17] Apparently this footnote was of great inspiration to Canadian Supreme Court judges, including former Justice Bertha Wilson, who wrote in *Andrews*:

> I believe also that it is important to note that the range of discrete and insular minorities has changed and will continue to change with changing political and social circumstances. For example, [American Supreme Court Justice] Stone J. writing in 1938, was concerned with religious, national and racial minorities. In enumerating the specific grounds in s. 15, the framers of the Charter embraced these concerns in 1982 but also addressed themselves to the difficulties experienced by the disadvantaged on the grounds of ethnic origin, colour, sex, age and physical and mental disability. *It can be anticipated that the discrete and insular minorities of tomorrow will include groups not recognized as such today* [emphasis added]. It is consistent with the constitutional status of s. 15 that it be interpreted with sufficient

flexibility to ensure the "unremitting protection" of equality rights in the years to come.[18]

This desire to include the minorities of tomorrow led the Supreme Court to adopt the "reading-in" doctrine in *Schacter v. Canada*,[19] another case in which LEAF intervened in favour of a healthy white male. In that matter, an adoptive father sought the same paternity leave benefits as a natural father. *Schacter* established that courts could "read in" provisions that weren't already in the Charter, to protect Wilson's ever-expanding list of "discrete and insular minorities." Possibly the most controversial use of this doctrine was to later read in sexual orientation as a prohibited ground of discrimination under section 15, as analogous to race, sex, religion or age.

Ironically, by the time of the *Andrews* judgment in 1989, the "disadvantaged groups" theory had long been abandoned by the U.S. judiciary.[20] One might ask why the Canadian high court based its interpretation of our brand-new Charter on a discredited American precedent, especially given the Left's supposed distaste for most things American. Could it be because there were suddenly many loud well-funded left-wing interest groups with clever lawyers clamouring for it do so? As Professor Michael Mandel puts it, "The rights in the *Charter* depart from the democratic rule of law in every important respect ... [i]t is clear we are closer to the rule of *lawyers* than the rule of law."[21]

Arming the Opposition ... Again

Which begs the next question: where did interest groups such as LEAF get the money to launch their legal challenges? Answer: from the Canadian taxpayer, courtesy of the Progressive Conservative government of Brian Mulroney. That's right: it was then-Justice Minister John Crosbie and Secretary of State Benoît Bouchard who expanded the Court Challenges Program (CCP) to extend funding to section 15 equality challenges.[22]

Interest groups had been pressuring the government's Committee on Equality Rights to recommend such a move, as they were "frustrated by ... Crosbie's unwillingness to adopt a substantive interpretation of the

Charter's Equality rights.[23] In 1985 Crosbie beat them to the punch and allocated $9 million to the CCP over five years. Five years later, the Tories renewed the program and upped its five-year budget to $12 million.[24] This was a bad enough move in good financial circumstances, but an inexcusable one given the size of the federal deficit at the time.

The CCP had initially been set up by the Trudeau government in 1977 to fund language-law challenges, in particular to Quebec's Bill 101. By 1984–85 the CCP's budget was $200,000 a year.[25] In other words, the Tories not only grew the CCP's mandate but increased its funding tenfold.

Worse yet, there was little government monitoring of how the money was spent. The funding process "operated autonomously,"[26] and after 1989, the government turned the entire administration of the program over to the Human Rights Centre at the University of Ottawa.[27] The inmates were now running the asylum.

One starts to understand why conservatism can't get ahead in this country. Even when they controlled the purse strings, the Tories enthusiastically armed their own ideological enemies!

Why on earth did they do it? We asked Crosbie himself. Twenty years after the fact, he admitted the decision was based completely on defensive grounds:

> It was political correctness. If we had discontinued the program we would have received very bad publicity. It would have led to the Liberal Party and opposition parties attacking on those grounds, saying we were not interested in human rights, and the institutions like *The Globe and Mail*, reinforcing our image as not being "with it" on social issues. Because of that, I thought it was not worth it to quash the CCP when it was just beginning, in addition to which the Charter was new and needed to be tested to see what it really meant. But that time is long past.[28]

According to Crosbie, the program has outlived its usefulness. "If the civil rights advocates want to, let them pay for their own challenges," he said. "Why should the government encourage it?"[29]

But as Milton Friedman once said, "Nothing is so permanent as a temporary government program." In 1992, the Tories did axe the CCP, but by then "the strength of the interest group networks the CCP had developed became clear."[30] These networks, together with powerful supporters including Supreme Court Justice Wilson and Max Yalden, chief commissioner of the Canadian Human Rights Commission, lobbied for the CCP's reinstatement and even turned it into a federal election issue. Liberal Leader Jean Chrétien vowed to re-establish the program and then-Prime Minister Kim Campbell promised to create a new Charter Law Development Fund.[31] After reducing Campbell's Tories to a tandem bicycle in the 1993 vote, Chrétien's Liberals inaugurated a new CCP in 1994 with annual funding of $2.75 million.[32]

The expansion of the CCP to fund equality challenges has come to haunt the conservative movement like few other policy decisions. Nine of the twenty-four equality rights judgments the Supreme Court handed down between 1984 and 1993 had a party or intervenor that was funded by the Court Challenges Program.[33] And as Brodie notes, "Overall, the Program has funded groups that supported a substantive approach to equality rights. In the cases it has funded the Supreme Court has generally followed a substantive equality approach."[34]

In other words, CCP money advanced the statist agenda and undermined principles of every kind of conservatism—social, neo and opportunity—at every turn. It is highly ironic that today, the only federal political party opposed to same-sex marriage was founded by the same people who funded the court battles that led to its legalization.

Don't misunderstand us: there is nothing wrong with any group using all the levers at its disposal, including the courts, to effect social change. Gays, lesbians and women's groups have a perfect right to make their case, but they don't have the right to make other people pay for it. They also don't have the right to have the state favour their side of the debate by funding it to the exclusion of other voices.

But under the CCP and other programs, that is exactly what happened. According to Ted Morton and Rainer Knopff, "The CCP has been a funding bonanza for LEAF and other equality seeking groups on the left."[35] In some cases, CCP grants appear to have had little to do with financial need and much to do with connections and ideology. Feminist lawyer Beth Symes received a CCP grant to challenge the fact that she couldn't deduct the expenses for her nanny. At the time, Symes was earning a six-figure salary and was one of the founders of LEAF.[36]

Conservative-minded litigants did not receive as warm a welcome from the CCP. "Non-feminist groups such as REAL Women and Kids First saw their applications for litigation funding either ignored or rejected."[37] Had LEAF, EGALE or other equality-rights groups had to raise money from non-governmental sources, would they have been able to launch as many challenges, and would their fights have been as successful?

Taking Action—Instead of Just Talking

To date, the most common conservative response to the left's triumphant use of the Charter has been to complain about "judicial activism." Elected politicians, not unaccountable judges, it is argued, should be making decisions on issues like voting rights for criminals, hate speech, gay marriage and abortion, all of which have been decided instead by the courts. Indeed, even the Charter's original framers are critical of its impact on the supremacy of Parliament. When the *Western Standard* magazine contacted the seven living former first ministers who negotiated the Charter, of the five that responded, "nearly all testified that the courts have done things in the name of the charter that astonish and in some cases infuriate them." Allan Blakeney, the former NDP premier of Saskatchewan, even went as far as to say that he hopes "to see parliaments and legislatures which will, in a robust way, contest the implied proposition that the courts are always standing on the side of the angels." Peter Lougheed, former Conservative premier of Alberta, has "repeatedly expressed dismay about the way the charter has been implemented."[38]

Decrying judge-made law is legitimate, but it is not enough. Conservatives must not simply criticize the courts—they must use them as well. Recently, when the Supreme Court struck down Quebec's prohibition against private health insurance in the 2005 case of *Chaouilli v. Quebec (Attorney General)*[39] on Charter grounds, many on the Right were overjoyed. Observed Andrew Coyne, "Conservatives ... are already citing the court's ruling in support of a parallel private health care system—so much for 'judicial activism.' ... "[40]

This decision is proof positive that Canadian conservatives must take action as their counterparts did south of the border. There, the activities of conservative groups in the legal system "grew more quickly than those of 'liberal' groups in the 1970's did."[41]

Indeed, America boasts dozens of legal foundations that successfully promote freedom and equality of opportunity through the courts. The National Legal Center for the Public Interest, founded in 1975, advocates for free enterprise, private ownership of property, balanced use of private and public resources, limited government and a fair and efficient judiciary. The Atlantic Legal Foundation, established in 1976, fights lawsuits against reverse discrimination, works with education groups to combat political correctness in academia and challenges regulations that hinder small business. The Landmark Legal Foundation was also set up in 1976 to fight for conservative principles, such as the protection of property rights and freedom of speech, in environmental and educational matters. The Criminal Justice Legal Foundation has been fighting to ensure that "crime doesn't pay" since 1982, while the Institute for Justice has been litigating civil liberties cases since 1991. And the list goes on.

The Long Arm of the Law

If conservatives want to stem the tide of enforced equality and shape a Canada in their image, they will have to learn from both the American Right and the Canadian Left. They must co-opt their tactics, set up their own litigation foundations and fight for their beliefs in the courts. The Charter is here to stay, which means conservatives should stop deriding it, make friends with it instead and use it to launch a thousand *Chaouillis*.

There are some precedents for this sort of activism in Canada. Advocacy groups supportive of small government, such as the National Citizens Coalition (NCC) and the Canadian Taxpayers Federation (CTF), have both gone to court on rights-based issues, ranging from freedom of speech to taxation challenges. Unlike EGALE, LEAF or other groups, however, neither the NCC nor the CTF received any government funding for these cases, directly from the CCP or indirectly through tax receipts, since neither is a registered charity.

Starting in 1983, the NCC led a series of legal challenges against so-called election "gag laws," invoking section 2(b) of the Charter, which guarantees freedom of speech and expression. Gag laws are prohibitions on third-party speech during election writ periods, both federal and provincial. For twenty years the organization successfully struck down laws passed by Liberal and Conservative governments alike, including the initial federal ban imposed in 1983 on all types of expression, including advertising and rallies, and subsequent bans that set spending limits for third-party groups. Unfortunately in 2003 the Supreme Court, in the case of *Harper v. Canada*,[42] ruled against the NCC and upheld the gag law imposed by the Chrétien government.

Despite this defeat, Gerry Nicholls, vice-president of the NCC, is proud of the organization's track record in the courts. By challenging election gag laws, the NCC postponed their effect for two decades, including the federal free trade election of 1988. This conservative-led fight for freedom of speech benefited all Canadians—at the left, centre and right—who got to speak their minds during what was arguably the most important Canadian election of the last twenty-five years.

The NCC was never conceived as a litigation vehicle, however. Nicholls points to the need for conservative legal associations and litigation foundations to promote a freedom-based view of the law and take up Charter challenges from a conservative perspective. "Right now the conservative movement in this country is not participating in this battle and is leaving the field to the left," he says.[43]

Nicholls is right. On law school campuses, many left-wing groups, including women's, environmental and native rights groups, actively organize law students and lobby for curricula on feminist legal theory, social diversity and the law and the like. At McGill University alone, human rights and social diversity courses comprise 38 percent of all elective courses offered to law students.[44] Few, if any, right-wing groups are active on campus. Conservative-minded lawyers and law students should get together to found such associations, encouraging students in particular to take up conservative legal activism.

And instead of being herded off to Bay Street, young conservative lawyers should have the option of pursuing their idealism and advancing the conservative cause at home-grown litigation foundations, like those that exist in the United States. Happily, the germ of such an idea has finally taken root in Canada, but it still has a long way to go.

In 2002 B.C. lawyer John Weston established the Canadian Constitution Foundation (CCF) "to explain to the role of the Constitution in [Canadians'] daily lives, to teach them how to recognize infringements and abuse of the Constitution in the world around them, and to help them defend its principles from improper decisions or actions of governments, regulators, tribunals or special-interest groups."[45]

Weston did not set out to create a legal foundation, but ended up doing so "as a result of a combination of dedication and frustration."[46] In 1997 he had read about the Nisga'a Treaty in the local press, which proposed to establish a third order of government for aboriginal people in British Columbia. Several prominent judges, including former Supreme Court justices Willard Estey and William McIntyre, publicly confirmed that it would be unconstitutional to create a virtual nation state that would prevail over federal and provincial laws in at least fourteen areas. Despite this evidence, in Weston's words, then-B.C. premier Glen Clark and former Prime Minister Jean Chrétien "shut down debate on the subject and rammed it through ... in a disgusting lack of commitment to the nation's welfare."[47] (Interestingly, unlike with same-sex marriage in 2004, the prime minister did not submit a Nisga'a Reference to the Supreme Court to see if it passed constitutional muster.)

After the treaty was endorsed by both the federal and provincial governments, a group of Nisga'a elders came to Weston and told him they shared his concerns. They asked Weston if he would go to court and challenge the treaty, but they had no money to fund the litigation. Weston believed so strongly in the Nisga'a case, and was so impressed by their courage, that he told them they wouldn't have to pay for it. He left his blue-chip law firm and set up the Access Law Group, which didn't share revenues among its lawyers, to immunize his colleagues and their spouses from liability.

Weston then pursued the onerous task of establishing a litigation foundation to fund the case. Worried that court activity might preclude charitable status, Weston's foundation committed itself to education on constitutional matters. He gave dozens of speeches about the Nisga'a to such organizations as the Empire Club, the Canadian Institute and the Donner Foundation. He applied for funding from the CCP, which initially awarded the CCF $10,000 for research purposes. When the foundation applied for more substantial litigation funding, however, the mood quickly changed. As Weston put it, "When the directors at the CCP found out our challenge would 'set back equality,' as they defined it, that door closed."[48]

Other entreaties to the provincial Legal Aid plan of British Columbia and the province's attorney general went unheeded. Weston worked on the case for two years without pay, continuing to apply for funding from other sources. By a serendipitous coincidence, Weston connected with a program official at the Donner Foundation who knew journalist Marni Soupcoff, who had worked with the Washington-based Institute for Justice (IJ). The Donner made a contribution to the CCF, enabling Weston to visit the IJ and learn the "ins and outs" of establishing and running a litigation foundation.

The CCF's goal is to litigate several major constitutional cases a year, in addition to commenting and presenting education information on constitutional issues. The foundation recently hired John Carpay, former Alberta director of the Canadian Taxpayers Federation, who had spearheaded the CTF's successful intervention in the case of *Benoit v. Canada*.[49] In that matter, the CTF had advanced an equality rights argument against a claim that aboriginal Canadians were exempt from tax on the basis of race.

Carpay believes the CCF could play an important role in defending many fundamental freedoms, including freedom of speech under section 2(b) of the Charter. Also, "[i]n the wake of the *Chaouilli* decision, promoting health care reform would be an obvious choice for litigation."[50] In addition, Carpay would like to see the CCF defend property rights. These rights are not explicitly protected in the Charter, but section 26 states: "The guarantee in the Charter of certain rights and freedoms shall not be construed as denying the existence of any other rights and freedoms that exist in Canada."

According to Carpay, there is therefore room for courts to confer constitutional status on property rights, though he is not aware of any litigation in support of this concept to date.

Carpay is also concerned that "a lot of court decisions talk about equality without defining it or recognizing the inherent conflict between equality of opportunity and equality of result." This is especially important on the next battlefront of enforced equality: the entrenchment of positive "social and economic rights." These include the "right" of disadvantaged groups to a certain minimum standard of living—and their right to force the rest of society to pay for it.

In the 2002 case of *Gosselin v. Quebec*,[51] the Supreme Court started treading down that dangerous path. Interest groups, including the National Association of Women and the Law and the Charter Committee on Poverty Issues, invoked section 15 rights to equality as well as section 7 rights to "security of the person." In its decision, the Court split five judges to four, narrowly upholding the constitutionality of a Quebec welfare law that reduced benefits for younger recipients who refused to participate in work-for-welfare programs. Of the dissenters, former Justice Louise Arbour went so far as to write: "This Court has consistently chosen instead to leave open the possibility of finding certain positive rights to the basic means of subsistence within s. 7. In my view, far from resisting this conclusion, the language and structure of the *Charter*—and of s. 7 in particular—actually *compel* it."[52]

According to the Fraser Institute, judgments like Arbour's might encourage "disadvantaged groups" to challenge similar work-for-welfare legislation in Ontario and time limits on collecting assistance in British Columbia.[53] They also open the door to establishing a "right to welfare" or a minimum income. In an article entitled "Louise Arbour's Economic Illiteracy," policy analysts Jason Clemens and Sylvia LeRoy review empirical evidence of the damage minimum-income policies can wreak. They found both Canadian and American studies show that, far from helping those in need, such policies reduce incentives to work, encourage dependency and lead to greater rates of family dissolution.[54]

Yet had one judge voted differently in the *Gosselin* case, the Canadian government might eventually have become compelled to provide such a program.

Thankfully, since rendering her decision in *Gosselin*, Justice Arbour has decamped to the United Nations as its high commissioner for Human Rights. But her judgment remains, and there are other Supreme Court justices who share her views. One of the latest additions to the Court, Rosalie Abella, is well-known for holding opinions that would leave Ayn Rand spinning in her grave: "[Through the Charter] we have added expectations that more needs will be treated as rights and not merely aspirations. ... [I]t will not be long before they spawn a deluge of repercussive rights demands, primarily about access—to health, to education, to physical and economic security, to privacy, and, of course, to justice itself."[55]

Patronage on the Highest Bench

This brings us to another important point for conservatives: the process of judicial appointments. When elected, a Conservative government must act to change the way judges are appointed in Canada.

Who sits on the Supreme Court is just as, if not more important, than who comes before it. This was clearly evidenced during the 1981 hearing of *Re Constitution of Canada*,[56] when Prime Minister Pierre Trudeau asked the Supreme Court to pronounce itself on his proposal to unilaterally patriate the Constitution. Seven of nine judges found the proposal legal; of these, all had been appointed by Trudeau.[57] The two judges who disagreed had been appointed by Diefenbaker. As Professor Mandel notes, "This was a transparently political decision and gave us a good idea, if we were paying attention, of what Canada could expect with the *Charter*."[58]

As *National Post* comment editor Jonathan Kay has written, judges are tremendously political people, and their ideological proclivities matter a lot. The widely held perception that Canadian judges are somehow non-political actors is bunk. "This fiction, obsolete even at the time the Charter became law more than two decades ago," Kay wrote, "has persisted in the face of blatantly political decisions challenging capital punishment, striking down our abortion law and reading gay rights into a Charter consciously drafted to exclude them."[59]

In Canada, the surest ticket to the High Court is to be on good terms with the prime minister. Unlike the United States, which has an open bipartisan judicial appointments process, Canada's Supreme Court judges are appointed at the sole discretion of the PM. Paul Martin attempted to make the most recent appointments in 2004 "more transparent" by including a review before a committee made up of MPs and legal experts, but under the new system, candidates aren't even compelled to appear before the committee and answer questions—a system Kay, himself a graduate of Yale Law School, calls a "fig-leaf consultation process."

Contrast this with the American experience, where Supreme Court nominees must face a grueling committee hearing, complete with thorough questioning in front of TV cameras, a Judiciary Committee vote and then a full vote of the U.S. Senate before being confirmed. And this is done after the president consults with senators on who is to be nominated. The U.S. Constitution obliges the president to seek the "advice and consent" of the Senate before nominating a candidate.

But it's not just the Canadian Supremes who are in issue. Our Federal Court appointments are also fraught with political bias. That's because under the current system, government does not have to pick the most qualified candidate, only the one who is not unqualified. The result is that "the federal system only ensures that the worst people don't get appointed."[60]

Here's how it works: Advisory committees composed of eminent members of the legal community rate the names of prospective Federal Court judges. The government then must choose a new judge from the pools labelled "highly recommended" or "recommended," which provides about five or six names per judgeship. The government is free to appoint a judge rated "recommended" instead of one rated "highly recommended" for whatever reason it chooses. According to Supreme Court Justice Jack Major, "The committee endorsement makes it much easier for the minister to appoint a friend."[61]

Even more damning were comments given by the former director general of the Liberal Party of Canada, Benoît Corbeil, to Radio-Canada on

April 21, 2005, that half of the twenty Quebec lawyers who volunteered on the party's 2000 campaign were rewarded by being named judges.[62] Corbeil said: "I am convinced that a person who wants to be named a judge ... has to have friendly ties with these people, who can influence the political apparatus and eventually ... the administrative apparatus."

Canadian conservatives need to demand real reform of the judicial appointments process. In the interim, conservatives should heed Gerry Nicholls' advice: they must "create a climate where there are more conservative voters, to elect more conservative politicians and thus appoint more conservative judges. They must also produce more conservative lawyers who become those judges."[63]

But as with the rest of our recommendations, none of this will happen without funding. If conservatives don't start opening their wallets, supporting organizations like the CCF, and founding more of them, they will continue to see the Charter used to undermine their views and increase the power of the state. To make a difference, conservatives must assert themselves as forcefully in the courts of law as in the court of public opinion.

Endnotes

1. This duality makes for a balancing act on the Supreme Court, where three of nine justices hail from Quebec, a point of contention for those who are not aware of the need to accommodate the bicameral nature of our legal tradition.

2. Michael Mandel, *The Legalization of Politics in Canada* (Toronto: Thompson Educational Publishing, 1994), 21 (hereinafter Mandel).

3. Mandel, 25.

4. House of Commons, Debates, May 21, 1980, 1264.

5. "Indeed, all the groups that Ottawa helped to organize during the 1970s lined up to support Trudeau's Charter-project in 1980-81. OMLG groups, multicultural groups, native groups, women's groups, disability groups, and human rights commissions—all came out in force to testify before the Joint Parliamentary Committee on the Constitution in 1980-81." R. L. Morton and Rainer Knopff, *The Charter Revolution and the Court Party* (Peterborough, Ont.: Broadview Press, 2000), 91 (hereinafter Morton and Knopff).

6. Morton and Knopff, 26

7. Morton and Knopff, 24–25.

8. Gregory Hein, "Interest Group Litigation and Canadian Democracy," reprinted in *Law, Politics and the Judicial Process in Canada*, ed. F. L. Morton, 3rd ed. (Calgary: University of Calgary Press, 2002), 349 (hereinafter Hein).

9. Hein, 349.

10. Morton and Knopff, 26.

11. Ian Brodie, "Interest Group Litigation and the Embedded State," *Canadian Journal of Political Science*, 34, no. 2 (June 2001): 375 (hereinafter Brodie, "Interest Group Litigation").

12. Women's Legal Education and Action Fund (LEAF) website. www.leaf.ca/about-work.html

13. According to LEAF's website, this model of equality is based on two basic ideas:

   • There are groups in our society (women, persons of colour, persons with disabilities, lesbians, to name only a few) whose members have historically been treated unequally.

   • The purpose of sections 15 and 28 of the Charter, the equality provisions, is to end their inequality and to help members of these groups overcome the results of their mistreatment.

   LEAF argues that, if laws or government practices contribute to the inequality of these groups, the courts must strike them down or require that they be changed. The reverse is true, as well, if laws or government practices promote the equality of these groups, they must be protected.

14. (1989) 1 SCR 143.

15. Christopher Manfredi, *Judicial Power and the Charter: Canada and the Paradox of Liberal Constitutionalism*, 2nd ed. (Toronto: Oxford University Press, 2001), 121.

16. Ian Brodie, *Friends of the Court, The privileging of interest group litigants in Canada*, (Albany: State University of New York Press, 2002), 2–3 (hereinafter Brodie, *Friends of the Court*).

17. 304 U.S. 144 (1938).

18. (1989) 1 SCR 152–53.

19. (1992) 2 SCR 679.

20. Brodie, *Friends of the Court*, 8.

21. Mandel, 43.

22. Brodie, "Interest Group Litigation," 366.

23. Brodie, "Interest Group Litigation," 365.

24. Brodie, "Interest Group Litigation," 367.

25. Brodie, "Interest Group Litigation," 364.

26. Brodie, "Interest Group Litigation," 366.

27. Brodie, "Interest Group Litigation," 367.

28. Author interview with John Crosbie, July 18, 2005 (hereinafter Crosbie).

29. Crosbie.

30. Brodie, "Interest Group Litigation," 368.

31. Brodie, "Interest Group Litigation," 369.

32. Brodie, "Interest Group Litigation," 370.

33. Brodie, "Interest Group Litigation," 374.

34. Brodie, "Interest Group Litigation," 374.

35. Morton and Knopff, 97.

36. Morton and Knopff, 97.

37. Morton and Knopff, 97.

38. Paul Bunner, "The Framers' Revolt," *Western Standard*, April 4, 2005. www.westernstandard.ca/website/index.cfm?page=article&article_id=694

39. (2005) SCC 35.

40. Andrew Coyne, "A Final Chance to Fix the System," *National Post*, June 10, 2005, A1.

41. Brodie, *Friends of the Court*, 9.

42. (2004) 1 SCC 33.

43. Author interview with Gerry Nicholls, July 13, 2005 (hereinafter Nicholls).

44. McGill Law 2005 curriculum. www.law.mcgill.ca/undergraduate/prog_bcl_llb-en.htm

45. Website of the Canadian Constitution Foundation. www.canadianconstitutionfoundation.ca/WhatWeDo.htm#WhatWeDoWhy

46. Author interview with John Weston, March 18, 2005 (hereinafter Weston).

47. Weston.

48. Weston.

49. (2003) FCA 236.

50. Author interview with John Carpay, July 26, 2005.

51. (2002) 4 SCR 429.

52. (2002) 4 SCR 429, paragraph 307.

53. Chris Schafer, "Gosselin Decision Forewarns of Right to Welfare," *Fraser Forum*, February 2003, 22–23.

54. Jason Clemens and Sylvia LeRoy, "Louise Arbour's Economic Illiteracy," *Fraser Forum*, May 2005, 29–31 (hereinafter Clemens and LeRoy).

55. Abella 2002, quoted in Clemens and LeRoy, 30.

56. (1981) 1 SCR 783.

57. Mandel, 26.

58. Mandel, 26.

59. Jonathan Kay, "The Right Way to Pick Judges," *National Post*, July 21, 2005, A16.

60. Retired political scientist and judicial appointments authority Peter Russell, quoted by Kirk Makin, "Appointment of Judges Too Political," *The Globe and Mail* May, 16, 2005, A7 (hereinafter Makin).

61. Makin, A7.

62. Terry O'Neil, "Justice for All?", *Western Standard*, June 27, 2005, 40.

63. Nicholls.

8 CHAPTER

ENGAGING THE NEXT GENERATION:
Issues, Ideals and Academia

"All State education is a sort of dynamo for polarizing the popular mind; for turning and holding its lines of force in the direction supposed to be most effective for State purposes."
— Henry Adams

If conservatives fail to capture the hearts and minds of young people, they can forget about ever retaking 24 Sussex Drive. So far, we've done a less than stellar job.

Conservatives must reach out and engage the next generation of Canadians in the development and marketing of conservatism. This presents certain challenges, as young Canadians are a rather quixotic bunch. On the one hand, they share many conservative ideals. Research has shown they accept an increased level of individual accountability for social services, health care and education.[1] Young people don't wish to entrust their well-being to others—they are more likely to be self-employed, and they want to save money for the future.[2] According to academic Matthew Mendelsohn, who researched the attitudes of youth and immigrants in the New Canada in 2003, "the connection between 'a large state' and 'social justice'" has broken down. ... The test of a social program today for Canadians is: Does it empower all

Canadians to make the most of their opportunities, and allow them to make their own choices?"[3]

In contrast, educators, the media and our self-appointed intellectual elites have relentlessly drummed the notions of enforced equality and the benefits of big government into the heads of our youth, whether in grade-nine social sciences class or in a university-level course on the Charter of Rights. This has borne fruit: young Canadians are more likely than older Canadians to think it is the government's responsibility to reduce difference between high and low incomes. And when asked to identify what things make them proud to be Canadian, 71 percent of people aged 18 to 30 named the Charter. The Charter doesn't even make the top five list of older Canadians.[4]

Young Canadians are bombarded with a variety of influences, all competing for their attention. These influences come from their families and other caregivers; the state, public schools and universities; from popular culture, such as films, books, music and fashion; and, ultimately, from their own peers. Except for the first influence, all tend to be liberal. And unlike their parents, today's young people are both tribal and global in their outlook. They spend time with their neighbourhood friends but also talk to other young people half a world away, thanks to the Internet. Technology has transformed their lives and broadened their outlook.

The Internet can be one of the most important vehicles for spreading the conservative message. This is especially true with regard to youth. According to polling by Ipsos Reid, eighteen to thirty-four-year-olds are spending an average of 14.7 hours a week on-line, compared with 11.7 hours of listening to radio, 11.6 hours watching TV and just 2.5 hours reading newspapers.[5]

Increasingly, youth are getting their news and information from the Internet. Sean MacDonald, the twenty-five-year-old editor of the news blog www.trickledowntruth.ca, says: "The Internet is on-demand ... It's a very free market, and what I think appeals to my generation is that it's immediate and it grows. ... Now with blogs and social networks, [news] develops into a much richer story and a much more firsthand story. Rather than having to wait all day until 6 [p.m.], you sort of feel you've seen the progression of the news."[6]

Technology is also challenging traditional power relationships between young people and adults. Technology-savvy youth no longer see adults as having all the answers, and they often prefer to start their own youth-led organizations rather than engage in adult-led ventures.[7] They are adept in using technology to mobilize others and organize communities. The events they organize may occur online or in the streets, as evidenced by the worldwide protests against the Iraq War in 2003.[8]

According to researchers at D-Code, a Toronto-based marketing and research company that studies the Information Age Generation (IAG), political movements must tap into this instinct for engagement, much like producers of successful interactive television programs. "Organizations that want to engage IAGs in political issues need to find ways to be more inclusive, interactive, and outcome-oriented," D-Code concludes.[9]

In 2003 the organization partnered with the Canadian Centre for Philanthropy to undertake a major study of citizen engagement among fifteen- to thirty-four-year-olds in Canada. They found that while IAGs seem to lack political knowledge, issue-based activist organizations have greater appeal.[10]

This finding is supported by other research that shows that young people are becoming more and more disengaged from the partisan political process. While 40 percent of Canadians are under thirty years of age, only 5 percent of members of political parties hail from this group.[11] Only 7 percent of those aged fifteen to thirty-four joined a political party, versus 20 percent of those aged thirty-five to fifty-four and 27 percent of those over the age of fifty-five.[12] In the 2004 federal election, only 38 percent of eligible voters between the ages of eighteen and thirty voted, compared with 60.9 percent of the general population.[13] It was even worse in the 2000 election: the turnout was twenty points lower for those born after 1970 than for those born before 1960.[14]

One problem is a serious lack of trust in politicians. According to a poll done by the Centre for Research and Information on Canada (CRIC), they are the least trusted of any social group. Only 36 percent of young people surveyed had a great deal of confidence, or some confidence, in political leaders. Sixty-four percent had not much or no confidence in them.[15] Young people are cynical about political parties, D-Code concluded, "and often see them lagging behind the courts and the media when it comes to effecting change on important IAG issues such as equality rights."[16]

Another reality conservatives must grasp is that Canadian young people are increasingly becoming less religious and socially conservative. According to polling by Ipsos Reid, 61.2 percent of men and 69.2 percent of women aged eighteen to thirty-four support gay marriage, compared with 55 percent of men aged thirty-five to fifty-four, and 24.6 percent of men over fifty-five, 62.2 percent of women thirty-five to fifty-four and 37.6 percent of women over the age of fifty-five.[17] Twenty-one point four percent of Canadian twenty-somethings say they have no religion, up from 6.4 percent in 1971.[18] D-Code reports that only 5 percent of fifteen- to twenty-four-year-olds attend a place of worship weekly, compared with 30 percent of older Canadians.[19] The aforementioned CRIC poll found that next to politicians, religious leaders were the group least trusted by young people; only 40 percent of youths expressed great confidence or some confidence in them, vs. 58 percent, who had low confidence or no confidence in them.

Coming to Conservatism

Conservatives—both big and small-c—must understand these new paradigms and work within them. An attempt at a mass partisan politicization of young people would be a waste of time. Rather than trying to draw thousands of youths into the Conservative Party, conservatives must draw them first into the conservative movement through non-partisan activist groups. And attempts to recruit young people into the conservative movement through religious means or on a social conservative basis will probably not bear long-term fruit.

The key is to reach, not preach. Conservatives must actively associate with young people in places where they learn, work and play. They must foster positive associations between conservatism and the issues that matter to them. This means focusing on the concerns of young people, the technology they use and the pastimes they enjoy. It means establishing a conservative culture within institutes of higher learning. It means providing outlets for activism and offering conservative solutions to problems that have traditionally been the preserve of the left. It means rising to the ultimate challenge: making it cool to be conservative.

A good start would be to develop a presence in a heretofore-neglected arena: environmental issues. Young people are very concerned about the environment. They also trust environmental organizations more than any other groups. The previously cited CRIC poll revealed that 83 percent of young people expressed either a great deal of confidence or some confidence in environmental groups—the highest level of confidence they had in any organization, and far higher than the 38 percent who trust politicians.[20]

Obviously then, the environmental movement provides an avenue for reaching young people. But, it is an area in which the left has a near monopoly and in which young people see government as the main actor. Therefore, involvement in environmental issues will draw young people into left-of-centre politics. Can conservatives overcome this challenge?

As we will see in Chapter 15, there are many conservative solutions to environmental problems. Free-market environmentalism is already being championed by a diverse cross-section of groups in the United States, such as the Thoreau Institute, the Competitive Enterprise Institute and on-line resources such as www.commonsblog.org. In Canada, the Fraser Institute, the Frontier Center for Public Policy and Environment Probe all publish research supporting free-market environmental policies. But they are think-tanks, not activist organizations. They are not out in the field mobilizing young people to this cause, and the Fraser Institute and the Frontier Center have other issues to focus on in addition to the environment. Conservatives must, therefore, launch organizations whose main focus is to actively promote free-market solutions to the environment among young Canadians, and involve them in the development and marketing of that message.

Conservatives should also blow their own horn on this issue. Who recalls that the Mulroney government got plaudits for its environmental record? In 1999, the Sierra Club's executive director, Elizabeth May, said a comparison between Mulroney and Chrétien's environmental records produced a result that "wasn't close." "The Mulroney record was one to be envied," May said, while Chrétien's was marked by a "total lack of concern" and "abject neglect."[21]

Not surprisingly, second to environmental groups, youth groups are those most trusted by young people, with 78 percent expressing a great deal or some confidence in them.[22] Conservatives should establish youth groups that promote good citizenship from a conservative perspective. They must also never forget the power of fun. Conservatives should organize groups and events that promote activities young people already enjoy, such as baseball leagues, theatre troupes and camping trips so that youths associate conservatives with good experiences.

The annual Liberty Summer Seminar in Orono, Ontario, which was founded by activist Peter Jaworski in 2001, is a perfect example of this.[23] Each August, thirty to forty young people pitch their tents on the grounds of a picturesque farm, complete with a swimming hole. In an atmosphere full of camaraderie, young people are exposed to anti-statist speakers and ideas in a supportive peer environment. The bonds of friendship forged at events like this one can produce a positive association with conservatism. Such events work more effectively than classroom instruction or reading a thousand policy papers ever could.

Conservatives should also mentor young people and expose them to conservative organizations. In this regard, they can take a page from the labour movement. Each year the Canadian Labour Congress organizes Solidarity Works, a youth-driven, three-week paid peer-to-peer summer training program, which consists of a week of classroom instruction and a two-week placement with a union and social-justice advocacy group. According to D-Code, "rather than telling young people what to think, Solidarity Works uses a popular education model, which draws on the life experiences of the participants. Participants are asked to question power and privilege in society, and encouraged to be self-critical and reflective. ..."[24] This kind of activity encourages interest in and adhesion to union philosophy, and these methods could easily be duplicated by right-of-centre organizations.

Providing opportunities for young Canadians to volunteer is another area to work on. Apart from the fact that encouraging voluntarism itself is a conservative value, such groups would allow young people to meet in an environment where they would be exposed to conservative beliefs. Projects might involve maintaining a database of links for a free-market environmental non-profit organization, or volunteering in a literacy program designed to "help people help themselves."

Volunteering is also viewed by young Canadians as a stepping stone to paid work. According to D-Code, 42 percent of Canadians aged fifteen to thirty-four volunteered in order to improve employment opportunities; 55 percent of those aged fifteen to twenty-four did so.[25] By providing opportunities for young people to hone their work skills, conservative groups would be seen as good places for young people to invest their time. Some provinces, like Ontario, also require students to work as volunteers for a set number of hours in order to graduate from high school, which provides conservative groups with another opening to connect with youth.

Another opportunity is—don't laugh—anti-poverty activism. This is an area where the left maintains a virtual monopoly through organizations such as the brick-wielding Ontario Coalition Against Poverty and the National Anti-Poverty Organization, which organized a youth-driven anti-poverty campaign in 2005. These groups appeal to idealistic young people who want to change the world, and such groups feed them a steady diet of anti-capitalist propaganda. While shrieking "make the rich pay" at G-8 leaders over a barricade may garner media attention, especially when police pull out the pepper spray, in the end it accomplishes nothing. Conservatives should provide an alternative by establishing youth-focused organizations that advocate free market means to alleviate poverty, both on international and local levels. These groups should engage in counter-demonstrations, disabuse the notion that the right is uncaring and present serious, non-statist solutions to poverty-related problems.

Young people are also readily influenced by television, film and other media. Conservatives should fund youth-oriented programming and documentaries that promote conservative points of view. Anti-corporate rants take up enough space on the big screen; think of *Supersize Me, The Corporation*, every movie made by American filmmaker Michael Moore, and *The Take*, Naomi Klein and Avi Lewis's documentary about Argentinean factory workers. Conservatives must provide a balance to these views. Why not establish a fund for young conservative filmmakers, or even an entire festival?

This type of action has already been undertaken in the United States, although it is a fairly recent phenomenon. The second annual Liberty Film Festival in 2005 billed itself as "Hollywood's premier event for conservative and libertarian film," showcasing films that celebrate free speech, patriotism and religious freedom.[26] The festival has already spawned a conservative film blog, *Libertas*, which provides a forum for conservative thought on the movie industry.[27] Another website, ProtestWarrior.com, was established to expose the lunacy of the anti-Iraq war movement by filming the antics of anti-war protestors. Activists Alan Lipton and Kfir Alfia attended anti-war rallies, challenged the protestors on tape and put the videos online for the world to see. The two recently produced a feature-length documentary called *Storming the Ivory Towers*, which, in their words, chronicles "the left's monolithic control" over America's universities.

A Blight on Academia

If Lipton and Alfia want to see monolithic control, they should come to Canada. The ivory towers of academia have tilted so far to the left up here that it's a wonder they haven't toppled over. Unless we "right" our Leaning Pisa of education, generations of students—and the Canadians who fund their education—will be gravely short-changed. With Canada becoming an increasingly educated country—18 percent of Canadian twenty-somethings now have a university degree, up from 8 percent in 1971[28]—it is imperative to expose these students to conservative thought.

As it now stands, our institutions of higher learning are left-wing indoctrination laboratories. Few on-campus outlets exist where conservatives may express themselves. If conservatives do speak out, they risk being mocked and even ostracized by both professors and peers. Some non-liberal students just remain silent rather than expressing their allegedly heretical views. We've experienced this first-hand. Tasha was once singled out by a professor in front of her Canadian literature class at McGill for wearing a pro-free trade sweatshirt during the 1988 election. At the high school level, Adam was called a "little Nazi" by a teacher in front of other students after writing an article in the school newspaper praising Mike Harris.

Lest one think campus political correctness had its heyday in the 1980s, be assured it is still alive and well in 2005. When *National Post* columnist Barbara Kay asked students to send her examples of left-wing bias in the classroom, she received 100 replies. She learned, for example, that a comparative politics teacher would not allow reports from the *Economist* to be cited as academic sources because of their "right wing, biased writers." Another wouldn't allow material from the Fraser Institute for similar reasons. A feminist political science profes-sor told her students they could not use statistics in their arguments because "mathematics is a male construct for a male-dominated world." Kay concluded that "[l]eft-wing ideologies have turned all but the hard sciences into hustings for the social empowerment of collectivities rather than groves of academic freedom."[29]

Today this anti-freedom attitude has spawned a campus chill, par-ticularly in relation to free speech. Nowhere is this phenomenon more evident than in issues relating to Israel and the Middle East. Students and professors who do not toe the orthodox Arabist line of various Middle East studies departments have felt too intimidated to speak out, especially since the events of September 11, 2001.

On September 9, 2002, raucous pro-Palestinian protestors forced officials at Concordia University to cancel a talk that was to be given by former Israeli prime minister Benjamin Netanyahu. The protest turned violent and police had to use pepper spray to bring the situation under control. The story made international headlines. Two years later, a group of Jewish students tried to make arrangements for another former Israeli prime minister (Ehud Barak) to visit Concordia. However, the students were told Barak could not speak because he posed too great a security risk. Under immense pressure the Concordia adminis-tration eventually backed down, although Barak has yet to speak there.

In January 2003, a visit to York University by Middle East scholar Daniel Pipes was nearly cancelled for similar reasons. York's faculty association wrote a letter to its members accusing Pipes of being "committed to a racist agenda and a methodology of intimidation and harassment." Amid an uproar Pipes was eventually allowed to appear, but the building where he was to speak had to be locked down for twenty-four hours beforehand, and those attending the event were frisked and passed through metal detectors.[30]

Left-wing bias is also amply evident in the area of curriculum. Too many courses are presented through gender, class and morally relativistic or anti-Western lenses. Entire disciplines have evolved to educate students about perceived injustices against various groups and to advocate the further imposition of enforced equality. Whether they provide a useful education or equip students for meaningful work is another story.

Our personal favourites are the "womyn's studies" programs. A product of the 1970s and state-sponsored feminism, today forty-one universities in Canada offer a BA in so-called women's studies,[31] while seventeen institutions offer master's degrees in the field.[32] Students can earn their degrees by taking such courses as "Mapping Masculinities"[33] and "The Dark Side of Sexuality."[34]

Other programs, chiefly in the arts, offer courses of similarly dubious academic value. The University of Windsor's course called "Gender, Space, and Time" is described as "An examination of sociological and anthropological approaches to the study of space–time relations within the field of gender studies, including a focus on the development of gendered environments and cultural practices." McMaster University offers an anthropology course called "Religion, Magic and Witchcraft," which is described as: "[a]n introduction to the cross-cultural study of the relationship between the natural and supernatural, and between ideology and social action." The University of Toronto has offered a first-year humanities seminar called "The Monstrous Imagination": "a study of monsters, perverts, and deviants in Western culture from the Middle Ages to the present." U of T professor Josiah Blackmore, who has taught the class, defended it after being criticized by the Ontario PC Campus Association, by saying, "[e]ven today you can see the monsterfication of a whole culture as a result of the [September 11] terrorist attacks."[35]

It's not that these types of courses have no place at all in university curricula. But their presence raises several questions.

First, in a country that spends $19 billion a year on post-secondary education,[36] should the taxes of working people fund schooling that will not equip students for the job market? While universities need not churn out a stream of dentists and engineers, in an atmosphere where resources are at a premium, are courses on gender and monsters really a priority? Student groups complain incessantly about the cost of higher education and the agony of paying back loans. They should realize that it's much easier to pay back a loan when your degree actually qualifies you for a job.

Second, many of these courses perpetuate statist notions that lead to a further call for redistribution of resources. For example, women's studies courses perpetuate the stereotype that women are perennially disadvantaged in Canadian society. Never mind that single never-married women earn 96 percent as much as their male counterparts,[37] or that "young women earn over 90 percent of what men do, and in some cases as much as 98 percent or more, in seven of the 10 occupations they are most likely to hold."[38] Or that men are now in the minority of university students, and are three to four times more likely to drop out of high school than women.[39]

Third, these courses give left-wing views a disproportionate amount of space compared with conservative perspectives. If the goal of a liberal arts education is to open students' minds and engage them in critical thinking, then they should be exposed to a variety of ideological viewpoints, not just those of Karl Marx. Too often this does not happen.

Case in point: in the fall of 1994, humanities professor Jeffrey Asher offered students at Montreal's Dawson College a course on men's lives, the only one of its kind in Canada at the time. According to Asher, he proposed the class because the college's three largest departments (humanities, English and the social sciences) offered more than eighty-three courses with feminist titles and content but with nothing objective about men. His course description proposed, among other things, to "examine men's values and experiences, and the cultural meanings for men of courage, duty, fidelity, success, family protection, career, and sexuality."[40]

After overcoming opposition from Dawson's women's studies professors, Asher taught the course for six years. During that time, he claims that he was accused of being paid by *Playboy* magazine, that he received anonymous accusations of sexual abuse and death threats and that his bulletin board was vandalized by none other than the chair of the women's studies program (the incident was captured by a campus security camera). The women's studies department finally had the course cancelled over accusations that students felt "belittled" if they expressed dissenting opinions in class. This, despite a lack of demonstrable complaints and many good student reviews: in class surveys over 85 percent of Asher's students reported that he treated them fairly and offered content and teaching that was "superior" and "outstanding," and 100 percent agreed that he treated them with "courtesy and respect."[41]

How many men's lives courses have there been since? According to Asher, in 2000, Canadian universities listed two courses on men, neither taught that year. At the same time, more than 1,617 feminist courses were offered in programs, ranging from undergraduate to Ph.D. degrees.

Asher's case was taken up by the Society for Academic Freedom and Scholarship (SAFS), an organization formed in 1992 to maintain freedom in teaching, research and scholarship, and to uphold standards of excellence in academic decisions about students and faculty.[42] SAFS president Clive Seligman wrote Dawson College demanding an explanation for its decision. Ultimately the intervention was unsuccessful and Asher retired from teaching.

But SAFS has made headway on another troubling aspect of campus politics, namely, preferential hiring policies.

Many universities openly exclude male applicants from applying for faculty positions. In 1999, SAFS spoke out when Wilfrid Laurier University posted an advertisement for a tenure-track position in the psychology department that read, "The department is attempting to address a gender imbalance, and therefore will hire a woman for this position." At the time, four of the department's twenty-two staff members were women. The head of the department told columnist Margaret Wente of *The Globe and Mail* that "everyone" wanted to increase the number of women on staff. As Wente discovered, however, it wasn't discrimination that accounted for the small percentage of women in the department, but rather the fact that other more prestigious schools had hired away the most qualified women.[43] In response, Laurier decided that it would discriminate against all men, qualified or not, and only hire a woman for the job.

In October 1999, Seligman filed a formal complaint with the Ontario Human Rights Commission (OHRC), disputing this discriminatory policy, but the university successfully challenged his standing to complain. In May 2001, the OHRC refused Seligman's final appeal on the basis that he hadn't applied for the position and had therefore not suffered discrimination, adding that the sole purpose of his complaint was to challenge a section of the Ontario Human Rights Code that allowed preferential hiring.[44]

Building an Academic Youth Movement

Unfortunately, there is only one SAFS in Canada, and it is just a small piece of the infrastructure needed to counter the prevailing culture of political correctness. So how else can conservatives bring balance to our universities? There are several approaches they can adopt.

For one, more "right-minded" people must be encouraged to earn Ph.Ds and to become professors and public policy researchers. This isn't an easy task. Above and beyond the enormous challenge of getting past the left-leaning faculty hiring committee, conservatives face another roadblock, one even more immovable than Michael Moore after a big lunch: mediocre pay. And let's be honest, money matters to conservatives.

Too many conservatives are busy earning a living to sacrifice themselves for the good of the conservative mass. For this observation, we rely on an informal survey Tasha conducted when attending a conference in Washington, D.C., hosted by the American conservative group Accuracy in Academia in the mid-1990s. After listening to a session extolling the importance of advancing conservatism on the campuses, she stood up and asked how many of the young delegates in the room intended to pursue a career in business or law. Dozens of hands shot up. Next she asked how many students wanted to go into academia or journalism. Maybe five hands went up. She then said to the audience, "There's your problem" and sat out the rest of the conference.

Conservatives' own philosophy of individualism works against them. So if the right is serious about levelling the playing field in academia, it will need to make it worthwhile for those who pursue academic careers. If professors earned as much as Robert Birgeneau, past president of the University of Toronto (who pulled in $304,077.00[45] in 2004), you can bet there would be conservatives lining for those jobs.

A successful conservative post-secondary initiative should include endowing chairs in major universities for research into small-c conservative issues, such as the promotion of liberty and market-oriented solutions to social problems. Liberals have done well feathering their own nests, with resources such as the bottomless well of taxpayer money at the Trudeau Foundation, which is available to fund the research of graduate students and scholars. There's also the Canada Research Chairs program, established in 2000 by the Chrétien government, which has a $900-million taxpayer endowment to fund 2,000 Canada Research Chair professorships.[46] All conservatives currently have is the University of Calgary political science department, a lone outpost of conservative thought. It must be made clear, however, that the donors will have some say over who gets these chairs; otherwise, we'll only see more situations like the 2005 awarding of the University of Toronto's Hal Jackman visiting professorship in human rights to putative Liberal-leader-in-waiting Michael Ignatieff.

Conservatives should also fund research grants to promote the study of market-driven solutions to social problems—and provide awards for those who succeed. The Donner Canadian Foundation Awards for Excellence in the Delivery of Social Services, administered by the Fraser Institute, provide $70,000 in awards annually to private groups that excel in delivering social services. Conservatives should establish more awards such as these through think-tanks and other non-partisan organizations. The United States has a similar, though far more generous, awards program: the Bradley Prizes. Annually, the Lynne and Harry Bradley Foundation presents four $250,000 awards to researchers, media figures and academics who promote liberal democracy, democratic capitalism and a vigorous defence of American institutions. Winners have included Princeton University professor

Robert George, conservative columnist George Will and scholar Heather MacDonald of the Manhattan Institute.[47]

Conservatives must also help start campus clubs that promote conservative interests, and fund the publication and distribution of materials that express conservative thought. Canadian youth may be a secular crowd, but conservatives can still take a page from campus religious groups: evangelize and convert! Campus clubs and publications can have the greatest impact on forming conservative thought in the shortest time. This is evidenced by the American experience. Rather than storming the Bastille of academe through its faculty, which is overwhelmingly left-wing,[48] American conservatives did an end run around it. They built a powerful network of campus and national conservative student organizations, conservative campus newspapers and internship/fellowship/mentorship programs. Much of this infrastructure has been driven by students themselves. This area has been one of the American right's biggest successes—while the lack of such infrastructure stands as one of Canadian conservatism's biggest challenges.

In the U.S., young conservatism has been the heart of the conservative revolution. Think of William F. Buckley's famous first book, *God and Man at Yale*, in which he chastised his alma mater for its hostility toward free markets and religion. Buckley also helped found Young Americans for Freedom (YAF), a conservative campus group that proved to be a key player in Barry Goldwater's Republican nomination for president in 1964.

Another group, Young America's Foundation, hosts national campus conservative conferences each summer at the bucolic ranch near Santa Barbara, California, that was once owned by the late Ronald Reagan. Here they learn about the life and legacy of the former president. But the foundation's most significant function is its ongoing effort to get conservative speakers on campuses. The foundation helps organize visits by such speakers as comedian Ben Stein, pundit Ann Coulter, former Congressman Jack Kemp, rocker Ted Nugent and dozens of others, all of whom bring the conservative message to campus crowds.

Probably the most important U.S. conservative campus organization today is the Intercollegiate Studies Institute (ISI). Founded in 1953 by Frank Chodorov, ISI also sponsors conservative talks on campus, hosts colloquia and publishes conservative pamphlets, books and academic guides. But most significantly, it helps young conservatives conceive, fund and publish campus newspapers through the Collegiate Network, an arm of ISI. About eighty-five newspapers across America are on ISI's roster.[49]

A newer group, Students for Academic Freedom, founded under the tutelage of conservative activist David Horowitz, now has 130 campus chapters and is pushing universities to adopt an Academic Bill of Rights, in order to guarantee an ideological balance on campus. SAF's motto is, aptly, "You can't get a good education if they're only telling you half the story."[50]

The American think-tanks have also grasped the concept of "get 'em while they're young." The Heritage Foundation spends $570,000 a year on its summer intern program, where sixty-four students come to Washington to learn about conservatism. In a recent profile of the interns in *The New York Times*, Edwin Feulner, the long-time head of Heritage, said "We almost think of ourselves as a college." A banner that reads "Building for the Next Generation" adorns Heritage's auditorium. Ralph Neas, head of the liberal group People for the American Way, admitted "[t]here's no question that the right wing over the last 25 years did a much better job of creating a farm system. ... They invested in young people. "[51]

The end result of all this is a vibrant and growing conservative youth movement in America. The number of campus Republican clubs has nearly tripled in the last six years, from 400 to more than 1,100 today.[52] Even the University of California at Berkeley, the nerve centre of the radical campus left in the 1960s, today boasts a strong conservative presence.

Indeed, it has gotten so bad for the left that in August 2005 *The Washington Post* reported that at least "80 wealthy Liberals" had pledged $1 million each to counter conservative activism on college campuses and activities in the American conservative movement.[53] Liberal heavy-hitters such as Bill Clinton have pledged to cultivate "a new generation of activists."[54] Their endeavours are funded by limousine liberals like left-wing billionaire George Soros, who created Campus Progress, an organization that promotes liberal activism in universities and colleges.

As Ralph Neas has said, the key to success is *investing*. Canadian conservatives have nothing comparable to any of these American groups. Apart from the SAFS, Canada does not have any organization committed solely to the defence of academic freedom. And as we mentioned in Chapter 3, thanks to the events that unfolded at the Montreal 2005 Conservative Party convention, the Tories don't even have a formal youth wing to promote activism on campus and to train their future leaders.

The other missing piece of the puzzle is the establishment of private universities. This is a more challenging prospect, but one that should also be pursued.

According to journalist Michael Taube, who has extensively researched the subject, private universities "decrease government involvement in education matters and increase freedom of choice in the education marketplace."[55] They foster competition between the public and private sector, which leads to improvements in the educational system as a whole. And contrary to the dogma that they are bastions of the well-heeled elite, they can also be less expensive than some public universities. Taube cites the examples of Buckingham University in the United Kingdom and Bond University in Australia, where fees averaged less than $2,500 a term. These institutions also boast student–staff ratios of ten to one. In Australia, Bond University has the lowest such ratio.[56]

Apart from private religious universities, such as British Columbia's Trinity Western University and Ontario's Redeemer College, Canada does not have a secular private university culture. This may change thanks to the establishment of the private University Canada West in Victoria, which opened its doors in 2005. This university offers a no-nonsense curriculum geared to academic excellence and career advancement. It will be interesting to follow the progress of UCW in the coming years, as it could provide a template for other institutions down the road.

Finally, a word of warning. Reaching the young doesn't just start in university or high school. Possibly the greatest threat to conservatives in the long term lies at the other end of the educational spectrum: the advent of national state daycare. As we will show in Chapter 13, the conservative movement has utterly failed to present an alternative vision on this issue. Conservatives must form their own advocacy groups to promote choice in child care, much as the labour movement has spearheaded groups that seek to park our children in unionized kiddy farms. This isn't even about conservatism; it's about the well-being of all Canadian children and families, who deserve the chance to raise their kids as they see fit.

So come on, conservatives, let's get out there and get organized! It's bad enough the left has its talons on the Boomer generation. Let's not let them snatch the cradle, too.

Endnotes

1. Robert Barnard, Denise Andrea Campbell and Shelley Smith, *Citizen Re: Generation: Understanding Active Citizen Engagement Among Canada's Information Age Generations* (Toronto: D-Code, 2003), 78 (hereinafter *Citizen Re:Generation*).

2. *Citizen Re:Generation*, 78.

3. Erin Anderssen, Michael Valpy et al., *The New Canada* (Toronto: The Globe and Mail / McClelland and Stewart, 2004), 281–282 (hereinafter *The New Canada*).

4. *The New Canada*, 25.

5. Simon Avery, "Calling and Clicking Like Never Before," *The Globe and Mail*, August 10, 2005, A1 (hereinafter Avery).

6. Avery.

7. *Citizen Re:Generation*, 96.

8. *Citizen Re:Generation*, 95.

9. *Citizen Re:Generation*, 4.

10. *Citizen Re:Generation*, 3–4.

11. Centre for Research and Information on Canada (CRIC) survey on the concerns and valucs of young Canadians, 1997 (hereinafter CRIC poll). www.cric.ca/pwp_re/cric_studies/citizen_participation_and_cdn_democracy_ aug_2003.ppt#337,3, Executive Summary.

12. *Citizen Re:Generation*, 54.

13. "Youth Vote Way Up, Says Elections Canada," *CBC News* Online, October 22, 2004. www.cbc.ca/story/canada/national/2004/10/22/youngvoters_041022.html

14. CRIC poll. www.cric.ca/pwp_re/cric_studies/citizen_participation_and_cdn_ democracy_aug_2003.ppt#310,34, Political Participation.

15. CRIC poll. www.cric.ca/pwp_re/cric_studies/citizen_participation_and_cdn_ democracy_aug_2003.ppt#261,28, Confidence in Groups.

16. *Citizen Re:Generation*, 3.

17. *The New Canada*, Appendix.

18. *The New Canada*, 18.

19. *Citizen Re:Generation*, 4.

20. CRIC poll. www.cric.ca/pwp_re/cric_studies/citizen_participation_and_cdn_ democracy_aug_2003.ppt#261,28, Confidence in Groups.

21. Transcript of Cable Public Affairs Channel Roundtable, "The Environment: How's Ottawa Doing," May 4, 1999. www.sierraclub.ca/national/es/cpaced.html

22. CRIC poll.

23. For more information see www.libertyseminar.org

24. *Citizen Re:Generation*, 63.

25. *Citizen Re:Generation*, 36.

26. Liberty Film Festival website. www.libertyfilmfestival.com/index.php?option= com_content&task=view&id=23&Itemid=46

27. The blog is accessible at www.libertyfilmfestival.com/libertas/

28. *The New Canada*, 17.

29. Barbara Kay, "Academic Freedom Is Under Attack," *National Post*, January 12, 2005, A14.

30. Daniel Pipes, "The Rot in Our [Canadian] Universities," *National Post*, January 30, 2003. www.danielpipes.org/article/1013

31. Canadian Women's Studies Online, Undergraduate Programs in Women's Studies. www.utoronto.ca/womens/under.htm

32. Women's Studies Programs, Graduate Schools in Canada. www.gradschools.com/listings/canada/womens_canada.html

33. Simon Fraser University, Women's Studies Course Offerings webpage. www.sfu.ca/womens-studies/courseofferings.htm

34. University of Waterloo, Women's Studies webpage. www.adm.uwaterloo.ca/infoucal/INTER/women_studies_inter.html#courseList

35. Joel Brown, "Vampires, Ghosts Not Educational," *UWO Gazette*, October 17, 2001. www.gazette.uwo.ca/2001/October/17/News5.htm

36. "The Price of Knowledge 2004," Millennium Scholarship Fund. http://64.233.167.104/search?q=cache:126JLidT_JAJ:www.millenniumscholar ships.ca/en/research/pokmill.asp+government+spending+post-secondary+educ ation+canada&hl=en

37. Marie Drolet, "The Persistent Gap: New Evidence on the Canadian Gender Wage Gap," Business and Labour Markets Analysis Division of Statistics Canada, 2001. www.statcan.ca/english/research/11F0019MIE/11F0019MIE2001157

38. Statistics Canada, Earnings of Canadians, 2001 Census Analysis Series.
www12.statcan.ca/english/census01/Products/Analytic/companion/earn/
canada.cfm#11

39. Mark Reynolds, "Where Have All the Boys Gone?" *The Reporter*, McGill
University, November 13, 2003, vol. 36, no. 5. http://64.233.167.104/
search?q=cache:p8Iyhp3ZMRUJ:www.mcgill.ca/reporter/36/05/gender/
+men+university+admissions+minority&hl=en

40. Jeffrey Asher, "The Matriarchy Rules," Montreal *Gazette*, October 6, 2001, B5
(hereinafter Asher).

41. Asher.

42. Society for Academic Freedom and Scholarship (SAFS) website.
www.safs.ca/about.html (hereinafter SAFS website).

43. Margaret Wente, *The Globe and Mail*, July 27, 1999, available on SAFS website
at www.safs.ca/issuescases/w1u2.html

44. SAFS website, "Update on the Complaint to the Ontario Human Rights
Commission Against Wilfrid Laurier University for Job Discrimination against
Men," June 2001. www.safs.ca/issuescases/wlu.html

45. Ontario's Public Sector Salary Disclosure, Ontario Ministry of Finance.
www.gov.on.ca/FIN/english/salarydisclosure/2005/univer05.pdf

46. See "Canada Research Chairs," Government of Canada.
www.chairs.gc.ca/web/about/index_e.asp for more information. This is not an
ideologically driven program.

47. Philanthropy Roundtable, March/April 2005, "Bradley Awards."
www.philanthropyroundtable.org/magazines/2005/marapr/brieflynoted.htm

48. A survey of Ivy League professors found that 84 percent voted for Al Gore in
the 2000 presidential race, while only 9 percent cast their ballots for George W.
Bush. This polling was done for the Centre for the Study of Popular Culture by
the Luntz Research Group.
http://studentsforacademicfreedom.org/reports/LUNTZ.html

49. Brian C. Anderson,"On Campus, Conservatives Talk Back," *City Journal*, Winter
2005. www.city-journal.org/html/15_1_campus_conservatives.html (hereinafter
Anderson).

50. Students for Academic Freedom (SAF) website.
www.studentsforacademicfreedom.org/

51. Jason DeParle, "Next Generation of Conservatives (By the Dormful)," *The New
York Times*, June 14, 2005. http://www.nytimes.com/2005/06/14/politics/
14heritage.html?ei=5089&ten=538dfa2e4e8234ca&tex=1276401600&partner=
rssyahoo&emc=rss&pagewanted=all

52. Anderson. www.city-journal.org/html/15_1_campus_conservatives.html

53. Thomas Edsall, "Rich Liberals Vow to Fund Think Tanks: Aim Is to Compete
With Conservatives," *The Washington Post*, August 7, 2005, A01.

54. Brian Faler, "Clinton and Other Democratic Leaders Urge Young Liberals to Get Involved," *The Washington Post*, July 14, 2005, A04.

55. Michael Taube, "The Case for Private Universities," *Ottawa Citizen*, January 6, 2000, A15 (hereinafter Taube).

56. Taube.

9 CHAPTER

UN-BLOC-ING QUEBEC:
Advancing Conservatism in *la Belle Province*

"Treat them as a nation and they will act as a free people generally do — generously. Call them a faction, and they become factious."

— Sir John A. Macdonald

Let's not mince words: Quebec has been the bane of the Conservative Party's existence for the past 100 or so years. With a few notable exceptions—R. B. Bennett's win in 1930, John Diefenbaker's 1958 majority and Brian Mulroney's victories in 1984 and 1988—conservatism has been a tough sell in *la belle province*. As Michael Bliss puts it, the Tory position in Quebec has been shaky "since at least the dithering over Manitoba schools, perhaps as far back as the execution of Riel or even the death of [Sir George-Étienne] Cartier."[1]

The death of Cartier? The hanging of Riel in 1885? That's harsh. It's also accurate. Apart from the Mulroney era, you have to return to the time of the Fathers of Confederation to find sustained Tory strength in Quebec. Macdonald actually won more Quebec seats than the Liberals in all the elections he fought but two: in 1874—the only election he lost—he still won a respectable 30 out of 65 seats; in 1891, the Tories won 28 out of 65 when Wilfrid Laurier, the first French-Canadian federal leader, arrived on the scene. Macdonald still won that election but died later that year.

So, to put it mildly, it has been a struggle. Those who have been involved in politics in the last decade know how tough it's been. The old PC Party, the Reform Party and the Canadian Alliance have had virtually no presence in Quebec for a decade, and the same die-hard party activists have been keeping the conservative cause afloat since the party's decimation in 1993. In fact, those few Quebecers who have stuck with the conservative parties all these years deserve a lot of praise. Those who joined the old Reform Party or Canadian Alliance deserve even more—maybe even a medal for bravery! It couldn't have been easy for them.

If you ask 100 people how the Tories can make a breakthrough in Quebec, you will get 100 different answers. Almost everyone has an opinion on why conservatives do so poorly. It's a favourite discussion topic in the hallways at Conservative Party conventions, right up there with how to get Stephen Harper to stop wearing golf shirts. Some say Quebec's political climate is just too left-wing. Others say Quebecers will never vote for a party with a leader who isn't from Quebec. Still others say the continued existence of the Bloc Québécois as the main non-Liberal option in the province prohibits any Tory growth.

All of these claims have merit, and the truth is probably a bit of all these put together. The Conservatives also have an image problem in Quebec, which dates back to the historical religious divide in which the Tories were associated with Protestantism and the British Empire while the Liberals were linked with Roman Catholicism. The Tories have been on the opposite side of Quebecers on so many issues. There was Sir John A.'s refusal to stop the hanging of Riel: "He shall hang, though every dog in Quebec bark in his favour," Macdonald said. There was the infamous Manitoba schools question in 1895, when English Protestant Tories supported the anti-French Manitoba Schools Act. And Quebecers opposed the draft in World War I, which resulted in Quebec being frozen out of Robert Borden's pro-conscription Unionist coalition in 1917.

As Stephen Harper and Tom Flanagan once wrote, "In the Progressive Conservative party, the predominant element has been centrist and eastern, anglophone and Tory, leaving western populists and Quebec nationalists feeling that the party does not represent their views or interests."[2]

What To Do About Quebec?

Great pains have been taken to remedy the schism. The Tories adopted the "two founding nations" view of Canada (*deux nations* in French, which has a slightly different meaning) under Robert Stanfield. At Stanfield's insistence the caucus backed Trudeau's official bilingualism legislation in 1969. The party has been desperately trying to improve its fortunes in Quebec ever since, with only Brian Mulroney, himself a Quebecer, having any success. Stanfield won 4, 2 and then 3 seats in the three elections he contested; Joe Clark won 2, 1 and 1; Kim Campbell won 1 and Jean Charest 5 in 1997. Reform or the Canadian Alliance never won any.

There are generally three views about how conservatives should go forward in Quebec. The first is that the Conservative Party should proceed like a tortoise and slowly win over the federalist vote, principally in the Montreal area. At times this approach has been advocated by Stephen Harper, and has won him friends in the Quebec anglophone community. In an ideal world, this strategy would be great. But the Liberal stranglehold on this bloc of voters goes back to Laurier and is showing no signs of loosening, even with the sponsorship scandal. This would also be difficult given how often the leadership of the Conservative Party seems to change.

The second approach is to give up on Quebec entirely, admitting that small-c conservative values are too out-of-sync with today's Quebec and that the big-c Conservative brand is too damaged. Peter C. Newman has argued that "Stephen Harper's best chance is to get a humour transplant, and stay out of Quebec."[3] David Frum has suggested that the Conservatives have no choice but to form a new political axis between Ontario and Alberta—two provinces that have more in common in terms of language and economics than either province has with Quebec.[4] Alberta and Ontario are both English-speaking provinces with low taxes and smaller government; Quebec is a French-speaking enclave with an expansive welfare state, fuelled by the highest taxes in North America.

The same point has been made by pundits George Koch and John Weissenberger (the latter a close associate of Stephen Harper), who wrote, "an Ontario-West electoral strategy is no longer laughable. With 201 of 308 seats, it's not even just barely feasible. It's entirely rational and, factoring in the two regions' converging social and economic interests, a potential winner."[5]

This path has merits, but it poses major problems. The most obvious is that the Tories would be automatically giving up on Quebec's 75 potential seats in the House of Commons. As much as we hate to use the word, it would also seem un-Canadian. The rest of the country, particularly Ontario, prefers strong pan-national parties that will keep Quebec in Confederation.

The third and most popular view is that the party must reconstruct the Quebec-West coalition that brought majority governments to Diefenbaker in '58 and Mulroney in '84 and '88, by courting francophone voters, including Quebec nationalists. Not only is this coalition difficult to build, but as the Mulroney experience showed us, it is even tougher to keep together. Quebec Premier Maurice Duplessis put it best when he said nationalists are "a ten-pound fish on a five pound line. They must be reeled in and let out with caution."[6]

It is true that Quebec and the West (particularly Alberta) share certain things, chiefly a suspicion of the federal government based on a variety of historical grievances, and a desire for more autonomy. But dislike for the national capital does not automatically make you suitable political bedfellows. Alberta and Quebec are much more different than they are alike. Economically, Alberta is the Canadian powerhouse, a "have" province that is debt-free, with a long tradition of conservative politics and provincial Conservative rule. Quebec is still a "have-not" province: its economic expansion is continually frustrated by high taxes, powerful unions and the machinations of the Parti Québécois, which holds the separatist sword of Damocles over any investors looking to do business there. The other obvious problem with this is that the Liberals and the media will pull out the unity card, pillorying the party for "working with the separatists." We saw this rhetoric in the lead up to the 2005 budget vote, when the Tories and the Bloc were seen to be working in tandem to force an election.

Apart from these three paths, there is the question of leadership—or, more precisely, the party leader's provincial pedigree. It is no coincidence that since the 1970s, and the rise of the separatist threat, the only prime ministers of importance—Trudeau, Mulroney and Chrétien—have come from Quebec. Clark, Turner and Campbell all served the equivalent of political internships before they were turfed in favour of another Quebecer. The only time it is possible for a non-Quebec leader to win nationally is when the other leader is also a non-Quebecer—hence the Diefenbaker win in 1958, when he faced Lester B. Pearson. With the continued presence of the Bloc, there will always be a Quebec leader on the ballot.

And it's not just about appealing to Quebec voters: it's about appealing to Canadian voters who think only a Quebecer can win Quebec. Unless you are born there or are at least a bilingual semi-Quebecer like Paul Martin (who, though born in Windsor, Ontario, has lived in *la belle province* since his twenties), it is assumed that you can't win the province, won't form government and won't be a credible voice in keeping the country together.

The result of has been to shut out other voices—mostly Western—from having a real say in running the country. This has corroded our sense of nationhood and fanned the prairie brushfire of Western alienation—alienation that threatens to turn into a separatist movement at any moment. The West is perennially outraged about what it sees as preferential treatment for Quebec. The Reform Party owed its rapid expansion in the 1980s in large part to the Mulroney government's bungling of a $1.3 billion CF-18 maintenance contract, which it handed to Montreal-based Bombardier, even though Winnipeg's Bristol Aerospace had put in a cheaper bid. According to Preston Manning, Reform helped to diffuse Western separatist momentum and to channel it into a federalist party: "I don't think to this day the political establishment in central Canada knows that, and if ... you'd had two full-blown separatist movements, one in Quebec and one in the West, it would have torn the country apart."[7]

Today, this tradition of Ottawa favouring Quebec continues. At the September 2004 First Ministers' meeting on health care, Premier Jean Charest negotiated a special "side deal" for Quebec that stipulated that

Quebec could set its own targets for waiting time reductions. No other province was afforded the same terms. Even when it comes to federal funding for Canada Day, Quebec gets a disproportionate share of the pie—40 percent for a province with approximately 25 percent of the country's population.[8] In 2005, for example, it received $3.2 million of the $7.5 million that was spent. Never mind that most Quebecers aren't celebrating Canada Day anyway—July 1 was declared Quebec's official "moving day" in 1973, the day on which rental leases expire and much of the populace is busy shuttling their belongings to a new home.

Is this the price of Canadian nationhood? For some politicos, it is—and no price is too steep to keep the country together. Despite mountains of evidence that money was diverted by unscrupulous Liberal bagmen and ad agencies, both former prime minister Chrétien and former Public Works minister Alfonso Gagliano testified that the corrupt federal sponsorship program had dented the separatist movement in Quebec.[9] The fear of Canada's disintegration has weighed heavily on every government since the Quiet Revolution and the not-so-quiet terrorism of the FLQ. It has exacted a heavy price, both in dollars and in energy, from the entire nation, which has struggled through the October Crisis of 1970, two provincial referenda in 1980 and 1995, one national referendum in 1993 and interminable debates about Canada's very existence.

Conservative Body Blows

The separatist shadow has also exacted a heavy toll on the conservative movement. Brian Mulroney's failures on the national unity front—the Meech Lake and Charlottetown accords—only served to reinforce the view that the Tories can't deliver on the Quebec issue. The fear of the nation's disintegration also makes the development of any kind of ideology secondary to saving the country. While countries such as the United States and Britain debated the merits of lower taxes and limited government, Canada debated whether it should stay together at all. Our intellectual and political culture has been stunted by the harsh reality of fighting separatism. Instead of a dialogue of ideas, we have a dialogue of fear, and it is the conservative movement that has paid the greatest price in this regard.

One person who realized this early on was Stephen Harper, who, according to his biographer William Johnson, was tremendously influenced by Peter Brimelow's 1986 bestselling book *The Patriot Game*. Brimelow's tome discussed several of the themes mentioned in this book, including the disproportionate amount of power wielded by Central Canada's liberal elite, which he called the "New Class." His analysis was years ahead of its time.

Brimelow ended his book with a set of six prophetic observations. Among them: He foresaw the rise of a "right-wing, fourth party in the west." (Reform was founded a year later.) He said, "Brian Mulroney will almost certainly fail to create a Tory electoral coalition" and that "new splinter parties will emerge." (Reform, the Bloc Québécois.) He said "a sectional party, probably from Quebec but possibly from the West, could hold the balance of power in the House and demand radical reform." (The Bloc formed the Official Opposition in 1993; the Reform Party in 1997.)[10]

But it is Brimelow's examination of Quebec's dominance in federal politics that is most trenchant. Brimelow observed that Canada was only "a geographical expression" and that Quebec was "emerging as a genuine nation-state." He observed that the Liberal Party had successfully convinced English Canada that whatever needed to be done to placate Quebec and keep Confederation intact should be done. As long as this attitude dominated, Brimelow said, conservative politics would not be able to succeed in Canada.

Twenty years after that book's publication, Brimelow now only casually follows Canadian politics from his perch in the U.S. In an interview, he said little has changed since *The Patriot Game* was written. "What I called in 1986 the Canadian Question has iterated itself in the last two decades but it remains unanswered: Canada is not a nation, but two (if not more) nations within a single state," Brimelow told us. "No purely ideological politics can succeed until the issues of national identity are resolved. Specifically, while Quebec is at the centre of every major government decision, and 'national unity' is considered the touchstone of all public policy, the natural conservative tendencies of the Anglophone majority will continue to be frustrated. For the Canadian Right, the road to power lies not through Quebec, but around it."[11]

From a purely practical perspective, it's tough to argue with this point. It would be much easier for conservatives if Quebec were not part of the equation. But you don't give up on a country just because of one party's electoral difficulties. For conservatives, accepting Brimelow's suggestion would mean choosing the Frum-Koch-Weissberger "door number two" and closing the book on Quebec, which as we discussed earlier in this chapter, would not wash in the rest of Canada.

An Action Plan for Quebec

So if they cannot win the existing federalist vote, work around Quebec or ally themselves with nationalists, what must the Conservatives do to break their "Bloc-age" in *la belle province*?

Quite simply, they must find a fourth way—and that way lies both with the Conservative Party and with the conservative movement. The party must outreach to existing conservative bases, while the movement must create a new conservative class in Quebec. This will necessitate an all-out effort, even more so than in the rest of Canada. But it is the only long-term solution. This would then allow big-c Conservatives in the rest of Canada to ally themselves with members of this new Quebec conservative class.

First, what the movement must do. If anything, there's an immense responsibility on the shoulders of the conservative movement to spread our ideas in Quebec. In recent years, the Quebec separatist movement has become more and more synonymous with socialism. The PQ is now a virtual arm of the Quebec unions, and the Bloc Québécois is no different. The PQ's current president, Monique Richard, formerly led the *Centrale des syndicats du Québec* (CSQ), the provincial union umbrella group. As more and more Quebecers become reliant on the state—the Quebec state, that is—their attachment to Canada dwindles. Quebec's separatist leaders use the province's infatuation with big government—usually called the innocent-sounding *"modèle québécois"*—to drive a wedge between Quebecers and the rest of Canada and reinforce differences. If a stronger emphasis on individual responsibility and less reliance on government can be brought to Quebec, its citizens will be less likely to support independence. Although the PQ is out of power at the time of this book's publication, there is a strong possibility that they will be back in office after the next Quebec election. At the federal level, the Bloc continues to hold a strong majority of Quebec seats.

Very little conservative infrastructure exists in Quebec today. The Montreal Economic Institute, a leading free-market think-tank, *Égards*, a small circulation magazine, and *Le Québécois Libre,* a libertarian on-line journal, are about it. The whole of the province's media and academic elites are a virtual carbon copy of the "Old Europe" social democratic left. They are nationalist, and in many—if not most—cases, separatist. Even the Conservative Party's troops in the province are more centrist: the Quebec delegates came to the March 2005 national convention to fight for, among other things, corporate welfare and government regulation of media ownership.[12]

Younger Quebecers are largely left wing and nationalist/separatist. Witness the mass student revolts in Quebec over Premier Jean Charest's ill-fated proposal to reduce university student bursaries by $103 million (despite the fact that Quebec's tuition remains about half those of the other provinces). Montreal's *La Presse* polled Quebecers of the 18-24 age group in September 2004 and found that 58 percent support Quebec sovereignty, 63 percent are in favour of unionizing McDonalds, 84 percent are pro gay-marriage, 85 percent are pro-choice on abortion and 70 percent favour less spending on the military.[13]

At the same time, on economic issues, there is some rightward movement, perhaps best incarnated in l'Action Démocratique du Quebec (ADQ), the third-place party in Quebec's National Assembly. In 2005, the party's 35-year-old leader, Mario Dumont, told *L'Actualité* magazine: "An honest and healthy social debate must take place. The Quebec social-democrat model is failing more every day. In the 1960s and '70s, we innovated, the state was an accelerant for young entrepreneurs. Today, it puts the brakes on innovation" (author translation).[14]

The next generation has had enough of being told what to do, whether by the state or, previously, the church. In the words of 27-year-old Montreal technology entrepreneur Benoît Jolin, "I'd hear it from teachers and grandfathers or aunts and uncles: It's okay to under-achieve. It was part of the Catholic education … It just left me infuriated.

Up in arms. That's exactly what distinguishes the old Quebec generation from the new one. With us, we can be whatever we want to be, the sky's the limit."[15]

As has been argued by the Montreal Economic Institute's president, Michel Kelly-Gagnon, Quebecers are a paradox. While appearing to embrace big government as they used to embrace big religion, they tend to not have the same kind of emotional attachment to social programs as English Canada. That's because Quebecers define themselves more along the lines of culture and language rather than social programs.

In an April 2005 poll, 52 percent of Canadians agreed that those who wish to pay for private health care for speedier access should have the right to do so as long as the universal system is maintained. But in Quebec, support for the idea was at 65 percent.[16] The case of *Chaoulli v. Quebec (Attorney General)*[17], which opened the door to private health insurance, didn't arise in Calgary; it was filed in Montreal. And let's not forget the massive endorsement the Quebec electorate gave Brian Mulroney and free trade in 1988, when left-wing English Canadian elites were unanimously panning the idea.

Quebec has shown a willingness to embrace free-market ideas. It now needs a massive dose of exposure for them to displace the popularity of socialism. According to Jean-Herman Guay, professor of political science at the Université de Sherbrooke: "The interest aroused by [the ADQ], its rise in the polls showed that the left-right dynamic can exist [in Quebec] like in the rest of the world."[18]

To spread conservative ideas, a Quebec-focused conservative infrastructure the likes of which we have advocated on previous pages must be constructed. That infrastructure must be seen as developing from within, with leadership from inside Quebec, and not be imposed by English Canada. It would involve the establishment of more conservative-minded think-tanks, which would put the accent on free markets as a way of protecting Quebec's culture and language. The message should be the stronger and more vibrant the Quebec economy, the easier it will be for French to flourish. At the same time, this puts a spoke in the wheels of the separatists who claim that Quebec must leave Canada for Quebecers to be "*maîtres chez nous.*"

It would also involve setting up more conservative media, including a Quebec media watchdog organization, which would churn out critiques of Quebec's overwhelmingly left-wing, separatist and anti-American mainstream press. (Note that most of Quebec's media is owned by non-separatist supporters of the free market, yet their views aren't reflected in their publications.) Conservatives would have to target young people through the university system and youth programs, much like in our chapter on the next generation. And new Quebecers, together with their second-generation children, would be another constituency with which conservatives must connect, as we discuss in Chapter 10.

Now for the Conservative Party's role in Quebec. The lip service Stephen Harper is paying to the province, occasionally dropping in to make a speech or to show up at a barbecue on St. Jean Baptiste Day, is not paying off. True, the number of Quebecers in the Opposition leader's office has increased dramatically. The new party held its first convention in Montreal. There have been attempts at getting Quebecers' attention with policy (remember the Belgian federalism proposal?). But at the time of this writing, the Tories are still hovering in the single-digit range in Quebec polls.

What to do?

First, the party must do a better job reaching out to the Quebec activists it already has. Belinda Stronach won more than 60 percent of the Quebec votes in the 2004 leadership contest. However, many of her organizers are today sitting on their hands. The same goes for many of the players from the Mulroney era. The Tories need to mobilize these people. They also need to treat the party's Quebec members better on big and small matters. For example, at the March 2005 national convention, the party failed to arrange for enough simultaneous translation headsets. As a result, when francophone delegates spoke to resolutions in French, most English delegates tuned out and francophones' points did not get made unless they switched languages. A small point, but one that tarnishes the Tory image in the minds of its Quebec supporters.

Second, the Conservatives must focus on raiding talent from Quebec's provincial parties. Both the ADQ and the Quebec Liberal Party held conventions in late 2004. Not a single Conservative MP, let alone

Harper, showed up at either event. These parties' activists are the Tories' target audience, and many are not involved federally. They are receptive to the Conservative view of decentralization, as well as its position on rectifying the so-called fiscal imbalance that is keeping federal coffers overflowing while the provinces are strapped for cash.

Third, the party must also capitalize on what few opportunities arise in Quebec. As mentioned, polls show Quebecers are the most open of any Canadians to private health care. On June 1, 2004, the Montreal Economic Institute commissioned a poll that showed that 51 percent of Canadians—but 68 percent of Quebecers—would accept allowing citizens to buy private health services to ensure faster service, provided the public system were maintained. Yet when the Supreme Court opened the door to change with its decision in *Chaoulli,* the Tories didn't applaud. Instead, Peter MacKay stood up in the House of Commons and blasted the Prime Minister for underfunding medicare. And as we previously detailed in Chapter 6, the party missed a great chance to ingratiate itself with francophones in Quebec City on the CHOI-FM issue.

Fourth, the party should advocate policies which resonate in the province yet are consistent with conservative ideals it advocates in the rest of the country. The overall message should be simple: "We're a pro-Quebec party that will cut your taxes." Some other concrete ideas, which we present in detail in Chapters 13 through 17, include:

- promoting pro-family policies which are not anti-gay or anti-abortion. As a whole, Quebec is more socially liberal than the rest of Canada. Guay is blunt: "Some Quebecers would agree with Harper to reduce the role of the state. But most are allergic to social conservatism" (author translation);[19]

- advocating real choice in health care and an increase in private services. As we have seen, significantly more Quebecers than other Canadians are prepared to purchase medical services on the private market;

- addressing the issue of national unity with a rebalancing of federal-provincial responsibilities for all provinces that want them. Conservatism cannot advance until support for separatism drops. This must be a priority for conservatives, not only for gaining support in Quebec but for the nation's welfare as a whole.

Polling shows that on law and order issues as well as immigration, conservative policies might also find traction in the province: According to a 2005 CROP-*L'Actualité* poll, 83 percent of Quebecers favour tougher sentences for criminals and 75 percent want tighter controls on immigration.[20]

Even if all this is done, the party may still not do well without a Quebec or fluently bilingual / sort-of-francophone leader (in the mould of Paul Martin, or for Conservatives, Bernard Lord). Quebecers will never elect a non-bilingual, non-Quebec Conservative leader as prime minister, especially if the Liberals have a Quebec leader on the ballot.

Quebec will always pose special challenges for conservatives. It is an entirely unique polity within Canada. The Bloc's failure to wither away will continue to hurt Conservative Party fortunes. But these problems are not insurmountable.[21] While the situation will not be remedied overnight, in the end, changing the culture will be worth it, for conservatives and Canadians. It will take the debate beyond the stale separatist "us vs. them" paradigm to "us and us—what is the best way forward together?" And that benefits all Canadians, inside and outside of Quebec.

Endnotes

1. Michael Bliss, *Right Honourable Men: The Descent of Politics from Macdonald to Mulroney*, (Toronto: HarperCollins, 1994), 72.

2. Stephen Harper and Tom Flanagan, "Our Benign Dictatorship," *The Next City*, Winter 1996-97. www.nextcity.com/main/town/6dictat.htm

3. Peter C. Newman, "To win, Tories need to learn from Dief," *National Post*, May 28, 2005, A23.

4. Author interview with David Frum, March 17, 2005.

5. George Koch and John Weissenberger, "You Can Win Without Quebec," *National Post*, May 25, 2004, A22.

6. Conrad Black, *Render Unto Caesar* (Toronto: Key Porter Books, 1998), 9.

7. Author interview with Preston Manning, March 31, 2005.

8. Peter Rakobowchuk, "Quebec's Canada Day Funding Slashed," *Canoe News*, June 7, 2005. http://cnews.canoe.ca/CNEWS/Canada/2005/06/07/1075586-cp.html

9. Testimony of Jean Chrétien, Gomery Inquiry Transcript, Vol. 72, Feb. 8, 2005; Testimony of Alfonso Gagliano, Gomery Inquiry Transcript, Vol. 67, February 1, 2005.

10. Peter Brimelow, *The Patriot Game* (Toronto, Key Porter Books, 1986), 289.

11. Author interview with Peter Brimelow, July 19, 2005.

12. See the blog of Laurent Moss for more.
www.polyscopique.com/blog/archives/000734.html

13. "Dossier: Qui sont les 18-24 ans?" *La Presse*, September 11, 2004, A31.

14. Isabelle Gregoire, "Y a-t-il une droite au Québec?" *L'Actualité*, 12 mars 2005.
http://72.14.207.104/search?q=cache:LZqAi0OpV90J:www.lactualite.com/homepage/article.jsp%3Fcontent%3D20050310_211115_4368+l%27actualite+%22droite+au+quebec%22&hl=en (hereinafter Gregoire).
Original French quotation: «Un débat de société sain et honnête s'impose. Le modèle social-démocrate québécois fait la preuve de son échec chaque jour un peu plus. Dans les années 1960 et 1970, on inventait, l'État était un accélérateur pour les jeunes entrepreneurs. Aujourd'hui, il est un frein à l'innovation.»

15. Ingrid Peritz, "The Language of Confidence," in Erin Anderssen, Michael Valpy et al., *The New Canada: A Globe and Mail Report on the Next Generation* (Toronto: The Globe and Mail/McCelland and Stewart, 2004), 210.

16. Montreal Economic Institute / Leger Marketing, "The Opinion of Canadians on Access to Health Care," April 12, 2005, 5.
www.iedm.org/uploaded/pdf/sondage0405_en.pdf

17. (2005) SCC 35.

18. Gregoire. Original French quotation: «L'intérêt que ce parti a suscité, sa montée dans les sondages ont montré que la dynamique droite-gauche pouvait exister ici comme ailleurs dans le monde.»

19. Gregoire. Original French quotation: «Certains Québécois seraient d'accord avec lui pour réduire le rôle de l'État, dit-il. La plupart sont cependant allergiques au conservatisme social.»

20. Gregoire.

21. As this book goes to press, even former Quebec Premier Lucien Bouchard is calling for Québécers to change their relationship with government. In a report bringing together both separatists and federalists, Bouchard and others criticize Québécers for working less and obtaining more social programs than other North Americans: "both individually and collectively, their credit cards are maxed out." The report calls for an increase in university tuition, reform of the tax system, and a reining in of the public debt. Graeme Hamilton, "New Manifesto for Quebec," *National Post*, October 20, 2005.
www.canada.com/national/nationalpost/news/story.html?id=1ccb68cd-3ad0-4412-92d3-652bd696b941

10 CHAPTER

CONNECTING WITH NEW CANADIANS:
The Ins and Outs of Immigration

*"Canada, having few indigenous prejudices, has been compelled
to import them from elsewhere, duty-free ... We are a nation of
immigrants, and not happy in our minds."*

— Robertson Davies

IT'S a cliché, but it's true: Canada is a nation of immigrants. We're
pretty sure that even First Nations originally crossed the Bering land
bridge from Asia and built their lean-tos in what became North America.
Whether for the wide-open spaces, refuge from war-torn Europe, sanc-
tuary from tinpot dictators or the fact they can't score a Green Card
south of the border, millions of immigrants have flocked to Canada in
search of a better life.

Unfortunately, they have yet to flock to the Conservative Party. The
Progressive Conservative Party, the Reform Party, the Canadian Alliance,
and its current incarnation are still (unfairly) viewed as the bastion of the
nation's white Anglo-Saxon elite. Meanwhile, the Liberals are generally
seen to be inclusive, socially progressive, less uniformly pale and, of
course, the champions of the Charter of Rights. Never mind that the Tories
were strong advocates of ending apartheid in South Africa, the first party
to elect a black member of Parliament (who subsequently became the

first black Cabinet minister and later the first black lieutenant-governor), or that today's Tories have the most ethnically diverse caucus in parliament. As is always the case in politics, perception has jelled into reality.

The Immigrant Vote—A Liberal Lock

During the debate on same-sex marriage in the spring of 2005, Stephen Harper tried to play to immigrant and religious communities by championing the traditional definition of marriage. While this did rally some ethnic troops to the Tories' side, the Liberals one-upped the Conservatives with their artfully timed changes to immigration rules. Knowing that the Conservatives were smelling blood before a potential election call, in April 2005 the Liberals craftily announced they would triple the number of applications processed annually for sponsoring parents and grandparents from 6,000 to 18,000.

According to *The Globe and Mail* columnist John Ibbitson, at the time 23 Liberal seats in Ontario and 4 in British Columbia were swing ridings based on immigration.[1] Knowing that the big electoral battleground in 2005 would be Ontario, the Liberals strategically positioned themselves to hold on to those constituencies. In the words of Martin Collacott, a former Canadian ambassador and immigration expert, "the move underlines once again the government's readiness to sacrifice the interests of Canadians in the hope of picking up a few extra votes in a handful of ethnically diverse urban ridings."[2]

Indeed, the Liberals have benefited from immigrant voting patterns in a big way—and so have the immigrant-heavy ridings that vote Liberal. In the fall of 2004, the Canadian Labour and Business Centre (CLBC) analyzed data based on the 2001 census. It revealed that immigrants form the majority of the population in 17 federal constituencies. Of the 20 ridings with the highest percentage of immigrants, 15 are in Ontario, 4 in British Columbia and 1 in Quebec.[3] All of the ridings lie in urban or suburban areas in and around the cities of Toronto, Vancouver and Montreal. In 14 of those ridings, a quarter of the population was composed of immigrants who have been in Canada only ten years or less.[4]

How did those 20 immigrant-heavy ridings vote in the 2004 federal election? Surprise, surprise: 19 sent Liberals to Ottawa, while 1 voted

NDP. And how did the Liberal Party reward these ridings? Twelve of the nineteen MPs were made ministers, filling just under a third of the entire Cabinet. Seven of those nineteen members were immigrants themselves; four of the seven made it to Cabinet.[5]

The message to new Canadians is clear: Vote Liberal, and you get a prime perch in the corridors of power.

This is no accident. The majority of immigrants (including our own parents) came here under Liberal rule, and many under the watchful eye of Pierre Trudeau. High immigration levels and state-sponsored multiculturalism weren't just a way of diluting the French-English fact, combating separatism and entrenching big government, they were also a way of winning elections. It would be naïve to imagine that newly arrived immigrants would not be grateful to the party that let them in, or that the millions of dollars in federal funding funnelled to ethnic groups by the Secretary of State did not increase immigrants' loyalty to the Liberals. Of course it did. And that loyalty remains undiminished today.

The Liberals are masters of ethnic politics. They have deep roots in most immigrant communities and continually reinforce those bonds. Pick up any of the ethnic newspapers in the Toronto area and see how many Liberal MPs have taken out ad space, or how many papers feature a picture of a Liberal (likely Immigration Minister Joe Volpe) hugging a smiling group of multicultural children. The Liberals have created a virtual monopoly in urban ethnic communities.

Multicultural Madness

As we explored in Chapter 4, state-sponsored multiculturalism was born in the Trudeau era, when the Department of Secretary of State first set up a multicultural directorate. In 1973, the policy got its own ministry, as well as the Canadian Consultative Council on Multiculturalism, eventually renamed the Canadian Ethnocultural Council. By 1982, multiculturalism grew up and graduated to the big leagues when the Liberals triumphantly enshrined it in the Charter of Rights and Freedoms.[6]

As with other bad Liberal ideas, the Mulroney Tories didn't challenge this policy when they came to office in 1984. Instead, they gave multiculturalism the keys to the family car. The PCs created a House of

Commons Standing Committee on Multiculturalism in 1985, which led to the 1988 Canadian Multiculturalism Act—making Canada the first nation in the world with a multiculturalism law. That legislation made it official government policy to "recognize and promote" multiculturalism because it is a "fundamental characteristic of Canadian heritage and identity." The government committed itself to providing support to "individuals, groups or organizations for the purpose of preserving, enhancing and promoting multiculturalism in Canada."[7]

Today, the impact of these policies is coming under increasing attack. Salim Mansur is an associate professor of political science at the University of Western Ontario and a frequent critic of Canada's immigration and multiculturalism policies. After the Liberals proposed their immigration reforms in the spring of 2005, he commented, "However noble the idea of multiculturalism was, and remains, its politics was invariably bent to suit the electoral requirements of the Liberal party, which was losing ground in Western Canada and Quebec. Moreover, the inherent paradox of multiculturalism is its loosening effect on national identity, of assisting the forces of fragmentation rather than binding a country already weakened by the politics of regionalism and separatism."[8]

Most conservatives today would agree with Mansur that state-funded multiculturalism is a divisive policy that should be scrapped. It has led to problems with integration, reinforced divisions between groups and ghettoized ethnic minorities, all while costing taxpayers plenty. Of course, immigrants should be allowed to maintain their own ethnic heritage and traditions if they choose—but not at the expense of national cohesion or the public treasury.[9]

But on the subject of immigration levels, conservatives are not all of the same mind. Some would like to see an unrestricted flow of immigration. In 2000, then-Canadian Alliance and now Conservative MP Rahim Jaffer proposed that Canada should have no immigration limits at all. Others argue for strict limits and think the number of immigrants entering the country each year should be cut, leading to charges that the party is "anti-immigrant" by Liberals and the left-wing media.

What is the ideal number of immigrants? It's hard to say. It is essential to attract them; Canadians simply aren't having enough babies (underlining the need for more family-friendly tax policies, as will be outlined in Chapter 13), and we need skilled workers to replace retiring baby boomers. But Canada's current immigration targets have no justification—unless you're a Liberal looking for a boost at the polls. A 2002 Fraser Institute study of Canada's immigration policy concluded that "The government's principal reason for promoting high immigration levels is the belief that most newcomers would vote for the Liberal Party in federal elections."[10] The study was unable to find a rational economic basis for Canada's stated goals on immigration, especially for its increase in family class admissions.

Today's immigration levels were arbitrarily set by the Liberal Red Book of election promises in 1993: "We should continue to target immigration levels of approximately one per cent of the population each year, as has been the case for more than a decade." In September 2005, the federal government announced that it was renewing its efforts to meet that arbitrary target—which means about 350,000 new immigrants a year. But why? According to James Bissett, a retired diplomat and senior public servant who helped shape the 1976 Immigration Act, Canada has never admitted that many immigrants. From 1960 to 1993, Canada's average annual intake of immigrants was 0.63 percent of population. From 1995 to 1998, it was 0.73 percent, or 215,000 people. In a speech to the Group of 78, an association which promotes peace and the role of the United Nations in world affairs, Bissett remarked: "To my knowledge, there has never been a rational explanation as to why it is believed that Canada should accept immigrants at the rate of one percent of our population. No other country, with the possible exception of Israel, accepts that many. The United States takes 0.40 percent and Australia 0.46 percent."[11]

Small- and big-c conservatives face a delicate balancing act on the issue of immigration. On the one hand, they must reach out to immigrant voters and involve them in the conservative movement and party if they are to win elections. On the other hand, they must respect the economic and social needs of our nation. This means questioning whether Canada needs as many immigrants as we presently admit, and acknowledging the difficulties in integrating large numbers of new Canadians.

In the 1990s, Australia faced similar problems with its immigration policy. Unlike Canada, however, it prioritized national concerns over those of newcomers. Australia set annual "benefit targets" to gauge the impact of immigration on its economy. It also adopted a "balance of family" test, under which at least half the number children of one family must already be in Australia before their parents are allowed to join them. These children must also post substantial bonds to offset their elders' potential medical expenses.

Canadian conservatives should learn from this experience, and undertake to set out policies of immigration at a level that will be of benefit to the country. They should also ensure that newcomers are able to integrate into and contribute to Canadian society. Bodies, even skilled bodies, are of no use to Canada if they end up on welfare, or sweeping floors because their degree isn't recognized by Canadian firms. According to Statistics Canada, six in ten immigrants took jobs other than those they were trained to do in 2000 and 2001.[12]

And today's immigrants are not doing as well financially as previous generations of newcomers. According to University of Toronto professor Jeffrey Reitz, in 1981, new immigrants earned on average about 80 percent of what native-born Canadians did. In 1996, that had dropped to 60 percent.[13] In 1996, employment rates for new male immigrants had dropped to 68 percent, compared to 85 percent for Canadian-born men.[14] Today, doctors and engineers wooed to our shores with the promise of a better life find themselves driving taxis to make ends meet. A study by the Conference Board of Canada estimates that failure to recognize immigrants' learning and credentials costs them between $3.4 and $5.0 billion annually in lost earnings, due to unemployment and underemployment.[15] This doesn't help anybody—the immigrants themselves or Canadian taxpayers. If these immigrants aren't making the money they could be, then they won't pay enough taxes to offset the costs of educating their kids or paying medical bills run up by elderly relatives, who won't be earning anything but will be costing our health system.

Striking a deal with the provinces and regulatory bodies that oversee professional qualifications should be a key plank in the Conservatives' platform. Short-term labour visas would be another solution. To Stephen

Harper's credit, the Tories seem to be on the right track in this regard with their campaign to "stand up for hard-working immigrants" and improve their ability to use their credentials to earn a living. However, the Liberals are already acting on this file. Minister Joe Volpe announced in April 2005 $269 million in spending to help ease immigrants into the workforce and get their credentials recognized (conveniently unveiled in Toronto and Vancouver by twelve Liberal MPs just when it looked like the Tories might force an election).[16] So it is the Grits, not the Tories, who will get credit from immigrant communities should any progress be achieved.

Immigration Balancing Act

Overhauling our refugee determination system is another must for conservatives—and the country. In the 1990s, smugglers made headlines when boatloads of illegal migrants were apprehended in Canadian ports. In the post-911 era, Canada's sieve-like refugee system has been accused of making us a haven for terrorists. According to Concordia University political science professor Stephen Gallagher, Canada is not only the easiest country in the developed world in which to secure Convention Refugee Status, it is also the easiest to move from being a refugee to gaining permanent residency and citizenship.[17]

Statistics bear this out. In the past twenty years, 600,000 people made a refugee claim in Canada. Over the same period, our government granted 500,000 refugees or people in "refugee-like" situations Permanent Resident Status.[18] In 2002, Canada granted refugee status to almost 60 percent of claimants, far in excess of any other "major destination country." Next highest was the United States, where 35 percent of claimants got status, followed by Austria and Belgium (20 percent). Fourteen percent of applicants got status in Australia, while only 2 percent did in Sweden.[19]

Our refugee determination system is slow and prone to abuse. Conservatives should call for a revision of refugee criteria to admit those truly persecuted, deny entry to bogus refugees and speed up processing times so unsuccessful claimants don't languish for years in Canada consuming public resources. These concerns were reflected in the Tories' policy statement coming out of the 2005 Montreal convention.

Then there's the thorny question of social integration. The United States and Australia have both recently emphasized immigration from communities which are more readily able to integrate into their societies, whose members espouse similar values of democracy and freedom and who possess the necessary skills, linguistic or otherwise, to find gainful employment. This shift is starting to happen in Great Britain as well, especially after the July 7, 2005 terrorist bombings in London. Prime Minister Tony Blair has announced plans to deport radical Muslim imams with no right to appeal and shut down extremist mosques. A commission on multiculturalism has been struck to look at ways to better integrate recent British arrivals. At a press conference Blair went as far as to say, "If people want to come here ... they play by our rules and our way of life" and that "coming to Britain is not a right." London's *Guardian* newspaper went as far as to call the reforms "a turning point in British postwar liberalism." [20]

Such policies would probably find similar traction here. Recent polling suggests that 69 percent of Canadians believe immigrants should be encouraged to integrate and become part of the broader society rather than maintain their ethnic identity and culture. That number rises to 85 percent in Quebec.[21] This flies directly in the face of Liberal claims that Canadians embrace their multicultural vision. While 71 percent of those surveyed believe that we should make no distinctions and accept immigrants from all countries, respondents were divided on whether immigrants from some countries "make a bigger and better contribution to Canada than others." Forty-one percent said they do; 50 percent said there is no difference in contribution based on country of origin.[22]

When it comes to discussing immigration, country of origin is probably the most volatile subject. Even raising the issue can lead to accusations of bigotry and racism. Why immigrants from some countries or cultures thrive while others founder is a taboo topic, yet it has to be addressed if governments are to design immigration policies that benefit our country.

It's a subject to which Torontonian Naresh Raghubeer has given considerable thought. Raghubeer came to Canada as a refugee from Guyana in 1984. Today he is the executive director of the Canadian Coalition of Democracies (CCD), a non-partisan, non-profit, multi-ethnic, multi-denominational organization which promotes democracy in Canada and abroad. According to Raghubeer, ability to integrate is not determined by immigrants' race or ethnic origin, but by their respect for the rule of law and ability to adopt Canadian values and culture, in particular political culture and respect for local laws.

Raghubeer believes that immigrants from countries which value individual freedom, the rule of law and parliamentary democracy integrate more easily into Canadian society than those coming from tribal or religious states, or non-democratic, lawless or oppressive regimes. Immigrants who are unwilling or unable to adapt to our language and social structures also are likely to have a tougher time. Mansur concurs: "For European immigrants, traditional Canadian values as an inherent part of western civilization are not entirely alien. But this does not hold for many non-European immigrants."[23]

Both at home and abroad, attitudes are starting to change. The governments of Ontario and Quebec both recently refused to allow the establishment of Muslim sharia tribunals to decide family law matters. In the wake of the 2005 London bombings and a push for Islamic law in Australia, its treasurer, Peter Costello, stated categorically, "If you can't agree with parliamentary law, independent courts, democracy, and would prefer Sharia law and have the opportunity to go to another country which practices it, perhaps, then, that's a better option."[24] Raghubeer is equally blunt: "Australia and America already give immigration preference to nation of origin and it is about time Canada does the same if we are to find the most suitable immigrants to build this country."

Turning New Canadians into New Conservatives

It is also important for new immigrants to be given a strong grounding in Canadian traditions when they get here. Conservatives should engender a new sense of patriotism among all Canadians. Democratic traditions, our linguistic heritage and symbols like the flag have been gradually co-opted by the Liberals for their own partisan advantage. They act as if they are the only ones who will protect Canadian values (read: their own) and that the Conservatives have a "hidden agenda." Part of that purported agenda, aside from banning abortions, making people mortgage their house to pay for hip surgery and breaking up Canada, is to send immigrants back on the boat they came in on, or to prevent their parents or relatives from joining them in Canada. Conservatives must counter this fear-mongering and directly appeal to immigrants by re-establishing Canada as a beacon of economic hope, peace and prosperity, not a place where the harder you work, the less you get ahead.

To communicate not only national values but conservative values to new Canadians, small-c conservatives must start programs and outreach efforts which appeal to immigrants' hopes and aspirations. For most immigrants, the values of home, family, education and hard work are paramount. These are also conservative principles—but what is missing are the mechanisms to connect them with immigrant communities.

What immigrant infrastructure does exist is run by government, faith-based organizations or left-leaning entities like labour and anti-poverty groups. These include the Ontario Coalition Against Poverty, whose website champions the stories of immigrants and refugees whom they claim are oppressed, exploited or have otherwise been denied their rights, and the Asian-Canadian Labour Alliance, which works to promote unionization and "generate a Labour-positive presence in Asian communities."[25]

Conservatives have to duplicate services currently offered by these groups, but provide them more effectively and from a conservative perspective. The underlying message should not be "what your new country can do for you" but "what you can do for yourself in your new country."

Immigrants are concerned with issues of employment, crime and the well-being of their children. Conservatives should build up organizations that respond to these needs. On a local level, activities for conservative-minded immigrant groups could include:

- Organizing job-search clinics for immigrants as well as seminars on how to start your own business, explaining and promoting free-market principles;

- Setting up community safety programs in immigrant neighbourhoods to help people protect themselves and their families from violence, while promoting a conservative vision of law and order;

- Organizing events at community centres featuring conservative immigrant speakers telling their story, and how conservative values helped them succeed in Canada;

- Teaching ESL classes with conservative-themed literature. Exposing immigrants to conservative texts would be a good start. Do you really think anyone's reading Ayn Rand, Friedrich Hayek, or the *Western Standard* in government-run ESL classes?;

- Organizing local "democracy clinics" to explain why democratic values are important and how conservatism has shaped those values;

- Starting a mentoring program for immigrant youth, which would expose them to conservative beliefs in the context of fun activities or assistance with schoolwork.

Because many of these activities would be deemed educational, it would be easier to get charitable status, which as we have already seen greatly facilitates fundraising efforts.

In fact, education itself is one of the best avenues to reach immigrant communities. Immigrants value education, particularly for their children, as a means to advancement. Conservatives should develop projects which provide scholarship assistance to immigrant families to improve their children's educational prospects.

In Ontario, the Children First School Choice Trust provides an excellent model for this type of program. In conjunction with the W. Garfield Weston Foundation, the Fraser Institute established this initiative in 2003 to help Ontario families afford the school of their choice. Children First funds 225 new tuition assistance grants annually for students entering junior kindergarten to Grade 8; each grant is worth 50 percent of tuition, to a maximum of $3,500 per year (parents pay the other half). The support continues until Grade 8 as long as the student remains in good standing.

The testimonials on the School Choice website illustrate the interest new Canadians have in such programs. In the words of one parent from Scarborough, "My son was a recipient of one of your Children First awards to facilitate entry into an Independent School. This opportunity was especially heart-warming as I am a recent immigrant to Canada and this reinforced the perception of this country as providing opportunities to all persons without consideration to ethnicity or income levels."[26]

Education can also be used to smooth the path to employment for immigrants, by informing native-born Canadians about the value of immigration. In 2005, the Canadian Council for Christians and Jews started a breakfast series entitled "Diversity is Good Business," designed to educate businesses on the benefits of hiring a multicultural work-force. But instead of presenting diversity as a Trudeauvian feel-good initiative, the series aims to show businesses how immigrants can be an economic asset. In the global marketplace, companies can increase their profitability by capitalizing on the foreign expertise of new Canadians. Using market incentives, instead of platitudes or quotas, is a more posi-tive way to increase immigrants' employment opportunities, and one which conservative groups could promote as well.

Critical to the success of all the aforementioned programs is that front-line workers come from the same cultural communities that they are serving. Immigrants will respond much more positively to a message deliv-ered by someone who has shared their experience and speaks their language, than to a sermon from a white guy who grew up in Etobicoke.

Conservatives must also blow their own horn about these initia-tives, and about conservative ideas, in the ethnic press. Whether it's conservative politicians posing for photo-ops at the local Chinese com-munity centre, conservative journalists producing a radio program on employment issues in the Somali community or conservative writers contributing editorial copy to the local Punjabi paper, ethnic media is a key venue for reaching the immigrant audience. Canada has more than 250 ethnic newspapers, representing over 40 cultures, including 7 non-English dailies. At least 14 radio stations provide programming for ethnic groups, while over 60 "mainstream" stations include ethnic programming on their roster. In Ontario, Toronto's CHIN media broadcasts in over 30 languages, while CFMT-TV provides programming in more than 22 languages. Similar stations and a host of digital specialty channels have also been licensed in British Columbia and Quebec.[27]

On a final note, reaching out to immigrants is not just about building a conservative culture in their communities, but about making urban Canada more conservative as well. Between 1996 and 2001, while the population of Canada increased by 4 percent, the "Big Four" urban regions (Toronto, Vancouver, Montreal, Calgary) grew by 7.6 percent. This urban growth was not fuelled by native-born Canadians, but by immigrants. Two-thirds of immigrants—657,520 people settled in big cities; at the same time, those centres actually lost 77,690 members of their existing populations, mostly to mid-size towns and cities. Making inroads into immigrant communities is a two-for-one deal: it would help turn around the ethnic vote and the big-city vote, both of which are increasingly elusive to conservatives.[28]

These urban voters also include a great number of second-generation immigrants. One in five Canadians in their twenties—730,000 people—have parents who were not born here. "Driven to make good on their parents' sacrifices, they tend to excel beyond their peers," writes journalist Erin Anderssen.[29] According to the 2001 census, 20-somethings who are members of visible minorities are twice as likely to graduate from university as their peers whose parents were born in Canada.[30] These young people want to continue building upon the foundations laid by their parents and achieve a better life.

The second generation's success-oriented attitude makes them a natural conservative constituency—if only conservatives connect with them. But that should not be as difficult as connecting with their parents, because new Canadian kids tend to be more integrated into Western cultural norms. According to polling for *The Globe and Mail*, "[t]heir attitudes are remarkably similar to people in their 20s with two Canadian-born parents."[31]

If the Conservative Party wants to grow it has no choice but to win over these voters. Realpolitik dictates the party must make a strategic shift from its rural base to becoming a more urban party. According to Statistics Canada, if current immigration trends continue, by the year 2017 more than 50 percent of the populations of Toronto and Vancouver will be visible minorities. More than a million Torontonians will be South Asians and 735,000 will be Chinese; half of Vancouver will be Chinese, and Montreal will be 27 percent black and 19 percent Arab. Overall, one of every five Canadians could be a visible minority.[32]

Conservatives must respond to this new reality—and soon. Continuing down the path of state-funded multiculturalism and untested immigration targets is a recipe for social and political disharmony, which serves neither the immigrants who come to our country, nor Canadians already living here. Conservatives must not only make inroads into immigrant communities but advocate for immigration reforms that are in the best interests of the nation, not of political expediency.

Endnotes

1. John Ibbitson, "Why the Liberals are focusing on immigration," *The Globe and Mail,* April 19, 2005, A4.

2. Martin Collacott, "Immigration reform, done badly," *National Post,* April 21, 2005, A16.

3. Canadian Labour and Business Centre, "Immigrants Now A Majority In Seventeen Federal Constituencies," Press Release, Thursday, October 7, 2004. www.clbc.ca/Press_Release_-_041007.asp

4. "Twenty Federal Ridings with the Highest Share of Immigrants in the Population, Canada, 2001 Census," Canadian Labour and Business Centre, October 7 2004. www.clbc.ca/files/Immigrants_now_a_majority_-_Table_1.pdf (hereinafter "Twenty Federal Ridings").

5. "Twenty Federal Ridings."

6. "Canadian Multiculturalism," Library of Parliament, Political and Social Affairs Division. Prepared by Marc Leman, February 15, 1999. www.parl.gc.ca/informa tion/library/PRBpubs/936-e.htm (hereinafter "Canadian Multiculturalism").

7. "Canadian Multiculturalism."

8. Salim Mansur, "Liberals' Ethnic Exploitation to be Tested," April 27, 2005. www.proudtobecanadian.ca/columnists/index/writergroup/comments/liberals_ ethnic_exploitation_to_be_tested/ (hereinafter Mansur).

9. The Conservative Party's March 2005 policy statement tiptoes around the topic, saying nothing of funding, only that Ottawa "must ensure that each [multicultural] community is able to enhance and contribute to Canada without discrimination and barriers."

10. Martin Collacutt, "Canada's Immigration Policy: The Need for Major Reform," *Public Policy Sources,* Vol 64, (February 2003), 5. www.fraserinstitute.ca/admin/books/files/immigration-2ndEdition.pdf

11. James Bissett, "Current Immigration Policy and the Crisis in Refugee Asylum," addess made to the Group of 78 Luncheon, June 20, 2000. http://64.233.167.104/search?q=cache:HXzPg6PF1dQJ:www.hri.ca/partners/ G78/English/Global/bisset.shtml+%22red+book%22+immigration+policy+numb er+reality&thl=en

12. Jennifer O'Brien, "Armed with degrees, they drive our cabs," *London Free Press,* January 17, 2004.

13. Jeffrey Reitz, "New immigrants find streets aren't paved with gold: study," University of Toronto, 2000. www.news.utoronto.ca/bin/000426a.asp

14. Jeffrey Reitz, "Why we need mentors to tap immigration skills," *The Globe and Mail,* February 9, 2005. www.theglobeandmail.com/servlet/story/ RTGAM.20050209.wiciz09/BNStory/Front/

15. The Conference Board of Canada, "Immigration: A New Deal for Newcomers," report by Michael Bloom, *Performance & Potential 2004–2005: How Can Canada Prosper in Tomorrow's World?,* October 2004, Chapter 5.

16. Marina Jiminéz, "Volpe unveils plan to approve immigrants' job credentials," *The Globe and Mail,* April 26, 2005. A11.

17. Steven Gallagher, "Canada's Dysfunctional Refugee Determination System," *Public Policy Sources,* no.78, December 2003, a Fraser Institute Occasional Paper, 3. http://64.233.187.104/search?q=cache:XIJXZUn74iMJ:www.frascrin stitute.ca/shared/readmore.asp%3FsNav%3Dpb%26id%3D614 +canada+refugee+system&thl=en (hereinafter Gallagher).

18. Gallagher, 5.

19. Gallagher, 18.

20. Patrick Wintour, "Blair vows to root out extremism," *The Guardian,* August 6, 2005. http://politics.guardian.co.uk/terrorism/story/0,15935,1543786,00.html

21. "Immigration Terrorism and National Security," The Strategic Counsel, August Survey for *The Globe and Mail* and CTV, August 7, 2005. www.thestrate giccounsel.com/our_news/polls/0805%20GMCTV%20August%20Poll.pdf (hereinafter Strategic Counsel).

22. Strategic Counsel, 15-16

23. Mansur.

24. "Muslims who want Islamic law told to leave Australia," AFP News on Yahoo news service, August 23, 2005. http://64.233.167.104/search?q=cache: NPZYN82XfWYJ:news.yahoo.com/s/afp/20050824/wl_asia_afp/australiaislama ttacks+%22Treasurer+Peter+Costello%22+sharia+law&thl=en

25. Website of the Asian Canadian Labour Alliance. www.buzzardpress.com/acla/goals.html

26. Children First website, "Children First Stories." www.childrenfirstgrants.ca/about_stories.html

27. "Ethnic Media in Canada." www.media-awareness.ca/english/issues/stereotyp ing/ethnics_and_minorities/minorities_ethnicmedia.cfm

28. Erin Anderson, Michael Valpy et al., "By the Numbers: A Graphic Look at the New Canada, Where We Live," in *The New Canada* (Toronto: The Globe and Mail / McClelland and Stewart, 2004), Appendix 1, (hereinafter *The New Canada).*

29. *The New Canada,* 67.

30. *The New Canada,* 79.

31. *The New Canada,* 79.

32. Study: Canada's visible minority population in 2017. Statistics Canada, *The Daily,* March 22, 2005. www.statcan.ca/Daily/English/050322/d050322b.htm

11 CHAPTER

PROFESSIONALIZING POLITICS:
Training Leaders, Generals and Ground Troops

"Leadership does not simply happen. It can be taught, learned, developed."

— Rudy Giuliani

JUST for a moment, imagine that the conservative infrastructure we've been talking about is built. Let's say that in ten years Canada has a much more balanced debate in the media, in the courts, on university campuses and in the public discourse in general. Would conservatism then take the voting public by storm, sweeping a truly right-of-centre Conservative Party into power at 24 Sussex Drive?

The answer could be yes, with one caveat: that party has to have the right people at the top. That means an inspirational leader, and the right team to back him or her up.

Politics is ultimately about leadership. And the Canadian right has seriously lacked it over the years. Without a strong, engaging and visionary leader, growing the conservative movement will be for naught. We can build the greatest political ship the world has ever seen, but without the right captain, it will run aground as it has in so many of the last elections.

Ideally, Canada needs its own Ronald Reagan or Margaret Thatcher. Someone who will capture the imagination of Canadians and bring the conservative movement to government in Ottawa. Someone who will not buckle under pressure when the combined weight of Ottawa officialdom, the media and every interest group in the country tries to block attempts at conservative change. Someone who possesses all the necessary elements of leadership: courage, vision, optimism, top-notch communications skills and the capacity to inspire. As Reagan himself said, "The greatest leader is not necessarily the one who does the greatest things. He is the one who gets the people to do the greatest things."

We have yet to find that person. But we must remember: great leaders aren't just born, they're also made. Conservatives must cultivate their potential leaders throughout all facets of the movement—media, academia, think-tanks, activism, law—and create a healthy pool of future prime ministers, thinkers, organizers and strategists. This will ensure that there will be inspiring people positioned to take the reins of political power when the time is right. It will also ensure that their support crew is in place, so that from the Leader's Office on down, communications people, campaign managers and advisers are all worthy of the titles they hold.

How can the conservative movement develop better, stronger leaders, generals and ground troops? The answer is by professionalizing our politics and arming political activists with the knowledge and skills necessary to beat the left and the Liberals in battle.

Learning to Lead

Like the other infrastructure we describe in this book, that training will not and should not come from the Conservative Party itself. According to Preston Manning, "The political parties in this country invest nothing in training people. If you were running a national service company and invested as little in human resources as the political parties do you'd be bankrupt in a year."[1] Yet this kind of education is crucial at all levels of political organization, from volunteer poll captains, to constituency organizers, riding executives, candidates and MPs. Manning believes that even political staff, such as legislative and executive assistants, would do their jobs better with formal training.

He's right. Politics is an art, but it's also a business, where having the latest skills, technology and know-how sets you apart from the fold.

No one understands this better than our southern neighbours. Though some may say the Americans can make an industry out of anything and money out of nothing, including politics, that's not the point. This is about *professionalism*.

In terms of professionalism, the business of Canadian politics is lagging behind. Much of this is due to economies of scale and the fact that we have fewer campaigns in which to hone skills and employ a professional political class. We have no senate elections, no open primaries. We elect MPs every four years, whereas the Yanks vote for Congressmen every two. But regardless of the quantity of politics in Canada, we can still improve its quality by replicating some of the successful training and leadership development programs that exist in the U.S.

The most notable of these is Washington, D.C.'s Leadership Institute (LI), founded by legendary Republican activist Morton Blackwell. A former executive director of the College Republican National Committee, Blackwell was the youngest delegate for Barry Goldwater at the 1964 Republican Convention and supported Ronald Reagan in his failed 1968 and 1976 bids for the Republican presidential nomination, long before conservatism was considered mainstream. When Reagan finally won the nomination in 1980, Blackwell ran his youth campaign. He later went on to work at the White House.

Blackwell established LI in 1979. Its mission is to identify, recruit and train conservatives in politics, government and media. Since its founding, more than 40,000 students have graduated from seminars on subjects ranging from media and public relations training, to the ins and outs of direct mail, to the effective use the Internet. One click on its snazzy website, www.lead-inst.org, will offer you everything from information on a workshop on "Effective Television Techniques" to a documentary entitled "The Roots of the Ultra-Left: What They Really Think" (no, it's not about the birth of the NDP). LI also runs www.conservativejobs.com, which helps young activists find employment in politics, think-tanks, activism and the press. The organization itself has a staff of fifty–seven and a $7 million revenue base–proof that conservative training can not only work, it can also pay.

One of LI's recurrent themes is the importance of reading conservative books. In his famous "Read to Lead" speech, Blackwell expounds on how all knowledgeable people are largely self-taught; how the surest way to acquire a wide range of useful knowledge is to read every day; and how important it is to read biographies and autobiographies of political leaders. He maintains a list of twenty–five suggested books for conservatives, including classics such as Friedrich Hayek's *The Road to Serfdom* and newer works like Dinesh D'Souza's biography of Ronald Reagan.[2] Blackwell knows that if people—especially the young—read books by and about great conservative thinkers, those who are already conservatives will become better ones, and those who are still finding their ideological compass will be more likely to embrace conservatism. Given the steady stream of socialist/leftist reading material fed to students today, getting conservative reading material into their hands is one of the best ways to win over converts. It's amazing the number of people who come to conservatism simply because they've been exposed to it.

Blackwell is also well-known for a forty-five point list he calls "The Laws of the Public Policy Process," in which he coined political axioms such as "Never give a bureaucrat a chance to say no," "Give 'em a title and get 'em involved," "You can't beat a plan with no plan," and, the most recognized and our personal favourite, "Personnel is policy,"[3] meaning that you should always expect policies to reflect the personal ideological proclivities of the people who write them. In other words, if you are a conservative in a government or policy job, you better encircle yourself with conservatives if you want to see your ideas implemented. It's all common sense, but Blackwell and his school's program lay it out in a simple, jargon-free way. A handful of Canadians have been fortunate enough to attend LI workshops, including some members of parliament. One Conservative MP's photo even hangs in LI's Arlington, Virginia office as a member of the organization's hall of fame.

LI is not just a model for Canada, but has been adopted by other groups in the U.S. In 1996, Ralph Reed, then-head of the Christian Coalition and himself an LI graduate, insisted that his organization launch and maintain "an ambitious training program modelled after the leadership schools of Morton Blackwell."[4] According to University of

Oregon professor Julia Lesage, "these training schools have proven vital to the [Christian Coalition's] ongoing practice, educating Coalition members as socially effective activists."[5]

In addition to the practical skills such schools impart, they also inspire a sense of team-building and solidarity. This would be incredibly useful in Canada at a time when conservatives often feel marginalized. Let's face it, for many, a political party is a social club. It provides a sense of family. There are probably as many ill-dressed, goofy nerds in politics as there are in the tech biz—why? Because if you're smart and have certain skills, such as polling or strategizing, you will be not only accepted but revered by your political peers. This creates a sense of belonging and organizational loyalty, which is critical to a political party's success.

Some conservative training, leadership and scholarship programs exist in Canada, but on a much smaller scale, and are geared almost exclusively to the younger set. One program where the right was well-represented was Magna International Inc.'s "As Prime Minister Awards" essay contest, the brainchild of Magna founder Frank Stronach. For several years, the program was chaired by daughter Belinda and run by George Marsland, a former staffer in Prime Minister Mulroney's Office. Finalists of the essay contest received a monetary prize as well as an internship with Magna, and had their submissions published in a book called *At Stake: As Prime Minister, I Would ...*[6] While by no means uniformly conservative, the annual competition was one of the only outlets available for young, non-liberal voices to be heard and published. Students with right-of-centre views were prominently represented among the ten finalists picked each year. Unfortunately, the program was disbanded soon after Belinda's departure from Magna for the political arena. In its place is a new reality TV program called "The Next Great Prime Minister" (and no, Belinda is not a contestant).

The Conservative Leadership Foundation

As far as conservative political training schools go, only one exists, the Ontario-based Conservative Leadership Foundation (CLF). The CLF was founded fourteen years ago by two young Tories: John Mykytyshyn, who went on to do polling for Mike Harris, and John Capobianco, a seasoned politico who has held many positions in the federal and Ontario Conservative parties.

Capobianco had been youth campaign chair for Mike Harris' successful run for the Ontario PC leadership in 1990. He used the race to build a core group of youth activists. Every weekend young Tories got together at Harris' Toronto leadership headquarters to learn election skills. The key, according to Mykytyshyn, was to make things fun while imparting the campaign savvy necessary to win. Capobianco went on to become president of the Ontario PC Youth Association, and the CLF was born soon after.

The idea for the organization came primarily from training schools that had been set up in the late 1980s under the auspices of the federal PC Party, National Campaign Colleges (NCC) and the National Leadership Institute (NLI). At the helm of the NCC and NLI were a group of young Tory turks who had worked in the Mulroney government. Among them were Nigel Wright, now a managing director at Onex Corp., Tom Long, a former Canadian Alliance leadership candidate and a key architect of the Common Sense Revolution, and Stewart Braddick, who went on to become principal secretary to Mike Harris. The group had heard of Blackwell's LI and wanted to emulate its success in Canada. Because the federal PC party was in government and had money, it was easy to plan events: an NCC the year before an election, the NLI in other years. The sessions were not only instructive but also exciting for young Tory trainees; perhaps too exciting, as when they made headlines for trashing the residences of Carleton University. But there was no doubting the schools' success. Unfortunately, they are now defunct, but the CLF continues to thrive.

At its inception, the CLF did not have the funds the NCC and NLI had. After the 1990 election, the Ontario Tories were in third place in the legislature and mired in debt. But in 1991 it held its first session, chaired by former Ontario PC Campus Association President Sandra Buckler, as a completely volunteer-run organization. It remains that way today.

The key to the CLF's appeal is a constantly-evolving curriculum geared to different levels of expertise, a system which avoided "the tyranny of the lowest common denominator," as Mykytyshyn puts it.[7] The current trend in parties reflects politically correct attitudes to make curricula as simplistic as possible, geared to the least knowledgeable person, so as not to make anyone feel out of place. While this may be an inclusive approach, it also ensures people won't bother to come back a second time. Once they've attended a school, perhaps for one and only one time, they think they know everything. The reality is that campaign techniques are constantly changing, especially with the rapid advancement being made in political technology and software. It is always possible to learn more and get better, as long as the program continues to challenge its participants.

With this in mind, the CLF created a "tiered system." Participants were initially assessed in a two-hour exam process. Based on their prior knowledge of campaign techniques and strategy, they were streamed and taught a variety of classes appropriate to their level. (These included Alister Campbell's famous basic "how to clap" course, as well as his more infamous class on how to run a recruitment table, in which he would throw a chair across the room to illustrate the fact that a successful recruiter never sat down.) Participants learned how to write brochures, knock on doors and much more.

As proof of the CLF's impact, there was a direct relationship between it and the genesis of the 1995 Common Sense Revolution. The CLF's founders and attendees were the ones who eventually conceived and wrote the platform, ran campaigns for PC candidates across Ontario and later staffed MPP and ministers' offices at Queen's Park.

After their electoral success, however, the CLF fell into inactivity for several years as activists were absorbed with the task of running the government. Then in 2000, Capobianco and Mykytyshyn were approached to restart the CLF, this time as an independent training school, not as an appendix of the PC party. It was refounded in 2001, with more than 130 students participating in its re-launch seminar in Hamilton, Ontario. CLF has had more events in recent years and hopes to continue doing more.

It is important for conservatives to invest in this type of organization and, most crucially, to replicate it at the national level. While the

Conservative party under Stephen Harper has done some training in the past year, it is not enough. No programs specifically dedicated to training young members exist. The party has campus clubs, a youth website, an annual summer internship program in Ottawa and a promising roster of MPs under the age of thirty, but little else. It is imperative that this change soon.

Mentoring the Next Generation

The Conservatives today do not have a national youth wing. A resolution to form one was shot down by a razor-thin margin at the party's 2005 Montreal convention, making it the only major party in the Western world without such an organization. This decision was a mistake, over which the Liberals crowed openly, handing out flyers on the convention floor exhorting disgruntled young Tories to join the Young Liberals. The Grits know the importance of organized youth groups. Paul Martin recruited heavily from his party's youth to create the inner circle of strategists that won him the leadership. Former Young Liberals of Canada president Véronique de Passillé is now a senior Martin aide. The Quebec Liberal Party regularly brings out 500 youngsters to its youth conventions—and the party pays for their delegate fees, transportation and accommodation for the weekend! Contrast that with the federal Tories. It's not hard to figure out who's investing in the future and who isn't.

Conservatives must revisit history and learn from it. For generations, party youth organizations have succeeded in training future leaders, both for the political front and back rooms. In the U.S., strategical geniuses Lee Atwater, Karl Rove, Ralph Reed and Grover Norquist all made their way through the ranks of the College Republican National Committee. Many of those in the group around Mike Harris in the early 1990s were graduates of the youth ranks—people like Tony Clement, Alister Campbell, Leslie Noble and Tom Long, who had been Ontario PC Campus Association president. John Tory, the Ontario PC Party's current leader, is a past president of the Ontario Progressive Conservative Youth Association. Ted Rogers of the Rogers media and communications empire was national PC Youth president under Diefenbaker. And lest we forget, both Brian Mulroney and Joe Clark served on the national PC youth executive.

It is especially crucial for the Conservatives to train the next generation because their party is so new. It doesn't have the institutional memory of the Liberals. The Liberals out-strategize, out-spin and out-do the Tories at every turn. Paul Martin's communications guru Scott Reid regularly slices and dices his Conservative opponent on TV. Warren Kinsella did the same thing for Jean Chrétien. The Liberals have better campaign managers, advisers and senior-level people than the Tories. And they make sure to pass on techniques and knowledge from one generation to the next.

The Conservatives aren't as good at this. This is partly because of carelessness, but mainly due to other factors. One is that Tories tend not to indulge in non-stop political hackery for their entire lives. They come and go as they please; often taking long breaks away from the game to make money in the private sector. Liberals do this too, but not as much. A second factor is that what successful Tory strategists do exist either no longer support the party or have moved on to something else in life. As an example, the Tory party's national campaign manager from the 1984 and 1988 elections, Senator Norman Atkins, opposed the 2003 merger and still refuses to support the new party.

This brings us to another yawning abyss: the Canadian right's lack of mentorship. As we have discussed, American conservatives have made fostering the next generation their priority for decades. It's almost as if the Republicans and the conservative movement have last wills and testaments, whereas in Canada it's a free-for-all after the funeral. In June 2004, William F. Buckley, Jr. used *National Review*'s fiftieth anniversary to turn over control of his storied magazine to a hand-picked board of directors. Buckley's careful succession plan was executed while he was still alive and on his own terms, ensuring the magazine will have a healthy life well into the future. While we have no *National Review*s to hand down here (yet), the conservative movement must incorporate succession planning into its infrastructure, to ensure that what is built up is properly passed down. Too often good initiatives and sound ideas are allowed to die, leaving a new group to come along years later to reinvent the wheel. Fostering the next generation has been one of the biggest failures of the conservative movement in Canada, and it must not continue for another generation.

Leadership training isn't just for youth, however. It's for activists of all ages. While little training exists in Canadian conservative circles, not surprisingly, there is a lot of it on the left. And it is effective, especially from a tactical perspective. According to Mike Harris, "A lot of [left-wing] activists go into training on how to make sure you get on TV, how to get your message to the media, how you can perform acts of civil disobedience that will get your message out, or make it difficult for police to enforce an injunction."[8]

Apart from party-sponsored training and mentorship within the Liberal Party, most non-partisan leadership schools in Canada are either funded by government, the labour movement or "progressive" organizations. These include programs run by the Maytree Foundation, First Nations Training and Consulting Services, the annual Aboriginal Women in Leadership Training Conference, the Pearson Seminar on Youth Leadership and Craig and Marc Kielburger's Leaders Today, a youth leadership training organization that runs seminars on topics like "social justice" and globalization.

In a similar vein, the Hollyhock Leadership School in Vancouver was established in 1997, and to date has trained more than 1,000 people from across Canada and the United States. It provides training and strategic support to people in the environmental and "social justice" sectors. Hollyhock's goals are to help activists "build relationships, create action plans and facilitate the development of winning campaign sessions on issues such as oil and gas, sustainable agriculture, ecoforestry, and coastal forest issues" and to "facilitate cross sector alliance building between environmentalists and scoial (sic) movements."[9]

In a newsletter from December 2004, it describes what it is really trying to achieve: clobbering conservatives in issue campaigns and elections:

> Progressive movements have often focused on issues, while conservatives have focused on values. This is a topic that came up a lot at our recent Organizing for Change conferences, and so we thought we'd pass along some of George Lakoff's wisdom ...

Lakoff explains how conservatives think, and how to counter their arguments. He outlines in detail the values that progressives hold, but are often unable to articulate. Lakoff also breaks down the ways in which conservatives have framed the issues, and provides examples of how progressives can reframe them.[10]

Without our own leadership schools to counter this kind of stuff, it's no wonder that Canada has trouble producing more than three qualified candidates for the leadership of the Conservative party, let alone the local community council.

Reclaiming Language

George Lakoff is a left-wing UC Berkeley linguistics professor who has argued that the American conservative movement has hijacked language to "frame" debates to their advantage. In 2000, he helped found the Rockridge Institute, which "offers its expertise and research on a non-partisan basis to help progressives understand how best to get their messages across."[11]

Lakoff"s claims are contestable, because the Left has had much success in this area as well. Columnist Thomas Sowell offers some prime examples:

- The innocent-sounding "people's democracies" is often used to describe oppressive Communist regimes;

- The word "swamp," once the name applied to smelly bogs, has been replaced with "wetlands." Restrictive legislation to protect all kinds of "wetlands" on citizens' private property have been introduced as a result;

- The word "bum" has been substituted with the far less negative "homeless," which engenders a feeling of the need to protect these people;

- An entire vocabulary exists to describe people who are denied "access" to things. Those who don't get jobs, for example, are seen as being denied something they are owed.

- The language of "rights" has been overused. As Sowell puts it, "rights" has "become an all-purpose term used for evading both facts and logic by saying that people have a 'right' to whatever the left wants to give them by taking from others."[12]

Canadian conservatives must work at reframing debates to favour their ideas. This is another example of what could be taught in a conservative leadership school. As of now the debate is severely slanted to the left in Canada. Some examples of where to start:

The Left uses	Conservatives should use
Medicare/public health care	government-run health care, or state health care monopoly
civil servants/public servants	government workers/bureaucrats
social services/social programs	government programs
investing tax dollars	spending taxpayers' money
regional development programs	pork barrel projects
government grants/loans to business	corporate welfare
budget surplus	amount Canadians were over-taxed
Quebec sovereignty	Quebec separatism

By reclaiming language, conservatives will help reclaim the dialogue on these issues, and can also impart their own take on words. Much like the American right demonized the word "liberal," rehabilitating the word "conservative" in Canada should be a priority!

The aforementioned Hollyhock is affiliated with the Sage Centre, a federally registered charity formed in 1990 focused on conservation, education and leadership development. It also has links to ACORN Canada, an offshoot of the same left-wing community activist group in the United States that delights in bashing President Bush (not to be confused with the Acorn Canada Christian Mission). Started in the summer of 2004, ACORN now has offices in Toronto and Vancouver and says its goal is "to be the most powerful membership organization representing low- and moderate-income Canadians on the critical issues of social and economic justice."[13] Further, it is "keen to work with our friends and allies in the labour movement and in other progressive organizations across the country." Just what Canada needs, another pro-labour front group!

Canadian unions don't require ACORN to train their troops, however, as they run their own leadership training programs. The BC Federation of Labour, the Canadian Auto Workers, the Steelworkers, NUPGE, the AFL and IWA–Canada, to name just a few, regularly hold leadership training sessions for their members and officials. Conservatives should learn from these models and start their own programs as well.

Apart from the lack of training schools, conservatives also suffer from a lack of communication. Aside from *Civitas*, a small conservative organization that holds an annual meeting to discuss conservative policy, there are no regular face-to-face meetings of Canadian conservative activists. There are no events to share knowledge of campaign techniques and leadership skills development. Preston Manning has a solution for this—the establishment of conservative trade shows. These would be forums for people in the "business of politics" to advertise products, trade ideas, hone techniques and just get to know each other and keep abreast of developments.

In the United States, these types of events are common. The most popular is the American Conservative Union's annual Conservative Political Action Conference (CPAC), which is held every winter in Washington. Hundreds of conservative activists (nearly half of them students)[14] converge in the American capital for a weekend to hear speakers, give out awards, learn about conservative causes and new organizations and simply network and exchange business cards. This event is popular even with high-ranking politicians: Ronald Reagan and Dick Cheney spoke at the conference.

The United States also has political trade magazines, such as *Campaigns and Elections*. Published in Washington by a company called Votenet Solutions Inc., *C&E* keeps a close watch on and is chock-a-block with the latest do's and don'ts from the campaign trail. It advertises the latest software and technology, reports on techniques, rates races and campaign consultants and provides just about any useful information politicos ought to know. Canadian conservatives would do well to subscribe and read this publication. While we may not have the market or the need to launch our own magazine of this mould here, *C&E* should be required reading for aspiring—and practicing—politicos.

By professionalizing our politics, conservatives will not only increase the chance of getting elected, but will perform better once in office. Leaders will have the supportive teams necessary to make their vision real. There's nothing worse than seeing great ideas fail for lack of proper communication or implementation. The message is clear: if conservatism is to succeed in Canada, conservatives must get in the training game, and groom the leaders of tomorrow, today.

Endnotes

1. Author interview with Preston Manning, March 31, 2005.

2. Website of the Leadership Institute
   www.leadershipinstitute.org/04RESOURCES/RTLlist.htm

3. Website of the Leadership Institute
   www.leadershipinstitute.org/04RESOURCES/Speeches-PublicPolicyProcess.htm

4. Ralph Reed, *Active Faith: How Christians Are Changing the Soul of American Politics* (New York: Simon and Schuster, 1996) 13.

5. Julia Lesage, "Christian Coalition Leadership Training." http://darkwing.uoregon.edu/~jlesage/Juliafolder/ChristianCoalitionTraining.html

6. "As Prime Minister Awards" website. www.asprimeminister.com

7. Author interview with John Mykytyshyn, March 2005.

8. Author interview with Mike Harris, July 5, 2005.

9. Hollyhock Leadership Institute website.
   www.hollyhockleadership.org/programs/stratservices

10. *ChangeMakers: The Newsletter of the Hollyhock Leadership Institute*, Volume 1, Issue 9, December 2004.

11. Bonnie Azab Powell, "Framing the issues: UC Berkeley professor George Lakoff tells how conservatives use language to dominate politics," *UC Berkeley News*, October 27, 2003.
    www.berkeley.edu/news/media/releases/2003/10/27_lakoff.shtml

12. Thomas Sowell, "The left's vocabulary," *Townhall.com*, August 6, 2004.
    www.townhall.com/columnists/thomassowell/ts20040806.shtml

13. Website of ACORN Canada. www.acorn.org

14. John Micklethwait and Adrian Wooldridge, *The Right Nation* (New York: Penguin Books, 2004), 172.

PART three
THE POLICIES

12 CHAPTER

VISION WANTED:
Tax Cuts Aren't Enough

"Where there is no vision, the people perish."
—Proverb inscribed on the Peace Tower

BUILDING a conservative infrastructure is the long-term plan for rescuing Canada's right. Conservatives must invest in ideas, build a conservative culture in media law, and academia, bring young people, New Canadians and Quebecers into the conservative family and "train the troops" to be the leaders of tomorrow.

But a political movement also requires something beyond the bricks and mortar of leadership schools, media monitoring centres and think-tanks. Something intangible, that will inspire people to come together and work for a better tomorrow, that will make Canadians actually care about politics and the conservative point of view.

That something is vision.

Here, we are speaking not just to small-c conservatives, but to the big-cs as well. Going into the next election, and the one after that, big-c Conservatives will have to offer Canadians something better than "we're not the other guys." While small-c conservatives are building the infrastructure to sustain the movement, big-c politicians will still be on the front lines fighting for votes and promoting the Conservative brand to Canadians.

But as it stands now, they suffer from the same problem as former U.S. president George H.W. Bush: a lack of what he called "the vision thing." Big-c Conservatives rarely speak of conservative principles: the morality of the marketplace, the value of freedom or the importance of opportunity. Talk too much about those sorts of ideas, and the lefties will accuse you of overdosing on Ayn Rand. Talk too little about them, and you end up where the federal Tories are today: a party without a true political foundation.

This isn't about defining conservatism by how much you cut taxes, or by how many civil servants you fire in a given mandate. It is about developing a vision based on the core principle of freedom: freedom of speech, choice and opportunity; freedom to enjoy one's property and the fruits of one's labours; and freedom from oppression and authoritarianism. It is about recognizing how free markets in particular are fundamental to our democratic way of life, and that respecting and encouraging the efficient operation of those markets is in everybody's interests. Preston Manning believes conservatism entails "the search for marketplace solutions to public problems rather than government intervention, through a limited role of the government."[1] William Thorsell, past editor-in-chief of the *The Globe and Mail*, echoes this sentiment: a conservative frame of mind "recognizes free markets as a fundamental expression of democracy, and values their power to generate technological change and productive work."[2]

Conservatives by definition respect tradition. In building on this link between markets, freedom and opportunity, Canadian conservatives would be drawing on ideas that have been present since Confederation (though, as we have seen, not necessarily those of the Conservative Party).

The origins of Canada are not statist. Our nation was built by capitalists trading in furs, lumber, gold and other natural resources. The great expanses of our country were opened up by entrepreneurs and adventurers, not bureaucrats and civil servants. And contrary to accepted conventional wisdom, from Confederation until the Trudeau era, "Canadians enjoyed smaller governments and a greater degree of economic liberty"[3] than our neighbours to the south.

In fact, the Americans brought in income tax, gas tax and sales tax before Canada did. America created a national bank first. Canada brought in family allowances, unemployment insurance and the Canada Pension Plan years after the United States implemented similar programs. And until the 1950s, the size of the public sector in both countries was similar—around 25 percent of GDP.[4]

In other words, from a "progressive" point of view, Canada lagged behind the United States in many areas. Yet the political chattering classes claim our country defines itself by social programs, setting us apart from our Darwinian neighbours. Canadians are said to be kinder and more caring than Americans—assuming that you define state dependency as a symbol of kindness.

Throughout the 1960s and 1970s, as we saw in Chapter 4, the federal government actively promoted the image of Canada as a "caring and sharing" nation more inclined to collectivism. It used millions of taxpayer dollars to fund programs, think-tanks and interest groups that reinforced this state-centred vision of Canada. And it did so under a banner that is, on its face value, impossible to oppose: that of "equality."

How the Liberals Enforced Equality

The notion of "state-enforced equality," to borrow a term used by the economist Frederic Bastiat, was carefully cultivated by Trudeau Liberals. It formed the cornerstone of Trudeau's "Just Society" and was enshrined in section 15 of the *Charter of Rights and Freedoms,* which reads:

(1) Every individual is equal before and under the law and has the right to the equal protection and equal benefit of the law without discrimination and, in particular, without discrimination based on race, national or ethnic origin, colour, religion, sex, age or mental or physical disability.

(2) Subsection (1) does not preclude any law, program or activity that has as its object the amelioration of conditions of disadvantaged individuals or groups including those that are disadvantaged because of race, national or ethnic origin, colour, religion, sex, age or mental or physical disability.

As we saw in Chapter 7, section 15 set Canada up for a massive in-crease in state intervention by mandating government to correct every inequity—real or perceived—under the sun. Perversely, it has become an advantage to be disadvantaged. Groups that are not named in the Charter, such as gays and lesbians, have pursued "disadvantaged" status through the courts to oblige the state act on their behalf. The unintended consequence has been a surge in rights-based litigation and the growth of an entire enforced equality industry: human rights commissions, pay equity legislation and all sorts of special-interest lobby groups, what legal scholars F. L. Morton and Rainer Knopff term "the Court Party."[5] The goal of these groups isn't to solve their problems by market means; rather, it is to attain special legal status to get the government to in-tervene and protect their interests. The government inevitably becomes more and more interventionist as it attempts to erase every new in-equality that arises.[6]

The result is to further embed the state in Canadians' daily lives. As Alan Cairns presciently pointed out twenty years ago, when Charter lit-igation was in its infancy, all of this has had unintended consequences for Canada's political and social unity: "By singling out particular groups or categories for individualized treatment, [the state] simultane-ously attracts those particular groups or categories to it as patron to client, accords political salience to some and not to others, and frac-tures the possibilities of a common citizenship focusing on more abstract and more general concerns."[7]

This notion of enforced equality—and the Conservatives' failure to repudiate it—has led our country to the mess we are in today. The result is a government that works around the clock to entrench statism in the national fabric.

At first blush, it seems only a troglodyte would oppose equality. The question that should be asked is: how is equality defined? Statists—both Liberal and Conservative—have a very different definition of equality than small-c conservatives. This difference is well illustrated by a Canadian twist on Aesop's timeless fable of the ant and the grass-hopper. This version (author unknown) has been circulated on the Internet, and we paraphrase it here.

In Aesop's original tale, the ant works hard in the withering heat all summer long, building his shelter and laying up supplies for the winter. The grasshopper thinks he's a fool, and laughs and dances and plays the summer away. Come winter, the ant is warm and well fed. The shivering grasshopper has no food or shelter, so he lies out in the cold, dying.

In the Canadian version, the shivering grasshopper doesn't expire. Instead, he calls a press conference and demands to know why the ant should be allowed to be warm and well fed while he and other unfortunate creatures are cold and starving. The CBC shows up to provide live coverage of the shivering grasshopper, then cuts to a video of the selfish ant in his comfortable warm home, where a table is laden with food. Canadians are appalled that in such a wealthy country, this poor grasshopper is allowed to suffer while others have plenty. The NDP, the Canadian Auto Workers union and various anti-poverty groups demonstrate in front of the ant's house. The CBC captures them singing "We Shall Overcome." Jack Layton argues that the ant has gotten rich off the backs of grasshoppers and calls for an immediate tax hike to make the ant pay his "fair share."

The Liberal government then goes to its enforced equality drawing-board and drafts the Economic Equity and Grasshopper Anti-Discrimination Act, retroactive to the beginning of summer. The ant's taxes are reassessed and he is also fined for failing to hire grasshoppers as helpers. As he is unable to pay up, the government confiscates his home. The ant moves to the United States and starts a successful ant-condo construction business.

The CBC later shows the now-fat grasshopper finishing up the last of the ant's food, though spring is still months away, while the government house he is in, which just happens to be the ant's old house, crumbles around him because he hasn't maintained it. Inadequate government funding is blamed for this state of disrepair, and Bob Rae is appointed to head a commission of inquiry that will cost $20 million. The grasshopper soon dies of a drug overdose. The *Toronto Star* blames his untimely death on the obvious failure of government to address the root causes of despair arising from social inequality.[8]

As we can see, policies based on enforced equality lead to all sorts of unintended consequences. In the short term, they punish the ant for being successful, and make it more advantageous for the grasshopper to seek government help than to overcome his problems on his own. In the long term, they end up killing the grasshopper and driving the productive ant out of the country.

As in George Orwell's *Animal Farm*, all Canadian animals are equal—but some are more equal than others. This isn't just true of interest groups; it is also true of entire regions of the country. In Canada, we redistribute income through federal transfer payments, in areas from health to corporate handouts. The goal is to "level the playing field" and equalize standards of living; the unintended consequences are to penalize wealth-generating provinces and to make it an advantage for poorer provinces to remain poor, or risk losing their benefits. Not to mention giving people an incentive to stay in economically depressed areas and discouraging them from moving to places where jobs can be found.

Witness what happened when Newfoundland and Nova Scotia struck a deal with Ottawa over oil royalties. The offshore revenues threatened to make them wealthier, thus resulting in a reduction in transfer payments. When Martin threatened to renege on his election promise to remove oil and gas revenues from the equalization equation, Newfoundland Premier Danny Williams became enraged, skipped out on a First Ministers' meeting and yanked Canadian flags from provincial government buildings. Eventually, the Martin government capitulated. The Atlantic Accord was included as part of the 2005 budget,[9] and Ontario and Alberta taxpayers will continue to send their eastern neighbours equalization cheques for years to come.[10]

Canadians' obsession with enforced equality is not ill-intentioned. Most socialists, liberals and even Red Tories genuinely believe they are helping people by having the government solve their problems for them. But their policies produce the antithesis of a society based on opportunity. They stifle social mobility and expand the role of the state, resulting in a rigid, classist society. In the name of equality, these policies generate a new type of inequality—namely, that people who work harder, are smarter, more talented or just more tenacious than others should not be allowed to achieve a better outcome than those who are less hard-working, less intelligent, less talented or less determined.

This is not to say that small-c conservatives do not believe in equality. But they define it as equality of opportunity, not of result. This critical distinction is not made enough in the public discourse, but it is the one that truly sets the Left apart from the Right. Where you stand on equality determines how you define the state's role in society. If you believe that the state should ensure the same outcome for all, regardless of ability or effort, you are an advocate of enforced equality, and by extension, a statist. If you believe the state should ensure the same opportunity for all, and leave the outcome to the individual, then you advocate less government intervention and are what we call an "Opportunity Conservative."

Introducing Opportunity Conservatism

Opportunity Conservatives frame the role of the state, and every policy it implements, through the lens of creating opportunity. The true "just society" is not about levelling, it is about lifting. It is about allowing maximum freedom and empowering Canadians to raise themselves up. It is not about redistributing the same pie into smaller and smaller slices. Former Tory Belinda Stronach got one thing right when she remarked in the 2004 Conservative Party leadership race that Canada must bake a bigger economic pie. The trick is to find the right recipe.

The Opportunity Conservative vision we prescribe combines free-market ideas and common-sense concepts in a blueprint for a better Canada. These include the following:

- reducing taxes, for businesses and individuals, to stimulate the economy and job growth;

- increasing free-market competition, and eliminating state monopolies in all sectors, including health care;

- ending subsidies to business, cutting regulation and red tape;

- strengthening the family through fiscal policies that encourage choice in child care and the formation of legally recognized family units;

- strengthening community by encouraging voluntarism as opposed to state intervention to alleviate poverty and social problems;

- preserving our environment through market-based environmental policies;

- reforming federalism by decentralizing power and encouraging freedom of action by the provinces;

- maintaining a positive and patriotic outlook that focuses on what conservatives stand for, not what they are against.

Opportunity Conservatism is a vision based on merit. It values and rewards—rather than punishes—excellence and achievement. As a nation, we must abandon the loser-worship that threatens to cripple us. Enough of lauding Robert Stanfield and Joe Clark! We are not a nation of losers. We are a country of winners—if only we can shake the shackles of statism that are holding us back.

For the various strains of Canadian conservatives to embrace Opportunity Conservatism, in author Linda Frum's words, "everyone will have to give something up."[11] Most people involved in the Canadian conservative coalition are used to this. This is a broad and diverse country, and no one in a political coalition can ever get everything they want.

Opportunity Conservatism challenges a number of concepts. It rejects *noblesse oblige*, where the rich redistribute money to the poor to keep them quiet and "in their place." It does not believe that the state should dictate personal morality. And it runs counter to the prevailing Liberal view, which is that who you know matters more than what you know when it comes to getting ahead.

But it is in sync with what many ordinary Canadians want and believe, including those who don't even define themselves as conservative. Polling done in April 2005 commissioned by the Fraser Institute and the Montreal Economic Institute found that:

- 52 percent of respondents said they think the Canadian economy would perform better if government allowed more freedom, vs. 37 percent who said it would do better with more regulation.

- 68 percent of those surveyed believed their standard of living would improve if their taxes were reduced; only 25 percent thought they would be better off if taxes increased.

- 70 percent of Canadians polled said they should be able to buy health care services from any provider they choose; only 26 percent disagreed.

- 51 percent said they are prepared to take more personal responsibility for their retirement, vs. 41 percent who said retirement should remain the government's responsibility.[12]

Clearly, a smaller government approach resonates with many Canadians. Yet neither the Liberals nor the Conservatives have come up with a policy platform that speaks to this view.

Adopting an Opportunity Conservative perspective would set big-c Conservatives apart from Liberals. Today's Liberal party isn't pro-opportunity at all. It is *pro-opportunist*. Liberals excel at giving your money to their friends. As Naresh Raghubeer, executive director of the Canadian Coalition for Democracies, quipped, "Canada has become the Guyana of the North." He would know: he was born and raised in Guyana! If you're pals with people in government, you benefit. If not, like the Canadian ant, you pay for the grasshoppers' well being. Today's Liberal Party is about power, not empowerment. And to quote Lord Acton, as seems to be a must for any political book taking the Liberals to task, absolute power corrupts absolutely.

Opportunity Conservatives would open the door to success, on the understanding that Canadians take the initiative and walk through it themselves. The Liberals and the NDP don't grasp this. The Liberals give free handouts to people they know and free passes to others who qualify because they belong to a special interest group. The NDP, in their obsession with enforced equality, would level society to such an extent that opportunity would simply cease to exist (for a case in point, time-travel to the former Soviet Union). The Liberal Party sees government programs as a way to buy votes, while the NDP sees them as a way of punishing achievement and making "the rich" pay for their success. Either path reduces opportunity while encouraging dependence on the state. Each approach strengthens the state to the detriment of the individual.

Accentuating the Positive

Of course, the crucial challenge will be selling this concept to Canadians. Conservatives, big and small-c, certainly won't have any help from the media or the country's self-appointed elites. But we would argue that this vision can be sold.

First, it is a vision—an actual alternative view of the how the country should look—not just the usual mish-mash of policies the Conservative Party has espoused for decades. It gives conservatives something to stand for. Conservatives do well when they have a vision and can champion bold ideas.

Secondly, it is inherently positive in nature. A big part of the problem with the current state of the Conservative Party and conservatism in general is that it is unrelentingly negative. Conservatives are seen as always opposing things instead of proposing. Ask the average Joe what he knows of the Conservative Party's policy today and he will say, "They're *against* gay marriage."

Worse, they are sometimes seen as unpatriotic or even as hating Canada. As just one example, MP Monte Solberg wrote on his Internet weblog just after the gay marriage vote in Parliament on June 28, 2005: "Gay marriage is now on the fast track to becoming the law in Canada. The new Canada. You can have it."[13] Solberg's frustration in losing the same-sex marriage vote is understandable, but bashing the country is not.

Unfortunately, these feelings are endemic of many in the Conservative Party and conservative movement. In response to two blog posts marking Canada Day 2005 on the *Western Standard*'s Shotgun (a home for conservative bloggers), numerous outrageous comments were made by readers. Among them:

- "Couldn't be bothered to think about celebrating a unified Canada. Instead, thought about how soon I can move to Alberta and get on the separation bandwagon!"

- "Canada is just a cheap imitation of the U.S. with none of the qualities and all of the liabilities."

- "I no longer feel patriotism or any kind of affection for this country, although I will continue to vote and otherwise participate in our political process and live my life to the fullest. I will continue living and working here but will leave this country without hesitation when the right opportunity arises."[14]

Well-known blogger Jim Elve (who is not a conservative) put out a call for what he called "the patriotic right" to rein in these Canada-haters. He wrote: "These malcontents are unwilling to listen to the left. It is only the right that can either reach out to these extremists and draw them back or distance themselves by actively denouncing the anti-Canada rant that is all too prevalent in the Canadian conservative blogosphere."[15]

Elve is right. Frustration with today's Canada is reasonable, but this is not the way to express it. Conservatives must stop the ultimatum talk. It makes them look mean-spirited and no better than the lefty Hollywood celebrities who threaten to move to France every time a Republican wins the U.S. presidency.

If the right is serious about installing a truly conservative government in Ottawa, it must be optimistic about the future and play the patriotism card. Ronald Reagan spoke of America as a "shining city upon a hill." Margaret Thatcher's platform started out with the sentence, "It is the task of the Conservative Party today to restore hope [and] confidence to a disillusioned British people."[16] Thatcher once said of Reagan: "If, at the deepest level, you have confidence in the talent and enterprise of your own people, you express that confidence, you give them faith and hope: Ronald Reagan did all these things—and it worked."[17]

During the time of the Common Sense Revolution (CSR) in the mid-1990s, Ontario Progressive Conservative leader Mike Harris talked about positive things, such as making Ontario "the best place to live in, work and raise a family." He constantly used positive language. Tellingly, the word "hope" appears in Harris' introductory letter to the CSR platform three times,[18] but it doesn't appear once in Stephen Harper's letters introducing the 2004 federal Conservative platform or the party's 2005 policy declaration.[19]

"Hope, growth and opportunity was in every stump speech," Alister Campbell, a senior Harris adviser and key architect of the CSR, told us. "Even the mandatory work for welfare text in our ads was supplemented by Mike's personal speech text 'a hand up instead of a hand out to break the tragic cycle of welfare dependency' to show the hope element of tough conservative policies."[20]

The federal Tories may not have figured this out, but the Liberals have. In a private address to the Liberal caucus on June 15, 2004, Prime Minister Paul Martin reportedly said "people see hope in us. Stephen Harper has never talked about hope."[21] Indeed, Harper seems to prefer marketing fear.

In an exclusive interview in August 2005 with the *Western Standard*, Harper commented, "The real issue is whether the country as we know it will survive. ... I think people are willing to make a change. I think if they are not willing to make a change, the long-term consequences for the country are devastating. ... I don't think it will survive this government."[22] Translation: vote for me or the country is finished. Not exactly the most uplifting message.

Conservatives must give people hope for a better life. They have to explain why conservatism is good for Joe Sixpack, Jane Lunchbox and their kids. The message of conservatism cannot just be about reducing the size of government and cutting taxes. Though these things are important, conservatives must offer more. They must show how their ideas will empower people and above all, improve their lives.

As the pages that follow will show, that's what Opportunity Conservatism is all about. We've chosen four areas where conservatives could innovate, and where big-c Conservatives could set themselves apart from the Liberals and from previous Tory platforms. These are family policy, health policy, environmental policy and that perennial favorite, national unity.

It's time to offer Canadians the recipe for a bigger—and better—economic and social pie, one they will bake themselves. So conservatives of Canada, let's get cooking!

Endnotes

1. Author interview with Preston Manning, March 31, 2005.

2. William Thorsell, "Conservatism Is About More Than Cutting Taxes," *The Globe and Mail*, September 27, 2004, A13.

3. Chris Leithner, "What on Earth Has Happened to Canada?" *Le Québecois Libre*, October 25, 2003. www.quebecoislibre.org/031025-6.htm

4. For more on the differences between Canada and the U.S. please see William Watson, *Globalization and the Meaning of Canadian Life* (Toronto: University of Toronto Press, 1998), and Mark Milke, *Tax Me, I'm Canadian* (Calgary: Thomas & Black, 2002).

5. F. L. Morton and Rainer Knopff, *The Charter Revolution and the Court Party* (Peterborough, Ont: Broadview Press, 2000) (hereinafter Morton and Knopff).

6. Morton and Knopff.

7. Alan Cairns, "The Embedded State: State–Society Relations in Canada," in Banting, Keith, ed, *State and Society: Canada in Comparative Perspective* (Toronto: University of Toronto Press, 1986), 67.

8. Thanks to James Lee, the communications director of the Canadian Council for Christians and Jews, for submitting the Canadian version of this classic tale. It has been circulated widely on the Internet, but its author is, to the best of our knowledge, unknown.

9. The campaign also benefited from an online effort by a Washington political consultant and Newfoundland native, Kevin McCann, who started the website www.fairdealfornewfoundland.com/
By bringing attention to the issue through his site, McCann showed how powerful a tool the Internet can be in obtaining political results.

10. Some may say this is only fair, as Alberta negotiated a similar deal years ago over its oil royalties, but our point is that no one should receive special privileges.

11. Author interview with Linda Frum, March 22, 2005.

12. "Exploratory Public Opinion Survey," The Fraser Institute / Institut Economique de Montréal, April 2005.

13. Monte Solberg's blog "[Its a route (sic)]," June 28, 2005, can be found at www.montesolberg.com/2005/06/its-route.htm

14. Comments to post by Ezra Levant at the *Western Standard*, Shotgun blog, July 1, 2005. http://westernstandard.blogs.com/shotgun/2005/07/but_what_does_i.html#comments

15. Jim Elve, "Calling on the Right to Quash Canada-haters," July 4, 2005. www.blogscanada.ca/egroup/PermaLink.aspx?guid=40e1adf4-3ea3-48c9-ab65-fd53449f3622

16. Margaret Thatcher Foundation, "The Right Approach" (Conservative policy statement), October 4, 1976. www.margaretthatcher.org/search/display document.asp?docid=109439&doctype=1
    It is important to note that this statement was drafted well before the 1978–1979 "winter of discontent," when it seemed that all of Britain was on strike.

17. Margaret Thatcher, "The Principles of Conservatism," address to the Heritage Foundation, Washington, DC, December 10, 1997. www.heritage.org/Research/reagan_lecture_thatcher.cfm

18. Mike Harris, introductory letter to the Common Sense Revolution, www.ontariopc.com/feature/csr/csr_text.htm.

19. "Demanding Better: Conservative Party of Canada Platform 2004 and Conservative Party Policy Declaration." www.conservative.ca/EN/policy_declaration/message_from_the_leader_of_the_conservative_party

20. Author interview with Alister Campbell, July 12, 2005.

21. Bruce Cheadle and Sue Bailey, "Stephen Harper to Spend Summer Bolstering Image, Showing Sunny Disposition," *Canadian Press*, June 14, 2005.

22. Terry O'Neill, "Standing his ground," *Western Standard*, August 8, 2005. www.westernstandard.ca/website/index.cfm?page=article&article_id=911

13 CHAPTER

STRONGER FAMILIES:
A New Framework for Social Policy

"Conservatives usually prefer twin beds, which may contribute to the fact that Canada has more Liberals."

— Peter C. Newman

FOR Canadian conservatives, social policy debates are like mud-wrestling matches—without the hot women. They're slippery, ugly, messy and everyone winds up flat on their back, while the media broadcasts the most embarrassing close-ups to a tittering public. Social conservatives, Red Tories and libertarians battle to see who will come out on top on issues such as gay marriage, euthanasia and abortion. In the end all conservatives lose by presenting an image of a movement divided, spiked with the spectre of a wild-eyed Elsie Wayne shrieking that pro-choice delegates were "in favour of killing babies" at the Conservative Party's 2005 national policy convention.

Historically, one of the main difficulties for the Conservative Party and the conservative movement has been designing a tent big enough to accommodate the views of both social conservatives—known as "so-cons"—and more "socially liberal" conservatives. So-cons usually take a traditional, heterosexual-only view of marriage, oppose abortion and euthanasia and often incorporate religion into their political world view. Socially liberal conservatives would rather leave religion out of these debates; they tend to support gay marriage and they believe the state should not get involved in moral issues.

In past Progressive Conservative Party policy debates, so-cons often felt marginalized by their more socially liberal counterparts. While so-cons' views were heard, they were rarely reflected in party platforms. In the 1990s, many so-con PC supporters left for the Reform Party, which was more hospitable to their views. When so-con positions do become party policy, as opposition to gay marriage did at the 2005 Conservative policy conference, their proponents are derided in the press as "extreme" and "out of touch" and denounced by members of their own party. (This even though the federal Liberals opposed gay marriage until close to the end of the Chrétien era.) Today the debate on the legalization of gay marriage still splits the conservative movement along regional and age lines: Central Canada and young conservatives tend to be more supportive, while older Tories and those from the West tend to oppose it.

How to reconcile the views of social conservatives and socially liberal conservatives is one of the most important factors in keeping the conservative coalition alive and taking both the movement and the Party forward. Failure to give social conservatives a seat at the table will mean another eventual schism and, along with it, a failure to offer Canadians a true political alternative to Liberal statism. At the same time, Conservatives must develop a vision that respects the views of socially liberal, fiscally conservative Canadians if they ever hope to win an election.

Let's be clear: an overtly socially conservative platform calling for implementing so-con ideas through legislative means—i.e., through laws restricting abortion, outlawing gay marriage, etc.—will not resonate with the majority of Canadian voters. Unlike the United States, we are not a socially conservative, God-fearing nation. A report of the Pew Global Attitudes Project found that of forty-four wealthy industrialized countries, America is unique in its embrace of religion. Fully 59 percent of Americans say religion plays a very important role in their lives, but in Canada the number is only 30 percent. (In Europe the numbers are lower still—even Italy, a strong Catholic bastion, was only 27 percent.) Demographic research shows this is unlikely to change: as we discussed in Chapter 8, the next generation of Canadians is increasingly secular and socially liberal in its outlook.

As Linda Frum observed earlier, if the Conservatives are to win power in Ottawa, every faction of the conservative family will need to add water to their whining. Abandoning the fight against gay marriage is not something so-cons want to hear about, but the time to stop gay marriage has passed.

Stephen Harper and the Tories spent a lot of time and energy in 2004 and 2005 opposing gay marriage—sort of. The party's position was actually more nuanced, a fact that was never properly communicated to Canadians. What the Tories advocated was keeping the traditional definition of marriage, while at the same time endorsing civil unions for same-sex couples. This would have given them the same rights and benefits as heterosexuals, but without the title. There was nothing politically wrong with taking that stance, especially given that most polls show the country split down the middle on the issue. But despite the party's relatively centrist position (Stephen Harper observed that the Tory position on marriage was the most liberal of any conservative party in the Western world), the party took a media beating for it. Now that same-sex marriage is a settled law, any attempt to undo it would seem like trampling on an established right.

Restricting the right to abortion would raise similar concerns. The Supreme Court's 1988 decision in *R. v. Morgentaler,* which struck down laws restricting abortion and created a legal vacuum. No limits on abortion have been legislated since. But Canadians' views on what to do are far from monolithic. For example, a 2000 poll by Environics found that 66 percent of Canadians agreed with the statement "Every woman who wants to have an abortion should be able to have one."[1] Yet other polls show Canadians want at least some restrictions. A survey done by the same firm, which was commissioned by a pro-life group in October 2004, showed that 33 percent of Canadians said legal protection for a fetus should begin at conception, and 24 percent said it should begin after three months of pregnancy. Of those questioned only

28 percent said legal protection should begin at birth (which is currently the status quo).[2] However, as the *Toronto Sun*'s Lorrie Goldstein points out, when Canadians are asked "without any qualifiers" whether they are in favour of a woman's right to an abortion, support tends to range from 55 percent to 78 percent.[3]

The Conservative Party adopted a resolution in Montreal that a future Tory government would not legislate restrictions on abortion. Harper is said to have supported the measure. The party also passed a resolution that "[o]n issues of moral conscience, such as abortion, the definition of marriage and euthanasia, the party acknowledges the diversity of deeply held personal convictions among individual party members and the right of Members of Parliament to adopt positions in consultation with their constituents and to vote freely." Spotlighting issues such as abortion and gay marriage is a recipe for continued shutouts at the polls, especially since the media, like pigs rooting for truffles, keep trying to uncover a "hidden agenda." As former premier Mike Harris told us in an interview, "I think there is the fear right now that there is some hidden agenda, or that there is a religious right that wants to take over the Conservative Party or the government of Canada. That's the fear, and that is a big barrier."[4]

Even if the Conservatives drop their opposition to gay marriage and end talk of abortion, however, this does not mean that social conservative values cannot shape the party's message. To the contrary, they should. The key contribution of so-cons to social policy is their belief in the importance of family and children. The Opportunity Conservative "third way" is that we're not talking only about the "traditional" family—a heterosexual couple with 2.5 kids where mom stays home—but about *all forms* of family. It is a principled position to value the family as the most important social unit in society—and as a counterpoint to the power of the state.

Pro-Family, Pro-Freedom

Unlike popular dogma, the greatest threat to statism is not the individual; it is the family. Communists and socialists understood this, and they have attempted throughout history to break up the family in every conceivable way. Karl Marx wrote:

Abolition of the family! Even the most radical flare up at this infamous proposal of the Communists.

On what foundation is the present family, the bourgeois family, based? On capital, on private gain. In its completely developed form, this family exists only among the bourgeoisie. But this state of things finds its complement in the practical absence of the family among proletarians, and in public prostitution.

The bourgeois family will vanish as a matter of course when its complement vanishes, and both will vanish with the vanishing of capital.[5]

In Soviet Russia, Lenin understood that the family was an impediment to communism. The government opened state-run nurseries, dining halls, laundries and sewing centres. Women were encouraged to work and children to be raised and educated away from their families. Anatol Lunacharski, the first Soviet education commissioner, wrote in the 1930s that the goal was to build "that broad public society which will replace the small philistine nook, that little philistine apartment, that domestic hearth, yes, that stagnant family unit which separates itself off from society."[6]

Reflecting on these sorts of anti-family policies sixty years later, former Soviet leader Mikhail Gorbachev wrote, "We have discovered that many of our problems—in children's and young people's behavior, in our morals, culture and in production—are partially caused by the weakening of family ties."[7]

Why do statists fear the family? One word: power. It is far easier for governments to maintain control over masses of disconnected individuals who depend on the state than it is to control families, who rely on their own members for support. Over generations, families are also more easily able to accumulate wealth than individuals. Since economic independence translates into political independence, leftists—including today's NDP—favour high inheritance taxes to prevent such accumulation of money. Finally, women who aren't married, don't have children or have fewer children are more likely to work full-time, pay more taxes and thereby feed the coffers of the state.

Liberals and some lefties claim to care about families. They talk of "supporting" families by creating program after program to do what families are supposed to do themselves, that is, sustain their members financially, raise their kids and care for aging parents. To do this, the state must extract more and more money from some families to redistribute to others. By increasing the redistribution of wealth, they remove personal choice from all families and place both faith and power in bureaucrats to decide what is in people's best interests. Most of the time, they haven't a clue. When asked how much state daycare would cost, Liberal Minister of Social Development Ken Dryden added, "You really don't know. In fact, you don't need to know because the future's going to decide it. ... That's how systems get created. That's how they evolve."[8]

Research shows that such policies actually encourage the breakup of the family. Case in point: the guaranteed annual income. This is the ultimate statist policy, by which the government "guarantees" all its citizens a minimum standard of living. Shockingly, PC leader Robert Stanfield actually campaigned on the idea against Trudeau in 1968. Both Canadian and American studies show that, far from helping those in need, such policies not only reduce incentives to work but also lead to greater rates of family dissolution.[9] Why? Quite simply because family members don't need to stay together for economic reasons. In fact, it becomes in their interest *not* to stay together, as members collect more benefits separately than when they reside in one household.

Think the guaranteed annual income will never come to Canada? Think again. As mentioned earlier in Chapter 7, the Left is already attempting to oblige governments to provide a minimum standard of living by invoking the equality guarantees in the Charter of Rights and Freedoms. Of course, instead of promoting the equality of opportunity to *earn* an income, they seek equality of result in *receiving* one.

Strengthening families is key to reversing the tide of statism in Canada. Opportunity Conservative social policy should be built around the family, whatever form that family takes. All couples—both opposite and same-sex ones—who want to marry should have the opportunity to do so. People should be encouraged, not discouraged, from caring for each other and formalizing bonds. Apart from questions of dignity, there is the pragmatic reality that the more people support each other within family units, the less of a role the state will have in supporting them. If both partners in a gay relationship wish to marry, form a household, sustain each other financially through good times and bad and raise children in a loving, stable environment, conservatives should applaud their efforts, not stymie them. Passing moral judgment on the nature of the couple's relationship undermines the ultimate objective: countering statism and promoting the family unit as a positive, desirable social norm.

Indeed, American studies show that children raised in two-parent households headed by same-sex couples are just as successful and well-adjusted as children from heterosexual married households. Just as importantly, children from both groups perform better on a wide variety of developmental indicators than children raised in single-parent families or by unmarried opposite-sex parents living in common-law relationships.[10] In Canada, however, legalized marriage is on the decline while common-law unions are increasing. The 2001 Census, the latest available, pegged the number of common-law unions nationally at 14 percent of couples. In 1981 it was only 5.6 percent. The problem is the worst in Quebec, where 30 percent of couples live in common-law relationships. The number of children being raised in common-law households is also going up, having risen from 3.1 percent in 1981 to 13 percent in 2001.[11]

This trend is not a positive one for families or society. Statistics Canada data show first common-law relationships are twice as likely to end in separation as first marriages.[12] Common-law partners are three times more likely to suffer abuse and violence than partners who are married.[13] Mothers living in common-law relationships are more likely to have adverse pregnancy outcomes, such as premature delivery, underweight or stillborn babies. These mothers are also more likely to miscarry than those who are married.[14]

That's not to say all marriages are perfect—far from it. Thirty-eight percent of Canadian marriages (49 percent in Quebec) now end in divorce by the thirtieth wedding anniversary,[15] producing an increase in single-parent families. Divorce is also detrimental, particularly for children. An endless stream of studies has shown how divorce negatively impacts children in their early and later lives, and how kids raised in two-parent families have better odds at success in a host of areas, including having a lasting marriage themselves.

Conservatives shouldn't worry that gay Canadians want to get married, rather they should be concerned that straight Canadians don't wish to marry or stay married. In terms of strengthening the family, it would be far better for conservatives to work on promoting the value of family and life-long marriage than to fight gay unions.

Pro-marriage and pro-family policies will pay dividends for conservatives down the road. Marrying and starting a family brings on responsibility and necessitates stability to maintain it. When people have families, by extension they become more conservative in their outlook. It is easy to be radical and left-wing when you're a carefree, footloose singleton. Factor in commitments such as a spouse, children and a mortgage, and it's a whole new deal. Providing for your family becomes paramount. Paying lower income taxes becomes more important, because it allows you to keep more of what you earn for your family. Property taxes become a concern, because you now need a house to shelter your family. Law and order are top of mind, because you want your kids to be safe. Accessing timely health care for your children jumps to the fore, etcetera, etcetera.

Family-friendly policies are attractive across the political spectrum and would help broaden the conservative coalition. Pro-family policies will be attractive to social conservatives, small-c conservatives and people with fiscally conservative values but liberal social beliefs. New Canadians who value the family will also support these policies. Who would say they are against families? No one.

Fighting for stronger families also sends a positive, upbeat message. Opportunity Conservatives are not anti-gay or anti-abortion, rather they are pro-family and pro-children. Couples should be encouraged to have kids and should have the opportunity to raise them as suits their family best. While Canada will continue to be a country of immigrants, it is in the national interest to increase the number of Canadians born here as well.

To sustain itself, the modern welfare state requires taxes from future generations of taxpayers. But at the same time, the welfare state's largesse is one of the contributors to the plummeting fertility rates in Western nations. Generous pension plans, for example, actually provide a disincentive to have children. When you can rely on the government for support, who needs kids? Children become an economic burden, not an advantage. Studies show that the lowest rates of childbirth are found in countries with the most generous pension systems.[16] This isn't recent news; as far back as 1986, sociologist Charles Hohm reported in the *Social Science Journal*, "After controlling for relevant developmental effects, the level and scope of a country's social security program is causally and inversely related to fertility levels." Hohm wrote further that "[r]educed fertility levels result in subsequent increases in social security expenditures."[17] Hohm's research was based on the study of eighty-one nations, both developed and developing ones.

This is yet another example of the unintended negative consequences of supposedly well-meaning social programs as well as an illustration of how the state has substituted itself for the bonds of family. The solution is to reduce the size of the state, improve families' economic position, encourage reliance of family members on one another and implement policies that remove economic penalties for having children.

What Opportunity Conservative policies are pro-family? They are policies that empower parents with the opportunity to provide the best quality of life to their children, to save money and get ahead and to offer their kids a brighter future than they themselves enjoyed. They are policies that would bring hope and opportunity and appeal to one of Canadians' most cherished desires: to have a family of their own.

A Prescription for a Healthy Family

In this regard, we propose an Opportunity Conservative prescription for family taxation and child care, which would make it an advantage, not a disadvantage, to marry and raise a family.

First of all, lower taxes! In its most recent survey of household spending, Statistics Canada reports that personal taxes are the largest family expenditure, ahead of shelter, food and clothing.[18] When you include all taxes, such as CPP, GST, PST, excise, gasoline, cigarette, liquor and import duties, the bill gets even bigger. In its annual Tax Freedom Day study, the Fraser Institute calculated that in 2005 Canadians worked until June 25 just to pay their tax bills.[19]

As a result, personal income has flatlined over the past fifteen years. A study by the TD Bank revealed that between 1989 and 2004, real after-tax income per worker rose just 3.6 percent. According to TD's Chief Economist Don Drummond, "Income growth would have fared far better were it not for rising tax burdens, which went from trimming back incomes in the 1970s to giving them a brush-cut thereafter."[20]

Worse yet, the study found that Canadians aren't getting value for all those taxes. Between 1975 and 1996, every tax dollar resulted in program spending of ninety to ninety-seven cents. Today, only seventy-six to eighty-four cents goes to programs, while the balance goes to paying down the debt of previous governments.

It doesn't take a rocket scientist to know that every dollar you take out of a family's pocket is one less opportunity for that family—one less chance for a child to play hockey or take piano lessons, one less bag of groceries in the cupboard, one less college fund or one less mortgage payment on a house. The incentive to work harder for your family is removed when more and more of your paycheque is stripped away.

Higher taxes also erode the connection between families and the community. Since so much money is paid in taxes, people expect the state to assume more responsibility. Families are less likely to volunteer their money or time to community activities, because they have less to give and because "it's the government's job" to do things like provide reading programs in libraries, visits to the seniors' centre or after-school activities for kids. The result is what socialists intend: a host of individuals who depend on the state and not each other for their well-being.

Tax policies should allow families to keep more of what they earn, save money and accumulate capital. They should also encourage them to value marriage, have children and raise them as they deem best. Tax policies should leave them greater room for charitable giving and activities. In the United States, the average family works until April 11 to pay their yearly tax bill. In Canada they're still toiling away until June 28.[21] Not surprisingly, Americans give two and a half times as much to charity as Canadians do.[22]

All this requires decreasing the tax burden on Canadian families. In addition to lower rates and a greater minimum personal exemption, governments should permit income-splitting. This could not only be done between married partners, so that single-earner families don't pay more tax than dual-earner families, but between all dependents in a household.

Ironically, one of the leaders in pro-family tax policy is France. While we certainly don't advocate adopting its expansive welfare state, the French family tax system is worthy of examination. In France, taxpayers combine all income earned by parents and children and split the income between all family members. Children are weighted half as much as parents. Individual tax schedules then apply to each of the split incomes. As a result, "a couple with two children would thus pay the same tax rate as a single person with one-third of their family income."[23] The result is a marriage bonus, as opposed to the marriage penalty Canadian families face under our own tax regime, in which a single-earner family pays more tax than a dual-earner family that pulls in the same total income.[24]

Family-friendly policies also means tax credits and vouchers to allow choice in child care—whether by a parent, relative, home care or daycare—rather than promoting the institutionalization of our children in state daycare. This is the position the Harper Conservatives seem to be adopting. If they can explain it clearly to Canadians, people should embrace it. Child care is one of the most important policy frontiers and one on which conservatives must stake out and defend a clear position. They are up against some formidable and well-organized adversaries. Advocates of state-run unionized daycares have been lobbying for their views for decades—at taxpayers' expense, no less.

It is instructive to examine just who is behind the push for a national daycare program in Canada. The major groups advocating state care all have strong ties to the labour movement. The Child Care Human Resources Sector Council is headed by three daycare unions and two organizations that advocate for publicly provided child care. It is funded by taxpayers to the tune of $500,000 a year.[25] The Child Care Advocacy Association of Canada (CCAA) receives federal funding from the Status of Women and the Social Development Directorate.[26] Jamie Kass, co-chair of the CCAA's Council of

Child Care Advocates, is with the Canadian Federation of Labour and is the child care coordinator for the Canadian Union of Postal Workers.

If you read the fine print, these groups are not calling for what's best for children, but rather what's best for their membership. In a position paper published in November 2004, the Ontario Coalition for Better Child Care states that "[I]t will also be critical to ensure that parents, communities, ECEs [early childhood educators] *and their unions* [emphasis added] play a key and ongoing role in planning and decision-making in the new operational model."[27] Meanwhile, the Canadian Labour Congress's priority for 2005 in the area of child care is to "work in coalitions to establish the national program we want incorporating the QUAD[28] principles, maintain a watchdog capacity on provincial governments, *and promote unionization* [emphasis added], work with labour councils to encourage municipalities to pressure the federal government."[29] "Honey, I forgot the kids!"

The union-run daycare lobby doesn't just want more daycare spaces; it wants more not-for-profit, state-run, unionized spaces. Why? In recent years, union membership has been declining. In 2004, about 31 percent of Canadian workers belonged to a union, down from 38 percent in 1981.[30] The only way of reversing that trend is to find new industries or businesses to unionize. State daycare is a natural market that would create legions of new members. Child care centres employ more than 100,000 workers in Canada and only 13 percent of these centres are currently unionized.[31] Daycare beats even Wal-Mart as a source of new recruits and new funding through the dues it will pay to unions.

Let's remember that the Left has never been about choice on child care, but about social engineering. To quote the late feminist Simone de Beauvoir: "No woman should be authorized to stay at home to raise her children. Society should be totally different. Women should not have that choice, precisely because if there is such a choice, too many women will make that one."[32]

Thank you for your opinion, Mme. de Beauvoir, but the key issue is indeed choice. And choice is exactly what's absent from the current federal Liberal proposals. Today's government is hell-bent on simply throwing money at government daycare, not enabling parents to choose their preferred means of child-raising with tax credits, vouchers or other mechanisms. Yet studies show that parents would rather have children cared for by a relative than an institutional daycare.[33] They favour tax breaks and direct assistance to families rather than creating more programs.[34] This is, in large part, a trust factor: parents are more naturally trusting of family than strangers to impart their values and provide a loving, caring environment for their children.[35] The assumption that all kids are better off being raised by the state is one made not by parents but by bureaucrats, educators and union reps.

In countries that do allow the choice, parents' preferences are clear. Australia introduced a voucher system in 1991, which produced a surplus of daycare spaces; in 2003, a survey of Australian families revealed that 94 percent were content with their access to all forms of child care.[36] Finland offers financial incentives to parents which enable them to either remain home to raise their children or place the child in daycare if they choose. Currently in Finland 10.7 percent of parents choose to put their children in municipal daycare; 42.7 percent choose a child home care allowance that allows parents of children from age one to three to remain at home; and 29.2 percent opt for the parenthood allowance, which covers parents with kids up to age one who stay at home. The stay-at-home parents receiving government allowances in Finland account for a whopping 72 percent of all children under three, while municipal daycare accounts for only 11 percent.[37] Someone tell that to the daycare pushers in Canada.

Promoting policies that support families—marriage, children and choice in child care—is the principled, positive way forward for the conservative movement. It would rally both social conservatives and socially liberal conservatives. It would strike a blow against statism and set the Conservatives apart from the Liberals. And most importantly, it would improve the lives of thousands of Canadians in a real and meaningful way.

Endnotes

1. Environics Research Group, "Support for Freedom of Choice on Abortion at an All-Time High," August 31, 2000. http://erg.environics.net/news/default. asp?aID=411

2. "Two-Thirds of Canadians Support Legal Protection for the Unborn," *LifeSite News*, October 26, 2004. www.lifesite.net/ldn/2004/oct/04102603.html

3. Lorrie Goldstein, "Extreme Views on Abortion," *The Toronto Sun*, April 3, 2005. www.canoe.ca/NewsStand/Columnists/Toronto/Lorrie_Goldstein/2005/04/03/980 963.html

4. Author interview with Mike Harris, July 5, 2005.

5. Karl Marx, and Freidrick Engels, *The Comminist Manifesto: A modern edition*, (London: Verso, 1998), 56.

6. Anatol Lunacharski quoted in Ferdinand Mount, *The Subversive Family* (London: Jonathan Cape, 1982), 35–36.

7. Mikhail Gorbachev, *Perestroika* (New York: Harper & Row, 1987), 117.

8. Sue Bailey "Dryden Has a Vision for Child Care," *Canoe News*, June 12, 2005. http://64.233.167.104/search?q=cache:e50_PUyg25YJ:cnews.canoe.ca/CNEWS/C anada/2005/06/12/1083778-cp.html+%22ken+dryden%22+child+care&thl=en

9. Jason Clemens and Sylvia LeRoy, "Louise Arbour's Economic Illiteracy," *Fraser Forum*, May 2005, 29–31.

10. Benedict Carey, "Experts Dispute Bush on Gay-Adoption Issue," *The New York Times*, January 29, 2005. www.contemporaryfamilies.org/media/news%20102.htm

11. "Common Law Relationships—A Dangerous Place to Be," *REALity*, July/August 2005, on REAL Women of Canada. www.realwomenca.com/newsletter/2005_july_aug/article_10.html

12. *Changing Conjugal Life in Canada*, Statistics Canada, 2001, summary. www.statcan.ca/english/freepub/

13. *Family Violence in Canada: A Statistical Profile 2005*, Canadian Centre for Justice Statistics, Statistics Canada, 2005, 18.

14. "Disparities in Pregnancy Outcomes According to Marital and Cohabitation Status" in *Obstetrics and Gynecology*, (Montreal: Statistics Canada/McGill University/ the Fetal and Infant Health Study Group of the Canadian Perinatal Surveillance System, 2004), summary.

15. "Divorces," *The Daily*, March 9, 2005, Statistics Canada. www.statcan.ca/Daily/English/050309/d050309b.htm

16. "[R]esults suggest that increased pension expenditures ... lead to lower fertility levels five or so years later. This lower fertility in turn implies increased pension expenditure." B. Entwisle and C. R. Winegarden, "Fertility and Pension Programs in LDCs: A Model of Mutual Reinforcement," *Economic Development and Cultural Change*, 32 (1984): 332, 348.

17. Charles F. Hohm et al., "A Reappraisal of the Social Security-Fertility Hypothesis: A Bidirectional Approach," *The Social Science Journal* 23 (1986): 163.

18. Statistics Canada, "Survey of Household Spending," *The Daily*, December 13, 2004. www.statcan.ca/Daily/English/041213/d041213b.htm.

19. Fraser Institute, "Canadians Celebrate Tax Freedom Day on June 26," news release, June 24, 2005. www.fraserinstitute.ca/shared/readmore.asp?sNav=nr&tid=672

20. Jacqueline Thorpe, "Fifteen Years of Stagnation: TD Blames Debt and Taxes as Take-Home Pay Flatlines," *Financial Post*, January 19, 2005.

21. Mark Mullins, "Higher taxes and spending make for later freedom day," *Budget and Tax News*, The Heartland Institute, August 1, 2004. www.heartland.org/article.cfm?artid=15478

22. Fraser Institute, "Manitoba Tops the Fraser Institute's Generosity Index for the Fifth Straight Year," news release, December 15, 2004. www.fraserinstitute.ca/shared/readmore.asp?snav=nr&tid=638

23. "Tax Breaks and Incentives," The Life Information Charitable Trust. www.life.org.nz/abortionpoliticalkeyissuesalternativestoabortion.htm

25. According to REAL Women of Canada, in 2003 a single-earner couple making $80,000 paid $2,743 more per year in tax than a dual-earner family in which each partner made $40,000. Source: www.realwomenca.com/newsletter/2005_may_jun/article_13.html

25. Peter Shawn Taylor, "National Day Care, Pay Care or No-Way Care?" Speech to the Fraser Institute, March 9, 2005, 6 (hereinafter Taylor Speech).

26. Child Care Advocacy of Canada, *Annual Report 2003–04*. www.childcareadvocacy.ca/resources/pdf/ccaac_annualreport04.pdf

27. Ontario Coalition for Better Child Care, "To boldly go ... towards a comprehensive child care system in Ontario," November 2004, 9–10.

28. QUAD stands for "Quality, Universality, Accessibility and Developmental," principles established by the federal government.

29. Canadian Labour Congress "Action Plan," as outlined at the CLC's 2005 convention, Montreal, June 13–17. www.canadianlabour.ca/index.php/Action_Plan

30. "Study: Diverging Trends in Unionization," *Statistics Canada*, April 22, 2005. http://66.102.7.104/search?q=cache:Kw6epzMmlW8J:dissemination.statcan.ca/Daily/English/050422/d050422c.htm+%22decline+in+union+membership%22+canada&hl=en

31. Taylor Speech, 6.

32. Simone de Beauvoir, *The Saturday Review*, June 14, 1974, 18.

33. In a COMPAS poll conducted on May 21, 2003, in advance of the Ontario election, subjects were asked: "Suppose it's not possible for a parent to stay home to take care of an infant or preschool child. Would it then be best for the child to be cared for by a relative of the family or in an institutional daycare setting." Sixty-two percent of respondents said the child should be cared for by a relative, versus 23 percent who preferred institutional daycare. Four percent volunteered that a home daycare setting would be best.

34. According to *CTV News* Online, polling by Ekos Research, conducted for the federal government in 2005, found that 30 percent of those polled were in favour of more and better programs; 28 percent were in favour of financial assistance; and 21 percent favoured tax breaks. See "No Deal on National Child Care: Dryden," *CTV News*, February 12, 2005. http://64.233.167.104/search?q=cache:7Yxs34zwvqgJ:www.ctv.ca/servlet/ArticleNews/story/CTVNews/1108079027793_21%3Fs_name%3D%26no_ads%3D+%22ken+dryden%22+child+care&hl=en)

35. Taylor Speech, 5.

36. Peter Shawn Taylor, "Private Sector Can Meet Child Care Demands," *Fraser Forum*, March 2004, 6.

37. "Trends in Social Protection in Finland 2004–2007," Ministry of Social Affairs and Health, Helsinki, 2005, 150. www.stm.fi/Resource.phx/publishing/store/2005/04/hu1113547327264/passthru.pdf

14

SUPERIOR HEALTH CARE:
Competition, Choice and Dignity

"If you think health care is expensive now, wait until you see how much it costs when it's free."

— P.J. O'Rourke

Picture this: Two patients limp into two different Canadian medical clinics with the same complaint. Both have trouble walking and appear to require a hip replacement. The first patient is examined within the hour, is x-rayed the same day and has a time booked for surgery the following week. The second sees his family doctor after waiting a week for an appointment, then waits eighteen weeks to see a specialist, then gets an x-ray, which isn't reviewed for another month and finally has his surgery scheduled for a year from then.

Why the different treatment for the two patients? The first is a Golden Retriever; the second is an elderly man.

Welcome to the Canadian health care system, where you can buy care for your pet, but not for yourself or a loved one. A system driven by rigid ideology, not results. A system that claims to guarantee equal access when it's really who you know, or who you are, that can determine how quickly you will be treated. Indeed, it's not only dogs who don't face queues, but prisoners, members of the Armed Forces and, in some provinces, beneficiaries of Worker's Compensation claims, all of whom get priority treatment in our supposedly "egalitarian" public health care system. And don't forget those who opt out of public care entirely: the very wealthy, from politicians to sports figures, who can jet off to the Mayo Clinic at a moment's notice. The notion that we don't have two-tier health care in Canada is laughable, or rather it would be if so many people weren't suffering or even dying as they wait for medical care.

And there are far too many examples of this. In 1999, Ontario teenager Joshua Fleuelling died of asthma while waiting for treatment, after being turned away from a hospital whose emergency room was full. In 2004, John Barnsley, a Saskatchewan farmer, finally underwent surgery to remove a fast-growing tumour on his adrenal gland. But not before protesting in front of the provincial legislature, where he made it known that he had already waited four months for treatment. In 2005, the family of four-year-old Ryan Oldford, who lived in Newfoundland, was told that it would be *two and a half years* before the boy could undergo a magnetic resonance imaging scan of his remaining kidney (he had lost the other one to cancer). This was because the province had only one MRI machine. (Mysteriously, after *The Globe and Mail* broke the story, Ryan received treatment within a few days.)

Our system denies middle- and lower-income Canadians the opportunity to access the health care system of their choice. In most of Canada, people who would obtain private insurance to cover themselves and their families, if it were legal and available, are prohibited from doing so. Governments find ways of preventing private clinics from operating and, in Ontario's case, even buy them out with public funds. Our system rations care and makes it unlawful for Canadians to spend their own money on better or faster services. Canada is a member of a depressingly exclusive club in this regard: Cuba and North Korea are the only other countries with universal health care that forbid their citizens from voluntarily spending their own money to remain healthy.

All this is due to the Canada Health Act, which obliges the provinces to respect the principles of universality, accessibility, comprehensiveness, portability and public administration—or face cuts in

Canada Health Transfers. In other words, allow private care to flourish on your soil, and Ottawa will turn off the taps. So instead of calling for real change, provincial governments, which are constitutionally entrusted with delivering health care, call for more transfusions of cash from their federal counterparts.

But increased state funding isn't the answer. The portion of provincial spending devoted to health care rose from 28.3 percent in 1975 to 38.6 percent in 2004.[1] That number continues to rise as baby boomers age. But as spending increases, the quality of care gets worse. Over the past decade, waiting times have risen by 92 percent. In 2005, it takes 17.9 weeks to see a specialist from the time you visit your family doctor.[2]

Compared with other nations, Canadians are not getting value for their money. The oft-heard claim that Canada has the "best health care in the world" has become so discredited that no one can believe it anymore. In the most recent ranking of 191 public health care systems by the World Health Organization, Canada lagged in thirtieth place, behind France, Germany, the Netherlands, Portugal, Spain, Greece, Morocco, Singapore, Japan, Australia and the United Kingdom, among other countries.[3] All of these countries allow private care to co-exist alongside their public systems.

In its 2005 report How Good Is Canadian Health Care? the Fraser Institute compared our system with that of twenty-six other OECD countries that provide universal coverage (this excluded the United States). Authors Nadeem Esmail and Michael Walker found that Canada ranks in the bottom half of nations in terms of patient access to mammograms, CT scanners and MRI machines, and last in terms of access to lithotriptors. Canada ranks twenty-four out of twenty-seven in the number of doctors per thousand people. (StatsCan says more than 1.2 million Canadians were unable to find a doctor in 2003; in reality, that number is twice as high, if you include those who weren't looking.[4]) Canada ranks twenty-second in life expectancy spent in full health and twentieth in infant mortality. All this despite the fact that we spend more money on health care than any other OECD country save Iceland and Switzerland. The authors of this study concluded that the Canadian system "produces longer waiting times, is less successful in preventing deaths from preventable causes, and costs more than any of the other systems that have comparable objectives." Countries that offer universal access but that also have user fees, private insurance, private hospitals and competition all fare better.[5]

In Canada, the lack of these elements breeds inefficiency at all levels, from those who use health services to those who deliver them. In his award-winning book, *Code Blue: Reviving Canada's Health Care System*, Dr. David Gratzer reviews the main structural problems. First, patients run to the ER for every sneeze, because health care is "free" and there are no fees to pay. Second, doctors don't spend as much time with each patient because the government remunerates them on a fee-for-service basis. Third, hospitals don't rush to get the latest technology, because it only means more patients will use it and strain their limited, block-funded budgets. Finally, politicians are loath to advocate anything other than public health care, because medicare has become enshrined as part of the Canadian identity.

All of these problems stem from one basic issue: health care in Canada is provided by a monopoly. A monopoly has no competition to keep costs or quality in check. Patients cannot vote with their feet and obtain better care at the hospital down the street. They're lucky if they receive care anywhere at all.

The fact that this monopoly is state-run and unionized only makes things worse. Government-run institutions are notorious for their bureaucratic, over-regulated and over-administered ways. Meanwhile, aggressive public-sector unions demand wages far higher than the private sector would pay. According to a 2004 study of Ontario hospital employee pay, mid- and lower-level unionized hospital workers receive relatively high wages in relation to workers in comparable private sector jobs; their wages are often 20 percent higher. For example, the average salary of a light-duty cleaner who works in a hospital is $30,433 a year—a third more than cleaners in other industries. And food counter attendants earn $29,709 a year—one and a half times the average wage for the same job in other sectors.[6] The result? Taxpayers get less bang for each precious buck.

This problem isn't unique to Ontario. British Columbia faced similar wage discrepancies, but unlike Ontario, it actually decided to do something about the situation. In 2004 Gordon Campbell's Liberal government outsourced a number of non-medical services to the private sector, including cafeteria food, security and cleaning services. Government unions denounced the move and staged a series of illegal strikes, which disrupted patient care and even resulted in the cancellation of surgeries. (So much for unions putting people first.) Campbell held firm, however, and the reforms ended up saving British Columbia's taxpayers $63 million a year, money that can be re-directed into purchasing drugs and equipment and improving facilities instead of being spent on inflated salaries.

Salaries in Ontario are also out of whack at the high end, especially when measured against performance. The Fraser Institute found that in Ontario, for example, hospital payrolls for high earners (hospital employees making at least $100,000) rose more than 18 percent in 2004. At the same time, inflation clocked in under 2 percent and the average wage gain in the province was 1.2 percent. During the same period, hospital deficits ballooned to $600 million, staff positions were cut, and the time patients had to wait between seeing a specialist and being treated in hospital jumped 15 percent. The study's conclusion? There exists "no statistical relationship between pay increases and nine measures of hospital performance."[7]

In a system where three-quarters of costs go to salaries and benefits, bringing wages in line with market norms would make a huge difference—and not a moment too soon. Health care is an ever-growing leviathan, swallowing funding for other political priorities such as education and infrastructure. According to the Canadian Taxpayers Federation, if the current trends continue, health care spending will consume 85 percent of some provincial budgets by 2035.[8] Of course, this would dramatically simplify government: we would have just two ministries left to deal with, Finance to collect revenue and Health to spend it.

Taking Health Care to the Courts

Apart from the economic implications, the human costs are staggering. Waiting times are not just statistics; they are a litany of personal tragedies. People lose their jobs, their relationships and their sanity as a result of protracted waiting times. To the patient, waiting means enduring unnecessary pain and suffering, decreased mobility, stress, deterioration in his or her condition and risking potential dependency on painkillers, a situation that is entirely preventable with timely care.

In Quebec, one such patient decided not to put up with waiting anymore. George Zeliotis, a seventy-year-old salesman, languished on a hospital waiting list in Montreal for nearly a year before receiving a hip operation. While on the list, Zeliotis inquired to see if he could undergo the surgery sooner by paying a private health facility, and whether he could purchase private health care insurance should he require similar treatment in the future. Both acts were illegal under provincial laws. Incensed, Zeliotis filed a lawsuit challenging these prohibitions on constitutional grounds. Specifically, Zeliotis claimed that the lengthy wait violated his right to life, liberty and security of the person under section 7 of the federal Charter of Rights and Freedoms and section 1 of the Quebec Charter of Human Rights and Freedoms. Together with Jacques Chaouilli, a Quebec doctor who had long advocated private care as a means of improving the Canadian system, Zeliotis went as far as the Supreme Court of Canada to defend his right to timely care.

On June 8, 2005 the high court ruled in favour of Zeliotis and Chaoulli and struck down Quebec's prohibition against the purchase of private insurance for procedures already covered by medicare. Four judges out of seven deemed it a violation of the Quebec Charter; three judges in that majority went further, finding a violation of section 7 of the federal Charter as well.

The case was a watershed—the first body blow to the state health care monopoly. It debunked one of the key arguments of pro-monopolists, namely, that private care would undermine the public system. Writing for the majority, Justice Marie DesChamps said, "It cannot be concluded from the evidence concerning the Quebec plan or the plans of the other provinces of Canada, or from the evolution of the systems of various OECD countries that an absolute prohibition on private insurance is necessary to protect the integrity of the public plan."[9]

The case of *Chaoulli v. Quebec (Attorney General)* gave a great boost to the cause of choice in health care, particularly in a province that is already the private health care capital of Canada. More than fifty private clinics are open for business in Quebec, including one run by none other than Paul Martin's personal physician. The court ruling had the effect of legitimizing the option of private care in the health care debate.

In the rest of Canada, calls for change began mounting as well. In November 2005, the Canadian Independent Medical Clinics Association held a conference to promote the co-existence of a European-style public and private system. In August 2005, delegates to the annual convention of the Canadian Medical Association, which had previously opposed increasing private health care, rejected by a two-thirds margin a motion calling on doctors to denounce a parallel, private health care system as a way to deal with long waiting lists.[10]

Where is the public on the issue? Even before *Chaoulli*, surveys done over the past few years show that Canadians are increasingly in favour of more private involvement in health care. An Environics survey published in 2004 found that 66 percent of Canadians say they strongly (31 percent) or somewhat (35 percent) support having health care services provided by the private sector, if patients do not have to pay out of their own pockets for these services and the services are covered by tax dollars, as they are now. Support for this concept was up from 54 percent in 2002.[11]

On the question of purchasing private care outright, the same study found that 50 percent of respondents said they agree that individual Canadians should be given the right to buy private health care within Canada if they do not receive timely access to public services, "even if this might weaken the principle of universal access to health care for all Canadians by making it possible for some people to have quicker access to services."[12] (A loaded aspect of the question if we ever saw one.) Polling done by Leger Marketing for the Montreal Economic Institute in 2005 produced similar results, with 52 percent agreeing that it would be acceptable "if the government were to allow those who wish to pay for healthcare in the private system to have speedier access to this type of care while still maintaining the current free and universal health care system." This percentage reached 65 percent of respondents in Quebec and 67 percent among those who said they would vote for the

Conservative Party.[13] A June 2005 poll conducted by Decima Research found that 23 percent of Canadians would be somewhat or very likely "to subscribe to a private health care service that charged $2,300 a year, with a $1,700 initiation fee, to screen for early signs of disease and manage chronic problems such as diabetes and pain."[14]

And where are our politicians? The Conservatives, like the federal Liberals and the NDP, still toe the doctrinaire statist line that private care is bad and public money cures all ills. Indeed, when the *Chaoulli* case was decided, the Conservatives responded in the House of Commons by accusing Paul Martin of underfunding medicare. Rather than being principled and embracing the groundbreaking decision, Conservative MP Peter MacKay got up in Question Period and demanded to know what the prime minister would do to preserve "Canada's universally accessible, publicly funded health care system." MacKay bemoaned the fact that, according to him, further court actions "could destroy the underpinnings of the *Canada Health Act*."[15] Instead of trumpeting *Chaoulli* as a breakthrough for Canadians, the Tory caucus, led by health critic Stephen Fletcher, spun it as an indictment of Liberal "neglect and mismanagement"[16] of the health file, as if there were no problem with the actual structure of the system itself.

Chaouilli is just the latest example of Tory pusillanimity. They've been trying to out-liberal the Liberals on the issue ever since the 2004 election. At the March 2005 policy conference in Montreal, the party endorsed a resolution allowing provinces "maximum flexibility to ensure the delivery of medically necessary health services *within a universal, public health care system*" (emphasis added).[17]

In April 2005, Preston Manning and Mike Harris made suggestions for improving the system. They penned a set of policy proposals called *A Canada Strong and Free*. Among their ideas on health care were removing federal restrictions prohibiting private health care in the provinces—in other words, respecting the Constitution, which makes health care a provincial responsibility. Cue the media smear: the Canadian Press was out the gates in minutes with a story saying the "right-wing" Fraser Institute had "tossed an electoral bomb into the lap of Conservative Leader Stephen Harper."[18] Harper's response? Despite having recommended that the Canada Health Act be scrapped when he was the head of the National Citizens' Coalition, a few days after the CP story broke, he told a Calgary crowd—at no less a venue than the Fraser Institute's annual meeting!—"I could not imagine a proposal that's more of a non-starter than that one."[19]

From Harper's past comments, it is clear that he doesn't actually believe in a state health care monopoly. Why not just be more forthcoming? Health care is a key area where the Conservative Party could distinguish itself from the Liberals, who are failing Canadians on what the polls show is their most important issue. It is an area where Conservatives should be vocal, direct and insistent in calling for an increase of private care in the system.

But since Conservative politicians refuse to write the necessary prescription, it's up to the non-partisan conservative movement to do it for them. The movement must step forward and create non-profit advocacy organizations whose sole focus is to get the message out about how the status quo is killing people. There are enough voices on the other side. The Tommy Douglas Research Institute, Friends of Medicare, the Canadian Health Coalition, Maude Barlow's Council of Canadians and other organizations administer a steady stream of pro-monopoly opiates to the press and the public.

The Need for Choice and Innovation

What would an Opportunity Conservative policy on health care look like? It would champion that key Opportunity Conservative principle: freedom of choice. It would maintain universal coverage but allow competition, which breeds innovation, which leads to efficiencies, which provide more and faster care at a lower cost.

From both a political and practical point of view, conservatives should advocate the adoption of a European-style health care system, such as is found in Sweden, Switzerland and France. Politically, this immunizes the right against the leftist bogeyman of wanting to import "U.S.-style" health care. Practically, European systems work. They have next to no waiting lists, maintain universal coverage and yet allow patients freedom of choice when they are selecting treatment.

What do these countries do that we don't? Sweden charges user fees for doctors' visits. Switzerland obliges all its citizens to purchase private health insurance. France allows patients to "top up" public care by paying for better hospital rooms and superior procedures. The list goes on. The basic point is that private health care is allowed to co-exist alongside public care. Private health care fosters competition and takes the pressure off the public system. Both systems work better and patients get superior care as a result. Everyone wins.

In Canada, conservatives should advocate the creation of a parallel private system, period. Not just half-measures, like contracting out public services to the private sector. (This is a practice government should engage in across the board anyway.) Let the provinces innovate and experiment, and don't interfere. That's where change will come from. In British Columbia and Quebec private clinics are operating effectively alongside the public system—and politicians are treading carefully around the issue. In Alberta, Premier Ralph Klein continues to bluster about private care. Others will follow. There is no time to lose on this issue. With the baby boomers getting greyer by the day, health care costs will only mount and so will people's frustrations with them.

Conservatives should insist that provinces that continue to ban private insurance, such as Manitoba and Ontario, repeal their laws to bring them in line with the Supreme Court's decision in *Chaoulli*, which technically only has legal ramifications in Quebec. It is only a matter of time before similar cases are litigated in the rest of the country. Apart from making sense from a policy point of view, changing these laws would pre-empt unnecessary litigation, saving taxpayers money, as well as ensuring the same freedoms to all Canadians as those enjoyed by residents of *la belle province*.

What benefits would such changes bring? They would reduce waiting lists and human suffering, as well as improving health care and quality of life. They would return dignity to patients, who would have control over their care and choice in how to manage it. There would be benefits to the economy as well. As mentioned earlier, the Canadian Independent Medical Clinics Association estimates that the creation of a domestic for-profit health care system would be worth $10 to $40 billion to Canada's economy, providing jobs, encouraging research and technological innovation.

Those who decry "chequebook medicine" should realize that its current alternative, "blank cheque medicine," is worse. Pouring more money down the black hole of the state health care monopoly won't make us healthier; it will only make us poorer. Perhaps the single greatest contribution Opportunity Conservatives could make to the welfare of this country would be to successfully advocate for true choice in health care. Let's make it our mission to ensure that no more Joshua Fleuellings die because an ER is full. And that patients like Ryan Oldford, John Barnsley and George Zeliotis aren't told they'll have to put their lives on hold while waiting for the care they need.

Endnotes

1. Mark Kennedy, "Medicare Summit Urged," *National Post*, January 28, 2005, A1.

2. Tom Blackwell, "Surgery Wait Times Soaring," *National Post*, October 21, 2004, A1, quoting the Fraser Institute's Nadeem Esmail.

3. World Health Organization, *The World Health Report 2000—Health Systems: Improving Performance* (Geneva, 2000). www.who.int/whr

4. Statistics Canada, Canadian Community Health Survey, *The Daily*, June 15, 2004. www.statcan.ca/Daily/English/040615/d040615b.htm

5. Nadeem Esmail and Michael Walker. *How Good Is Canadian Health Care? 2005 Report: An International Comparison of Health Care Systems* (The Fraser Institute). www.fraserinstitute.ca/admin/books/files/HowGoodIsCanHealthCare2005.pdf

6. Mark Mullins and Andrea Mrozek, "Where Does the Money Go? A Study of Worker Pay in Ontario's Hospitals," *Fraser Alert*, September 2004, Ontario Policy Series, 4. www.fraserinstitute.ca/admin/books/files/WhereTheMoneyGoes.pdf

7. "Ontario's High Earner Hospital Payrolls Up 18 Percent But No Boost to Outcomes," Fraser Institute, May 9, 2005. www.fraserinstitute.ca/shared/readmore.asp?snav=nr&tid=661

8. Tasha Kheiriddin, *2004–05 Ontario Pre-Budget Submission: A Twelve-Step Program for Ontario's Fiscal Recovery* (Toronto: Canadian Taxpayers Federation, April 2004), Appendix II. www.taxpayer.com/pdf/2004_Ontario_Pre_Budget_Submission.pdf

9. *Chaoulli v. Quebec (Attorney General)* 2005 SCC 35, opinion of J. Deschamps.

10. *CBC News* Online, "CMA Backs Private Parallel Health Care," August 18, 2005. www.cbc.ca/story/canada/national/2005/08/18/health_care_2005_08_18.html

11. "New Poll Shows Private Health Care Not a Taboo for Canadians," Environics Research, June 22, 2004. http://erg.environics.net/news/default.asp?aID=556 (hereinafter Environics Research).

12. Environics Research.

13. Montreal Economic Institute / Leger Marketing, "The Opinion of Canadians on Access to Health Care," April 12, 2005, 5. www.iedm.org/uploaded/pdf/sondage0405_en.pdf

14. "Canadians Would Subscribe to Private Care: Poll," *CTV News* Online, *Canadian Press*, August 11, 2005. www.ctv.ca/servlet/ArticleNews/story/ CTVNews/1123791335477_119200535/?hub=Canada

15. House of Commons, Hansard, June 9, 2005. www.parl.gc.ca/38/1/parlbus/ chambus/house/debates/112_2005-06-09/HAN112-E.htm#Int-1335922

16. "Fletcher: Supreme Court Ruling Proves Liberals Have Damaged Health Care," press release by Stephen Fletcher, MP, June 9, 2005. www.stevenfletcher.com/archives/000392.php

17. "Conservative Party of Canada Policy Declaration," March 19, 2005, 19. www.conservative.ca/media/20050319-POLICY%20DECLARATION.pdf

18. "Harper Given Electoral Bomb on Health-care," *Canadian Press*, April 14, 2005. www.ctv.ca/servlet/ArticleNews/story/CTVNews/1113482081408_105/?hub=Health

19. Thomas Walkolm, "Harper Backs Medicare Law," *Toronto Star*, April 30, 2005. www.thestar.com/NASApp/cs/ContentServer?pagename=thestar/Layout/ Article_PrintFriendly&tc=Article&cid=1114813812969&call_pageid=9683321884 92&DPL=IvsNDS52f7ChAX&tacodalogin=yes

15 CHAPTER

FREE-MARKET ENVIRONMENTALISM:
Greening the Conservative Movement

"The best thing that could happen to the environment is free-market capitalism."
— Robert F. Kennedy Jr.

When one pictures defenders of the environment, conservatives are probably the last group that springs to mind. Images of environmental activism range from the predictable, such as former Ontario NDP premier Bob Rae being arrested for trying to block loggers in Temagami, to the annoying, like those Greenpeace fundraisers who accost you on city street corners, to the bizarre, like activist Julia Butterfly Hill, who lived in a 1,000-year-old tree named "Luna" for two years to save it from loggers. Despite his desire to appear more *au courant*, it's still hard to picture Stephen Harper sporting a bandanna and chained to the top of a giant redwood.

Yet in Canada, previous Conservative administrations have been at the forefront of environmental protection—they just never got the credit for it. The Progressive Conservative Party had a first-rate record on the environment in the 1980s under ministers Tom McMillan and, believe it or not, Lucien Bouchard. The Mulroney government negotiated the Acid Rain Treaty with the U.S., massively reduced sulphur dioxide emissions, and created the National Roundtable on the Environment and the

Economy. Compared with the Chrétien Liberals, whose environmental record was dubbed a "disaster"[1] by Sierra Club executive director Elizabeth May, Mulroney's achievements were considerable. But because he was a conservative, we rarely heard him toasted by the environmental community, which is dominated by left-wing interests. Former Ontario premier Mike Harris also did a tremendous amount for the environment. In 1999, Harris announced Ontario's Living Legacy, an initiative to protect 2.4 million hectares of Crown lands and create 378 new parks.[2] It was the biggest expansion of parks and protected areas in Ontario's history. Not surprisingly, he received few accolades.

Today's federal Conservative Party, however, is failing to take the lead on the environment. In the 2004 election, the Tories dedicated a measly one and a half pages of their forty-five-page platform to environmental issues. It's not that the proposed ideas were bad, but they were not detailed enough and were buried on page thirty-four. Some of the policies included negotiating new power plant emissions limits with the United States, increasing fines against companies for oil spills, working with the provinces to develop strategies for energy conservation and, lastly, "redirect[ing] federal spending aimed at fulfilling the terms of the increasingly irrelevant Kyoto Protocol to concrete programs to ensure clean air, water, and land, and to promote energy conservation."

It was this last point that got all the attention, mainly because the liberal media considered any criticism of Kyoto as being tantamount to wanting the Earth to overheat and explode like a Gremlin in a microwave. The focus on the Tories' anti-Kyoto stance has increased the perception that only the left cares about the environment and that if it were up to the Conservatives, Banff National Park would be paved over and turned into another West Edmonton Mall.

The Conservatives' principled stand on Kyoto should not be denigrated; it should be applauded. The accord, signed in 1997, is an economic disaster for Canada. The Liberals have made a commitment to spend $10 billion in order to implement the accord's provisions, which call for a reduction of greenhouse gas emissions to an average of 6 percent below 1990 levels by 2012. The Canadian Taxpayers Federation estimates that the price increases and wage reductions needed to bring energy consumption down to meet Kyoto's requirements would reduce annual real net household income by $3,000. According to the Federation's federal director, John Williamson, "it will mean making drastic changes to our way of life without a corresponding reduction in global emissions or an improvement in our quality of life here at home."[3]

That's because under the accord, countries such as the former Soviet Republics will be able to sell clean air "credits" to nations like Canada. This is not because their industries are cleaner, but because they have such a limited industrial base after the fall of communism. Meanwhile, developed Western economies will buy the credits and continue to pollute. Adhering to Kyoto targets will not reduce smog in Toronto, improve the health of the Great Lakes or halt contamination of the Arctic tundra. All it will do is dig a hole in Canadians' wallets.

To make matters worse, the Liberals have no serious plan to reach the accord's emission reduction targets. Add to that the fact that so-called developing countries like China and India are not bound by the same restrictions, and that the U.S. has not signed on at all, and you have an environmental deal that is the equivalent of unilateral disarmament. Kyoto is objectively a bad accord. It is not even being enforced—indeed, it may be unenforceable.[4]

But because the Conservatives have failed to offer Canadians a full alternative vision to Kyoto, they have left themselves open to attacks that they are environmentally uncaring, or worse, Neanderthals who disregard modern science. Their approach to environmental issues since the 2004 election has been haphazard and piecemeal. They've mused about a Clean Air Act and a Clean Water Act; they voted to support policies on aquifer mapping and aquatic invasive species at their Montreal convention; and in August of 2005, they unveiled a plan to offer transit tax rebates to city commuters in order to encourage people to leave their cars at home.

Though the latter plan was a good idea, it went over like a lead balloon. Harper was pilloried in the press, in particular by the *Toronto Star*, which ran an editorial denouncing the proposal and claiming the proposed savings would not be significant enough to change commuters' habits. The plan would give taxpayers a 16-percent federal income-tax rebate for buying a transit pass, thus saving the average urban taxpayer $153 annually if he or she spent $80 a month on a transit pass (ironically, the savings would be just enough to pay for a one-year *Star* subscription). Toronto Go Train commuters would save even more, to the tune of $485 a year.[5]

Like much of the media, the *Star* can never find anything good to say about the Tories on the best of days. But what the party should take away from this incident is that it needs to give more consideration to the big picture in order to make headway on green issues. Free-market alternatives to statist environmentalism are about more than bus passes. A holistic vision is required, one that presents a broad spectrum of policies based on common sense and private solutions that work.

Another reason the Tories must make headway in relation to the environment has to do with the growth of the Green Party. In the 2004 federal election, the Greens garnered 4.3 percent of the vote. Under new federal political finance rules, this entitles them to receive more than one million tax dollars per year, which will allow them to mount a much stronger campaign next time around. Though they haven't captured any seats yet, this could change if they use their new resources to target specific ridings and attract star candidates. A likely spot for a Green seat is British Columbia, where the party has done well provincially.

If the Greens were successful in electing MPs and the Tories were in a minority government situation, finding common ground could be the ticket to a coalition government. (It would also confuse the heck out of the left, which alone would make it worth the effort). This may not be as far-fetched as it first sounds. The Greens' leader, Jim Harris, is a former Progressive Conservative. In the last election, the Green platform actually proposed income tax reductions and some other small-c conservative policies. While the Greens' support for Kyoto is an obvious stumbling block, if the Tories present a sensible free-market alternative, this could open the door to co-operation and turn an electoral liability into an advantage.

To do this, the Conservatives need a strong, comprehensive and well-developed environmental message. They need a vision that will resonate with regular Canadians who care about these issues. As a starting point, they should turn to activists already in the field and craft a plan of action based on existing research and programs.

Free-Market Solutions

Opportunity Conservative environmental policies are based on the tenets of free-market environmentalism. Free market environmentalists believe that non-governmental tools such as user fees, incentives, private property and markets will alleviate environmental problems more effectively than centralized, state-directed tools, such as subsidies, bureaucracy and regulation.[6]

In the United States, the Property and Environment Research Center (PERC) has been advocating free-market solutions to environmental problems since 1980. Its credo is:

- Private property rights encourage stewardship of resources;
- Government subsidies often degrade the environment;
- Market incentives spur individuals to conserve resources and protect environmental quality;
- Polluters should be liable for the harm they cause others.[7]

PERC's starting position is that protecting property rights is key to protecting the environment. The organization examines "how property rights evolve, how they are defined and enforced, how they are traded, and how they affect incentives for environmental stewardship."[8]

One of the policies PERC advocates that could be applied in Canada is called "homesteading the oceans." The goal is to replace regulation with private ownership of ocean resources in order to avoid the so-called tragedy of the commons, whereby a common resource like fish is inevitably overexploited and depleted, because no one has a vested proprietary interest in protecting it. Homesteading involves the allocation of individual transferable quotas (ITQs), which give fishers ownership of a portion of the annual catch. According to PERC researcher Donald Leal, in New Zealand, where ITQs have become genuine property rights, they are "increasing the value of fisheries and encouraging cooperation among owners in protecting the long-run future of the fishing areas."[9]

Declining fish stocks are achingly familiar to Atlantic Canada, where, despite government regulation, decades of overfishing finally caused the complete collapse of the cod fishing industry. If the Conservatives were to champion an ITQ-based policy for the eastern provinces, it would not only be an innovative step but a positive one in preserving a traditional way of life by market means. It would do a lot to re-ingratiate the Tories with Newfoundland fishermen, many of whom have never forgiven the Mulroney government for the 1992 cod fishing moratorium and its $225-a-week aid package for the affected fishers.

An additional policy change that would help wildlife—this time endangered species—is championed by the Thoreau Institute, another U.S. environmental think-tank. Founded in 1975, the organization bases its philosophy on that of Henry David Thoreau, who believed that "in wilderness is the preservation of the world" and "that government is best which governs least." Sounds good to us, but don't just take our right-wing word for it; read what former Democratic presidential candidate and vice-president Al Gore says on the Thoreau Institute's website: "Free market capitalist economics is arguably the most powerful tool ever used by civilization. As the world's leading exemplar of free market economics, the US has a special obligation to discover effective ways of using the power of market forces to help save the environment."[10]

The institute makes a compelling case for why endangered species acts actually harm the very creatures they are designed to protect. The regulations they impose on land use often lead private landowners to simply destroy species habitat before government officials learn that a species is living on their land. The Thoreau Institute advocates compensation instead of regulation to encourage landowners to safeguard these habitats.

It also promotes creative policies to safeguard parklands. The institute does not promote privatization but what it terms *marketization*. The organization advocates four principles:

1. Public land managers should be allowed to charge fair market value for all resources, including recreation.

2. National forests, national parks, and other public lands should be funded exclusively out of a share of the net user fees they earn.

3. Public land permits, which are now all written on a *use-it-or-lose-it* basis, should allow users to *use it or conserve it.*

4. A share of gross user fees should be dedicated to trust funds designed to protect biodiversity, historic sites and wilderness.[11]

With Parks Canada's giant $500-million annual budget, the Conservatives could present an intelligent alternative along the lines of what the Thoreau Institute suggests. The Fraser Institute released a study in April 2005 entitled *Can Markets Save Canada's National Parks?* which reported that about 87 percent of income at Canada's national parks is coming from government appropriations rather than internally generated revenue. Ten years ago that figure was 91 percent.[12]

In Canada the lion's share of environmental advocacy organizations are still located on the left of the political spectrum. These include Greenpeace, the Sierra Club, the David Suzuki Foundation, Friends of the Earth and Paul Watson's Sea Shepherd Conservation Society, a group founded in 1977 that became infamous for ramming boats engaged in whale and seal hunting. So who can the Conservative Party go to for green free-market advice and to build political alliances?

A few groups exist that promote a vision for the environment that is more in line with Opportunity Conservative principles, although these groups would probably not call themselves conservative. The foremost is Ducks Unlimited, a privately funded non-profit group founded in 1938 whose mission is to "conserve, restore and manage wetlands and associated habitats for North America's waterfowl."[13] Like free-market environmentalists, Ducks Unlimited doesn't constantly look to government to take over private land. It raises private money and works with private landowners to maintain the land's natural beauty.

Two other groups that don't take knee-jerk leftist positions on environmental issues are Environment Probe and Energy Probe. These are Toronto-based organizations that have brought forward innovative ideas on the environment and energy production. Each is run as a division of the Energy Probe Research Foundation, which has a stable of several divisions focusing on the environment, consumer rights and urban issues. *Financial Post* columnist Lawrence Solomon was a co-founder of the organization in 1980. The foundation "has always championed property rights and market mechanisms to protect consumers and the environment, has been a critic of foreign aid and other forms of unaccountable international lending, and believes that an informed public can best ensure lasting environmental protection."[14] On its board of directors the foundation boasts such luminaries as columnists Andrew Coyne and Margaret Wente as well as University of Toronto professor Clifford Orwin.

The key to Environment Probe's work is "the promotion of property rights and decentralized decision making to empower individuals and communities to protect natural resources."[15] In the past, the organization has championed community and privately based solutions to environmental problems rather than looking to the government for help.

Energy Probe has a similar mandate focusing on the energy sector. It promotes more environmentally friendly alternatives like wind energy, which it believes can be better sustained on the free market and doesn't need governmental bailouts.

Opportunity Conservatives will need environmental advocacy groups to help spread this type of message. Other than the above-mentioned groups, few conservative lobbying or public-relations-oriented environmental groups exist in Canada. The Fraser Institute does put out a sizeable number of environmental studies and reports. It also runs partnerships with groups such as the Foundation for Teaching Economics. In October 2005, the Fraser Institute helped to sponsor teachers so they could attend a three-day program in Florida, the focus of which was to present "an understanding of how market forces may be used to solve environmental issues."[16]

The Winnipeg-based Frontier Center for Public Policy has also taken on the environment file, arguing that "wealth creation is the wellspring for environmental improvement,"[17] and that "property rights encourage conservation and environmental improvement."[18] It promotes "modern environmentalism," which is similar to free-market environmentalism.

As this book goes to press, a new organization is being launched called the Natural Resources Stewardship Project (NRSP). This group plans to run proactive grassroots information campaigns against bad (read: big government) environmentalism and advocate pro-freedom alternatives. It plans to promote responsible environmental stewardship by individual Canadians and will also serve as a watchdog to monitor the effects of government environmental regulation.

The Conservative Party and groups like the ones mentioned above must aim to debunk the myth that economic growth, free markets and conservatism are incompatible with protecting the environment. The two go hand in hand. The image projected by the left is that conservatives all shill for big business and that they want to clear cut forests, melt the polar ice caps and kill off endangered animals. The truth is exactly the opposite.

The Benefits of Being Green

The best way to encourage environmental protection is to promote private property rights. When you own land, you want to take care of it. When the land is owned by the government, you have less interest in it. Why do you think people spit and throw cigarette butts on the sidewalk but not inside their own homes? It's the message the left doesn't want you to hear: Ownership encourages righteous behaviour. And the more private land we have, the better off the environment will be.

And enterprise can do more to help the environment than any single government regulation. Just look at the market for fuel-efficient and hybrid automobiles. Consumers demanded more environmentally friendly cars, so car-makers responded. Toyota and Honda have developed new hybrid vehicles, which operate on a mixture of gas and electricity. North American auto-makers like Ford are now following suit. With gas prices skyrocketing, these cars are selling so well that manufacturers can't build them fast enough. According to J.D. Power and Associates, American purchases of hybrids increased 146 percent in the first four months of 2005 from the same period a year earlier.[19]

Conservatives need to develop and get this pro-market, pro-environmental message out. One of conservatives' biggest problems in the environmental realm, as in so many other areas, is that their ideas are not accurately represented in the media—if they are presented at all. Most Canadians are not exposed to alternatives of the statist vision of environmentalism. If they are, it is usually a negative caricature. More groups like NRSP must be founded, especially on university campuses where the doctrinaire leftist "enviro" groups usually have a monopoly. Because young people care about these issues so much, they might come out to a teach-in on free-market environmentalism just out of sheer curiosity.

A huge opportunity exists for the conservative movement and the Tory party on the environmental file. But it means devoting significant attention and resources to the issue. In the end this strategy will pay enormous dividends, especially among urban and young voters where the Conservative Party must make gains if it is to create a more enduring electoral base. An April 23, 2005, cover story in the *Economist* asserted, "market forces could prove the environment's best friend—if only greens could learn to love them." We believe the environment can be the right's best friend—if we can succeed in convincing Canadians that conservatives can be conservationists too.

Endnotes

1. Elizabeth May, "The Environment: From Local to Global in a Cosmic Blink of 25 Years," *Policy Options*, March–April 2005. www.irpp.org/po/archive/mar05en/may.pdf

2. Ontario Ministry of Natural Resources, "Ontario's Progress on Living Legacy." www.mnr.gov.on.ca/MNR/csb/news/apr13fs00.html

3. Canadian Taxpayers Federation, "Ottawa's Latest Multi-Billion Dollar Boondoggle—It's Not the Firearms Registry But the Kyoto Protocol," News Release, April 13, 2005. www.taxpayer.com/main/news.php?news_id=1977

4. For a hard-hitting look at the Kyoto Accord, see Ezra Levant's book *Fight Kyoto* (Calgary: JMCK Publishing, 2002).

5. Steve Erwin, "Federal Conservatives Propose $400-Million Tax break for Commuters," *Canadian Press*, August 4, 2005. www.recorder.ca/cp/National/050804/n080465A.html

6. Thoreau Institute website. www.ti.org/faqs.html#1

7. Property and Environment Research (PERC) website.
www.perc.org/aboutperc/index.php

8. Terry L. Anderson, "Reasons to Celebrate," PERC website.
www.perc.org/publications/percreports/june2005/celebrate.php

9. Donald Leal, "Federal Government Can't Stop 'Tragedy of the Commons' in U.S.
Fisheries," PERC website. www.perc.org/publications/policyseries/homestead.php

10. Thoreau Institute website. www.ti.org/faqs.html

11. Thoreau Institute website. www.ti.org/faqs.html#1

12. Sylvia LeRoy with Kenneth Green, "Can Markets Save Our National Parks?",
Fraser Institute Digital Publication, April 2005, 3.
www.fraserinstitute.ca/admin/books/files/canmarketssaveparks.pdf

13. "Ducks Unlimited Mission and Vision," Ducks Unlimited Canada website.
www.ducks.ca/aboutduc/who/mission.html

14. Energy Probe Research Foundation, "Our Foundation's Background."
www.eprf.ca/eprf/index.cfm?DSP=content&ContentID=1693

15. Environment Probe, "About Environment Probe."
www.environmentprobe.org/enviroprobe/about.html

16. Fraser Institute, "The Environment and the Economy Program."
www.fraserinstitute.ca/shared/readmore.asp?snav=ev&id=291

17. Robert D. Sopuck, "Smart and Green: An Environmental Policy for the 21st
Century," Frontier Centre for Public Policy Series, No. 25, October 2005, 8
(hereinafter Sopuck).

18. Sopuck, 10.

19. "Free Market Environmentalism," editorial, New York Sun, July 18, 2005, 6.

16 CHAPTER

THE FUTURE OF FEDERALISM:
Keeping Canada Together

"There are two miracles in Canadian history. The first is the survival of French Canada, and the second is the survival of Canada."

— F.R. Scott

Where is Canada heading? Will it survive? Will Quebec separate? Will the West? What of aboriginal Canadians? How can a central government respond to the needs and aspirations of so many regional political forces and still keep Canada together?

These questions and others relating to Canada's existence have been and continue to be examined non-stop in an endless litany of newspaper columns, books, TV documentaries and dissertations. Indeed, in researching this book it has been revealing to see how little the issues affecting Canada have changed since the 1960s. It's like the Bill Murray movie *Groundhog Day*—you just wish you could wake up and not have to deal with the same scenario over and over again.

As F. R. Scott observed, it's remarkable that Canada has stayed together this long. In the past hundred years we've been through two conscription crises, the FLQ crisis, two Quebec referendums, three failed attempts at constitutional reform and endless bouts of federal–provincial wrangling. Canada continues on because of the resilience of its people and their love of this country. Canada was created through an act of will, and it has taken several more of them to keep it going.

Even so, national unity is the issue that won't go away. It has become as Canadian a pastime as hockey. And as we mentioned in Chapter 9, it has been terribly destructive for the conservative movement. While other countries engage in debates on economic issues, foreign policy and other social concerns, Canadians are constantly figuring out how to keep the country together. Who has time to talk ideology when the nation is falling apart?

The Rise of Quebec Nationalism

Since the Quiet Revolution of the 1960s and the immense changes it brought to *la belle province*, the federal government has jumped through hoops to make Quebecers feel more welcome in Canada. Much of that has involved the withering away of the symbols of our British heritage. Lester B. Pearson's 1965 introduction of the maple leaf flag, which removed any reference to the Union Jack, is a prime example. The size of the federal government ballooned, as Canadian citizenship became more and more defined by Ottawa mandarins, as we reviewed in Chapter 9. The greatest changes came after the report of the Royal Commission on Bilingualism and Biculturalism in 1969. Reforms like the Official Languages Act, which passed with the support of Stanfield's Tories, were supposed to stem growing nationalist/separatist sentiment in Quebec.

It didn't work. Trudeau's vision of a pan-Canadian multicultural nationalism based on linguistic duality has failed. Rather than French expanding across the country, the language has become increasingly ghettoized inside Quebec. The only interaction most English Canadians have with the French language is when they see it on their cornflakes box at breakfast.

And as French-speaking Canadians have become more confined to Quebec, Anglophones have continued to leave the province. About 400,000 English-speakers left between 1976 and 1996, including 130,000 in the period between 1976 and 1981, the time of René Lévesque's election, the introduction of the Charter of the French

Language (Bill 101) and the first referendum.[1] Today the English population of Quebec stands at 8 percent, and, according to *La Presse*
editorialist André Pratte, the province experiences an annual net loss of
5,000 more Anglophones each year. Few francophone communities exist outside of New Brunswick, where the population is about a third
French-speaking, and in Ontario, which has a francophone population
of about 5 percent.[2] Despite Governor General Michaëlle Jean's contention that Hugh MacLennan's two solitudes are over, the reality is they
are thriving and the country is more regionalized than ever.

Mark Steyn aptly dubbed the drive for Quebec independence "the
world's dumbest secessionist movement" because separatist politicians
are always trying to explain to Quebecers why they should establish a
new country that is exactly the same as the one they'd be leaving.[3] Yet
the movement lives on. Trudeau promised to renew federalism in 1980
to get Quebecers to vote No in the first referendum. When 59.5 percent
opposed sovereignty-association (a term that suggests Quebec could
have its *gâteau* and eat it too), the repatration process began. This
hardly qualified as a renewal, and when a new deal was struck in 1981,
Quebec's National Assembly didn't give its blessing. Twenty-four years
later, it still has not done so. In the second referendum in 1995, the
country came within a whisker of being lost when 49.4 percent of
Quebecers voted Yes. The separatists won't give up. The threat of a third
referendum looms. Jean Charest's Quebec Liberal government has struggled, and the Parti Québécois has renewed its leadership, girding for the
next round of battle.

Why do we keep going around in circles on the unity question?
Mainly because Ottawa refuses to take the necessary steps to quell the
separatist threat—starting with respect for provincial jurisdiction. Poll after poll shows that while a substantial number of Quebecers desire
"sovereignty," they want to remain Canadian as well. The media worked
themselves into a tizzy about a poll taken at the height of the sponsorship hysteria in April 2005 that showed 54 percent of Quebecers would
vote Yes to the 1995 referendum question if it were asked again. But of
those 54 percent who said they would vote Yes, 56 percent said they still
wanted Quebec to remain part of Canada.[4] "Renewed federalism remained

the preferred option for a sizable portion of the population, according to the poll, but voters are still deeply divided over the issue," the front-page story on the poll in *The Globe and Mail* read. Comedian Yvon Deschamps' old joke that Quebecers want an independent Quebec in a strong Canada was not just funny—it was true.

The result of this constant dalliance with separatism, as phony as it may seem, is that the feds bend over backwards to appease Quebec. Almost every major decision in Ottawa is tested, if informally, against the question of whether it will hurt or help the separatist cause. It was undoubtedly the prime motivator behind two recent decisions in foreign policy: Jean Chrétien's choice to stay out of the March 2003 invasion of Iraq, and Paul Martin's February 2005 announcement that Canada would not participate in the U.S. missile defence system. Both decisions were popular in Quebec, a province where anti-Americanism is rampant.[5] And let's not even discuss the appointment of Michaëlle Jean as Canada's Governor General, a journalist previously best known in the rest of Canada for her two-minute introductions of CBC documentaries. The Liberals must take seats in Quebec if they want to win majority governments. The result is that the province wields tremendous influence over government decisions whether it sends a lot of Liberals to Ottawa or not.

But national unity is not just about Quebec anymore. Canada's economic power and population base are shifting. British Columbia, Alberta and Ontario continue to grow, while the proportion of Canadians in Quebec and the Maritimes is shrinking. Quebec used to make up 25 percent of Canada's population, but it will only be around 20 percent of Canada by 2025. This is partly due to Quebec's chronically low birth rate, which has gone from 3.85 in 1951 to 1.49 in 2004.[6] So as Quebec's population relative to the other provinces decreases, any future demands it makes relative to constitutional concessions may be tougher to bargain for.

In Western provinces, people's discontent with their position in Confederation has been simmering for years, and has threatened on more than one occasion to become a full-blown separatist movement. According to a poll commissioned by the *Western Standard* magazine in August 2005, 36 percent of Western Canadians—including 43 percent of Albertans—agreed with the statement "Western Canadians should begin to explore the idea of forming their own country."[7] Not a particularly strong-worded question, but the result is nothing to scoff at. This anti-Ottawa sentiment, particularly in B.C. and Alberta, was spawned even before Trudeau gave the finger to protestors in Salmon Arm. In the 1980s and '90s, the Reform Party provided a federalist outlet for this angst, but the issue never completely went away. In February 2001, a group of Alberta scholars, including Stephen Harper, wrote an infamous letter proposing to create a "firewall" around Alberta, exhorting the province to wrest from Ottawa many powers that Quebec already enjoys. The growing strength of Alberta's economy poses new challenges for Confederation. In light of booming oil revenues, the province is forecasting a surplus in the billions of dollars for the fiscal year 2005–2006. Already, people in have-not parts of the country are grumbling that this should be "shared" in the grand Canadian tradition of enforced equality. But Premier Klein is standing his ground, declaring that Albertans are "doing more than our fair share, so keep your hands off."[8]

In the middle of the country, workhorse Ontario is in danger of being worked to death. A study by the Ontario Chamber of Commerce predicts that the province could become a "have-not" in five years if it continues to fund the rest of the country at its current rate. Premier Dalton McGuinty has called for a national commission on the so-called fiscal imbalance he claims is bleeding his province dry.

This is a significant development in federal–provincial relations. Ontario has historically played the good cop of Confederation. Now Queen's Park has joined the ranks of the complainers. McGuinty's motives are debatable, as Ontario's stuttering economy is more to blame on his government's unwillingness to trim spending than on overly large equalization payments. But, in fairness, Ontario has been sending cheques to Canada's have-not provinces for years.

The fiscal imbalance is one issue that all provinces—rich and poor—should be able to find common ground on. It is a huge issue in Quebec. There does seem to be something wrong when the feds rake in billions of dollars in surpluses each year while the provinces run deficits. And rather than returning their surpluses (read: amount Canadians were overtaxed) to the people, the Liberals are more likely to use that money to create grandiose new spending programs, often in areas of provincial jurisdiction such as education (Millennium Scholarships, anyone?)

And what of Atlantic Canada? For years on the receiving end of government transfers, grants and subsidies, its economy continues to languish. The cod moratorium and the collapse of its coal and shipping industries have only exacerbated the region's dependence on transfer payments for its survival. Its biggest export today is Atlantic Canadians, who migrate to the rest of the country looking for better opportunities. When those opportunities finally arose at home in 2004, with the advent of offshore oil exploration, Newfoundland whipped itself into a nationalistic fervour when it appeared Ottawa would claw back equalization payments.

Factionalism, whether provincial, regional or linguistic, has become a hallmark of Canadian political life. This is perhaps not surprising when you consider that for the past forty years big-state governments have been entrenching a culture of special-interest politics in this country. It is a natural extension of the attitude that it's only by setting yourself apart that you get what you want, as opposed to the country pulling together in a common direction. But it is something that has to be stopped if Canada is to thrive and move forward. And conservatives are the only ones who can put on the brakes.

Required: A Pan-Canadian Vision

Opportunity Conservatives must pursue a vision that encompasses the whole country. This vision must acknowledge regional differences, but it must not make Canada simply a collection of regions. It must respect the constitutional jurisdictions of the provinces, but not abdicate the function of instilling common values in Canadians. It must increase the economic independence of aboriginals, but not create a third order of government.

What is a country for if it doesn't have a common purpose? What is a central government for if it doesn't shape that purpose? Canada is not merely a collection of warring special interests strung along the forty-ninth parallel. Canada has a soul, and our leaders have a responsibility to nurture that soul.

While Opportunity Conservatives believe wholeheartedly in limited government, that government still plays a key role in defining the national character. But that doesn't mean the usual course of action: throwing money at problems, creating big-government programs and spending tax dollars on flags and special interest groups. In fact, it means the opposite. As we explained previously, the bonds of society are forged by its citizens, its families, its local communities. Government provides the framework within which people are either free to do this or are fettered by the state. The Opportunity Conservative policies we propose in terms of social policy, health care policy and environmental policy will not cost taxpayers more money than they are spending now—in fact, they will cost less. Yet through them, the federal government will shape Canadian society. It will encourage the values of responsibility, self-reliance and freedom. It will create a more competitive, entrepreneurial, achievement-oriented society, which champions equality of opportunity.

To accommodate the demands and realities of its disparate communities, the Canadian government should get out of the way in some areas and step forward in others. The feds should keep within their constitutionally mandated boundaries and return to the Laurier/St. Laurent style of running a modest national government, one that competently manages the affairs it is supposed to, such as the military, foreign affairs, currency and the regulation of trade and commerce, among others. Instead of creating unnecessary new programs to increase reliance on the state, surpluses should go to tax relief for families and business, as well as to debt reduction.

Preston Manning and Mike Harris, in their Fraser Institute publication, *A Canada Strong and Free* (2005), lay out the case for what they call a "rebalancing" of the Canadian federation. Aside from altering which level of government does what, this means adjusting the percentage of GDP that is held by government through public ownership and tax collection—currently about 40 percent of the economy—versus the amount that is privately held, about 60 percent. The two propose a 7 percent cut in taxes and spending over six years. As the authors put it:

Expansion of the federal role in areas of provincial jurisdiction through the arbitrary exercise of the federal spending power violates the spirit of the constitution and creates needless strains in federal-provincial relations. It runs counter to the principle that essential social services are best delivered by the level of government closest to those receiving the services. And by increasingly dividing responsibility for the outcomes of social policy, it diminishes the ability of Canadians to hold any one level of government democratically accountable for social policy failures.[9]

Manning and Harris propose a devolution of power, but they don't equate it with weakening the federal government, because it would be accompanied "by a parallel strengthening of the federal role in its constitutionally assigned areas of responsibility such as defence, foreign affairs, and ensuring free inter-provincial trade."[10] Manning has been beating this drum since he entered public life. The Reform Party's 1998 New Canada Act called for the feds to focus on foreign affairs, criminal law, national standards, equalization and trade, while leaving social services, health, education, social assistance, employment training, language and culture to the provinces. With the right messenger this plan would go over well in Quebec, too.

The ideas contained in the New Canada Act would be a good basis to start the discussion. Another would be the much-maligned and now almost-forgotten *Allaire Report*, the 1991 paper that columnist Andrew Coyne called "the most extreme entry in the long catalogue of [Quebec] nationalist audacity."[11] Produced by the Quebec Liberal Party's Constitutional Committee in response to the failure of Meech Lake, the report was adopted by the Liberal Party in convention, but it was disavowed by then-premier Robert Bourassa. The report's author, Jean Allaire and the Quebec Liberal Party's youth president, Mario Dumont, left shortly after to found the Action Démocratique du Québec.

Allaire proposed that Quebec claim full sovereignty in the twenty-two areas of jurisdiction: the eleven already given to the provinces in the current Constitution, plus eleven new ones. The feds would keep authority in only five areas: defence and territorial security, customs and excise (tariffs), management of common debt, money and equalization.[12] Given the radical decentralist approach of the report, it is highly unlikely that its recommendations will ever be implemented. They would require a massive overhaul of the Constitution, and, even if these powers were given only to Quebec as Allaire wanted, the other provinces would never accept them.

But it is important to note that Allaire's proposals are in sync with the views of a wide swath of Quebec francophones. Peter White summed it up well when introducing Allaire at the first United Alternative convention in February 1999:

> Most francophone Quebecers remain profoundly attached to Canada—after all, they first settled the country and have greatly prospered here—but not at the price of risking the gradual marginalization or loss of their language and culture, or of their role as partners in the Canadian enterprise as a whole. These moderate Quebecers, highly conscious of their vulnerable position as a gradually shrinking minority in Canada, want other Canadians—the permanent majority—to formally recognize their linguistic and cultural differences, and they want the guaranteed right and ability to manage and develop their own society based on these differences—within Canada if possible, but outside it if necessary.[13]

Simple respect for provincial jurisdiction by Ottawa would go a long way to quell the country's unity problems, but a rebalancing of powers may be inevitable if the issue is to be sidelined for a long period. This could necessitate an eventual renewal of the Constitution. When this could happen remains an open question. Nobody seems in the mood to do anything right now, and they may not be for a long time. The country is still suffering from a constitutional hangover as a result of the Meech/Charlottetown/Quebec referendum trifecta of the 1990s. And of course, changing the Constitution is notoriously difficult to do: the general amending formula adopted in 1982 requires the consent of the House of Commons, the Senate and two-thirds of the provincial legislatures representing no less than 50 percent of the population.

Reservations Not Required

One cannot discuss national unity without addressing another Pandora's box: the future of aboriginal Canadians. It is unacceptable that in twenty-first century Canada, an entire class of people be segregated from the rest of society based on race. Yet, today, the federal Indian Act continues to isolate native Canadians by placing them on reserves and preventing them from fully participating in the national economy. Tanis Fiss, director of the Centre for Aboriginal Policy Change, has gone so far as to call the situation "Canada's apartheid."[14]

Across the country, native land claims are quietly working their way through the courts and the backrooms of federal and provincial bureaucracies. The residential schools settlement saw millions of dollars go to "survivors" many of whom did not even have to prove that they had suffered damages. The Nisga'a Treaty and the creation of the territory of Nunavut have increased political autonomy for native Canadians, but have done nothing to relive their economic dependence on Ottawa.

According to Fiss, the result is "a system which relies on the perpetual dependency and poverty of native Canadians to survive." Funded by the state and fuelled by white guilt, the "Indian industry"—lawyers, bureaucrats, advocates and band chiefs—has consumed $86 billion in federal tax dollars over the past fifteen years alone. Yet for all this money spent, the welfare of aboriginal Canadians has barely improved. First Nations people continue to suffer greater rates of poverty, health problems and substandard living conditions than non-aboriginal Canadians.

This state of affairs cannot continue. While there would be tremendous resistance to change on the part of some natives, others are more open to reform, and Opportunity Conservatives should work with them to make it happen. We must propose policies that would enable aboriginal Canadians to have equal access to the opportunities that all Canadians enjoy. This means abolishing the Indian Act, ending the reserve system and giving natives the key to control of their own future: property rights.

For centuries, their status as wards of the federal Crown has kept native peoples in an economically dependent position. Aboriginal land is held in trust by the government; natives enjoy common usage, but they do not have rights or title. They cannot mortgage, transfer or use their land as collateral for business loans or other purposes. They are at the mercy of band governments that receive funds from Ottawa, not their local communities, and that are not financially accountable to the people over whom they exert authority. This must change, and the first step is to grant aboriginal Canadians title to the lands currently held in trust.

The second step is to accord bands the same status as municipal governments. Aboriginal municipalities would then be able to raise revenue from their residents like any other city or town, and community members would want to hold their officials accountable for this taxation. This would encourage more responsible use of aboriginal funds than is currently the case. Since native peoples do have a special place in the Canadian Constitution, however, powers might be delegated directly from Ottawa as opposed to through provincial governments.[15]

What the Conservatives should not advocate is aboriginal self-government. Further fractioning of Canada's polity is the last thing this country needs if it is to move forward as a unified whole. There is also no evidence that this right exists; the Constitution does not explicitly grant the right for aboriginals to establish a third order of government in Canada. A self-government clause was proposed in the Charlottetown Accord in 1992; the Accord was opposed by many members of the aboriginal community, specifically native women's groups, due to the "uncertainties of self-government and concern of collective rights overriding individual rights."[16]

The key point in all the foregoing is that conservatives must tackle the national unity issue and do whatever they can to bring it to a point where it no longer dominates federal politics. The future of the federation is like the proverbial elephant in a room. It must be dealt with before it tramples the country to pieces—and before it crushes any chance of developing a full-fledged Canadian conservative ideology.

Endnotes

1. Louise Marmen and Jean-Pierre Corbeil, *New Canadian Perspectives: Languages in Canada.* (Ottawa: Minister of Public Works and Government Services Canada, 1999). www.canadianheritage.gc.ca/progs/lo-ol/perspectives/english/census96/census96.pdf

2. Statistics Canada, "Profile of Languages in Canada, Provinces and Territories." www12.statcan.ca/english/census01/Products/Analytic/companion/lang/provs.cfm

3. Mark Steyn, "Mordecai Richler: 1931-2001," *The New Criterion*, 20, no. 1 (September 2001). www.newcriterion.com/archive/20/sept01/mordecai.htm

4. Rhéal Séguin, "54% in Quebec Back Sovereignty," *The Globe and Mail*, April 27, 2005, A1.

5. Polls showed the 1991 Gulf War was unpopular in Quebec too, but then-prime-minister Mulroney showed admirable resolve in bringing Canada into the coalition.

6. "Taux de fécondité, selon le groupe d'âge et indices globaux, Québec, 1951–2004." www.stat.gouv.qc.ca/donstat/societe/demographie/naisn_deces/naissance/402.htm

7. Kevin Steel, "A Nation Torn Apart," *Western Standard*, August 22, 2005. www.westernstandard.ca/website/index.cfm?page=article&article_id=928

8. Jason Fekete and Tony Seskus, "Hands Off Our Oil Cash," *Calgary Herald*, August 26, 2005, A1.

9. Preston Manning and Mike Harris, *A Canada Strong and Free* (Vancouver: Fraser Institute, April 2005), 20. (hereinafter Manning and Harris).

10. Manning and Harris, 20.

11. Andrew Coyne, "Start the Revolution without Him," *National Post*, September 25, 2002, A23.

12. Peter G. White, "Summary of the *Allaire Report*," Address to the United Alternative Convention, Ottawa, February 20, 1999. www.petergwhite.com/content/allaire-E.htm (hereinafter White).

13. White.

14. Tanis Fiss, "Apartheid: Canada's Ugly Secret," Canadian Taxpayers Federation, Centre for Aboriginal Policy Change, April 14, 2004. www.taxpayer.com/pdf/APARTHEID_Canadas_Ugly_Secret_April_2004.pdf

15. Tanis Fiss, "Dividing Canada: The Pitfalls of Native Sovereignty," Canadian Taxpayers Federation, Centre for Aboriginal Policy Change, March 15, 2005. www.taxpayer.com/pdf/Dividing_Canada_(Centre_for_Aboriginal_Policy_Change).pdf (hereinafter Fiss).

16. Fiss, 18.

CONCLUSION

A CALL TO ARMS FOR CONCERNED CANADIANS

"All that is necessary for the triumph of evil is that good men do nothing."

— Edmund Burke

So there you have it: a road map for rescuing Canada's right.

Conservatives stand today at the beginning of that road. Ahead lie speed bumps, pitfalls and potholes. It's easy to take a wrong turn and end up lost in the liberal wilderness, as we have on more than one occasion. Or to run out of gas, if funders for the new conservative infrastructure turn off the taps. So many things can go wrong, it seems daunting to even start.

But if conservatives do not try, we will never know what might have been. The Tories will sigh and chalk up loss after loss at each federal election. Conservative MPs will stare longingly across the floor of the House of Commons as the Liberals form yet another government and as Canada travels even further down the statist path to the land of enforced equality.

Conservatives cannot allow this to happen. That's why we wrote this book; because we couldn't just sit there and do nothing. The conservative movement has made some progress in the last decade, especially in building new think-tanks. That momentum must be built on so that electoral success can be had, too. Too many people are clamouring for change; many others are already taking action. We wanted to chronicle their stories and inspire others to join them or follow their example. We hope you feel that way too, that you will put down this book and put yourself out there to do your bit to build this movement.

It's not as difficult as you might think. Michael Walker grew the Fraser Institute from a 1970s pipe dream to the powerful ideas machine it is today. Organizations like the Canadian Taxpayers Federation and the National Citizens Coalition run their operations purely on public donations, and they score impressive achievements, influencing public policy through the media and the courts. Sheer will and determination drove George Zeliotis and Jacques Chaoulli to successfully sue the Quebec government over access to health care. Individuals can make a difference, but they have to take that first step.

So to recap, what must conservatives do?

First, we must examine the past and learn from our mistakes. The lack of coherent policy and ideology, the lack of infrastructure and lack of leadership must all be remedied. The Tories shouldn't just sit around and wait for the Liberals to screw up—they must give voters a reason to mark that "X" beside the Conservative Party. As we've seen by their dismal record, they can't do it alone.

Second, we must build a broader, non-partisan conservative movement. This pyramid will have donors and foundations at the base, thinks-tanks and policy institutes at the next level, media outlets and pundits above that and politicians and the Conservative Party at its apex. These actors must work together to challenge the statist status quo in all areas by:

• Seeding a thousand think-tanks to develop and disseminate conservative policy and counter the propaganda of the left. Amending charities regulations so that privately funded conservative advocacy groups can play a greater role in the political process and bring balance to the political dialogue.

- Rebalancing the media by getting the conservative message on-line and innovating in television, radio and print. Eventually, the Tories must amend the Broadcasting Act and abolish the CRTC in order to remove restrictions on freedom of speech.

- Making friends with the Charter of Rights and Freedoms by using it to defend conservative ideals instead of undermining them. Starting legal defence funds to promote conservatives' interests through the courts and changing the way judges are appointed.

- Engaging the next generation by reaching out on university campuses and at the local 4H club. Helping expose students to conservative thought. Appealing to young people on the issues they care about, including the environment, and attracting them through media they use, such as the Internet and video entertainment.

- Breaking the Bloc's stranglehold on Quebec by creating a conservative culture in that province that builds on its nascent entrepreneurial spirit. Promoting policies that respond to the cultural aspirations of Quebecers while respecting those of the rest of the country.

- Connecting with new Canadians by developing a presence in immigrant communities and appealing to those conservative values that emphasize family, hard work and education. At the same time, developing immigration policies that are in the best interest of Canada as a whole.

- Professionalizing politics by training the leaders, generals and ground troops of the conservative movement and party. Establishing leadership and campaign schools to teach activists the latest techniques and groom the prime ministers of tomorrow.

Third, conservatives must develop and advocate policies that take Canada forward. We must move beyond the tax-cuts mantra and embrace an inherently positive, optimistic and patriotic Opportunity Conservative vision for the country. This includes:

- Pro-family and pro-marriage policies that make it an economic advantage to wed and have children. These policies should include all families, both opposite and same-sex ones, with the goal of establishing strong families as a counterpoint to dependency on the state.

- Health care policies that permit the development of a parallel private health care system. Ironically, this is the only way to maintain medicare, which will otherwise collapse under the crushing weight of its costs. Conservatives must end the state monopoly on health care and promote mixed-delivery systems, like those that exist in Europe.

- Greening the conservative movement. Free-market environmentalism is the way of the future and provides a stark counterpoint to the interventionism of Kyoto. Canadians care about their environment and conservatives should offer them a better alternative to preserving it than the Liberal statist model provides.

- Keeping Canada together. This is possibly the greatest challenge for any federal political party, and it is imperative that conservatives resolve it so Canadians can move on to debate real ideological issues. The conservative movement will continue to struggle if public policy is constantly dominated by discussions of national unity. Conservatives should advocate a rebalancing of powers that takes into account the concerns of all parts of the country, not just Quebec.

In sum, from the media to the law to academia, conservatives must infuse our principles into every aspect of Canadian life. We must reach out to the young, to immigrants, to Quebecers. We must professionalize our politics and present a policy vision that inspires Canadians. We must fight for stronger families, superior health care and a better approach to protecting the environment. We must not only make it cool to be conservative, we must make it uncool *not* to be conservative. And we must keep Canada strong and united. The sum of these efforts will be a robust new electoral coalition that keeps Canada on a conservative path.

We know what you're thinking: this sounds like a lot of work. Well, most things that are worth it aren't easy. The Berlin Wall didn't fall overnight. One thing's for sure: the ways of the past don't work. Waiting for Liberal screw-ups or a Messianic leader is a recipe for continued losses. While our plan hasn't been attempted at home, facsimiles of it have worked in other places, such as the United States and Britain. So we think it has a pretty good chance of making a real difference, if conservatives take it seriously and pursue it with vigour and enthusiasm.

Naysayers may still claim that even if small-c conservatives do everything we suggest in this book, it is for naught, because the big-c Conservative brand is tainted beyond repair. They should remember that the same point was made to Mike Harris when he was in third place in the Ontario legislature in the early 1990s. He was told he couldn't win because the PC name had become too tarnished after Mulroney left office. But in 1995, he won a majority.

"If you are consistent, and you're disciplined and focused I think people are able to differentiate the leader and the team and the party without saying 'well that brand is tarnished or damaged,'" Harris says. "I'm not sure it's the party that's tarnished or damaged, it's individuals or perceptions of the party with a certain team of people involved."[1]

We believe the Conservatives not only can be, but must be, rehabilitated. For the good of Canadian democracy, our country needs more than one viable governing party. A one-party state is a recipe for arrogance, corruption and bad government. It leads to the seamy tale that played out at the Gomery Inquiry, where Canadians saw just how dishonest their government could be if given the chance. The 2003 merger of the PCs and the Canadian Alliance returned Canada to having two national parties, the best structure for British-style parliamentary democracies.

As conservatives we sometimes try to make things more complicated than they need be. It really isn't that difficult. During a 1983 visit to Canada, Margaret Thatcher was asked by CBC's Barbara Frum about how she won an election running as an unabashed conservative. Her response? "Because we had clear goals, and clear ways of getting there. I think people much prefer that. They like to know what we want to do, why we want to do it, how we're going to do it. That's what we set out to do."[2] It's not rocket science.

If conservatives follow the prescription outlined on the preceding pages, Canada will have a real choice to make. Canadians will be able to choose between the shackles of the statist status quo and the opportunity of the future. Canada will be free to become the great nation we were told it would be last century.

Conservatives of Canada, it's time for a revolution. It's time to work together instead of against each other. It's time to put our money where our minds are, build a vibrant conservative movement, and leave a proud legacy for the next generation of Canadians.

It's time to rescue Canada's right.

Endnotes

1. Author interview with Mike Harris, July 5, 2005.

2. "Britain's Iron Lady," Barbara Frum interview with Margaret Thatcher, CBC Online Archives, September 27, 1983.
   http://archives.cbc.ca/IDC-1-74-368-2029/people/frum/clip8/

CONSERVATIVE CONTACTS

The following is a list of current groups and organizations already fighting the good fight. Some of them might dispute being labelled "conservative," but they all generally promote freedom, less government, classical liberal or small-c conservative ideas. We've included contact information in case you would like to learn more about them, get involved or even make a donation!

Atlantic Institute for Market Studies
2000 Barrington Street, Suite 1006
Cogswell Tower
Halifax, Nova Scotia B3J 3K1
Tel: (902) 429-1143
www.aims.ca

AIMS, as it is commonly known, is a public policy think-tank that focuses on policy issues in Atlantic Canada. In recent years, it has been responsible for scintillating studies on the damaging effects of equalization and corporate welfare, as well as the need for health care and education reform. The organization was founded in 1995 by Brian Lee Crowley, who is also the president.

Canadian Coalition for Democracies
P.O. Box 72602
345 Bloor Street East
Toronto, Ontario M4W 3J0
Tel: (416) 963-8998 or 1-877-383-8320
www.canadiancoalition.org

The Canadian Coalition for Democracies (CCD) focuses primarily on international affairs, promoting "a Canadian foreign policy that supports our democratic allies and democratic values around the world." Founded in 2003, its president is Alastair Gordon and its executive director is Naresh Raghubeer.

Canadian Constitution Foundation
C/O Box 118, 970 Burrard Street
Vancouver, British Columbia V6Z 2R4
Tel: (604) 683-7006
www.canadianconstitutionfoundation.ca

The Canadian Constitution Foundation (CCF) aims to explain the role of the Canadian Constitution in citizens' daily life, teach people how to recognize infringements and abuses and help them defend its principles from improper decisions or actions of government, regulators, tribunals or special interest groups. Established in 2002, its executive director is John Carpay.

Canadian LabourWatch Association
Suite 205, 125A-1030 Denman Street
Vancouver, British Columbia V6G 2M6
Tel: (604) 631-3323
www.labourwatch.com

The Canadian LabourWatch Association strives to educate employees and employers about their rights and responsibilities during union drives and de-certifications. Founded in 2000 by Vancouver's John Mortimer and Jamie McCallen, LabourWatch has become an important part of the labour relations community in Canada—to the great disappointment of unions.

Canadian Taxpayers Federation
105-438 Victoria Avenue East
Regina, Saskatchewan S4N 0N7
Tel: 1-800-565-1911
www.taxpayer.com

The Canadian Taxpayers Federation (CTF) is Canada's only non-profit, non-partisan, taxpayer watchdog and advocacy group. It is at the forefront of the fight for lower taxes, more accountability and less waste in government. Areas of research and activism include income taxation, gas taxes, property tax, electoral reform, health care and corporate welfare. Founded in 1990, its federal director is John Williamson.

C.D. Howe Institute
67 Yonge Street, Suite 300
Toronto, Ontario M5E 1J8
Tel: (416) 865-1904
www.cdhowe.org

The C.D. Howe Institute is a non-profit public policy think-tank that aims to improve Canadian living standards by fostering sound economic and social policy. A precursor organization began in 1958 under the name the Private Planning Association of Canada, and the current name was adopted in 1981. Its president and CEO is Jack Mintz, who will retire in 2006.

Centre for Aboriginal Policy Change
1580 Guinness House
727-7th Ave SW
Calgary, Alberta T2P 0Z5
Tel: 1-800-565-1911 / (403) 263-1202
www.taxpayer.com

The Centre is a branch of the Canadian Taxpayers Federation that specifically deals with aboriginal issues. It advocates equality for all Canadians, regardless of race, and supports abolishing the Indian Act, giving property rights to aboriginal Canadians and granting municipal status to aboriginal communities. The Centre's director is Tanis Fiss.

Citizen Centre for Freedom and Democracy
Suite 203, 10441-178 Street
Edmonton, Alberta T5S 1R5
Tel: (780) 481-7844
www.citizenscentre.com

The Citizen Centre for Freedom and Democracy is a non-profit organization that promotes responsible government. It is headed by Link Byfield, a long-time Albertan conservative activist, who is currently one of the province's senators-in-waiting.

Conservative Leadership Foundation (CLF)
c/o 2020–120 Adelaide Street West
Toronto, Ontario M5H 1T1
Tel: (416) 848-8171
www.clftraining.com

The CLF is a political training school for young conservatives, founded in 1990 by John Capobianco and John Mykytyshyn, who continue to run it.

Donner Canadian Foundation
8 Prince Arthur Avenue, 3rd Floor
Toronto, Ontario M5R 1A9
Tel: (416) 920-6400
www.donnerfoundation.org

The Donner Canadian Foundation is a grant-giving organization that "seeks to encourage individual responsibility and private initiative to help Canadians solve their social and economic problems." The chairman is Allan Gotlieb; the executive director is Helen McLean.

Energy Probe
225 Brunswick Avenue
Toronto, Ontario M5S 2M6
Tel: (416) 964-9223
www.energyprobe.org

Energy Probe is a consumer and environmental research team, which works on issues such as fighting nuclear power, breaking up energy monopolies and promoting environmentally friendly energy alternatives like wind power. Its executive director is Tom Adams.

Environment Probe
225 Brunswick Avenue
Toronto, Ontario M5S 2M6
Tel: (416) 964-9223 ext. 232
www.environmentprobe.org

Founded in 1989, this group works on environmental issues, striving to develop and promote "alternative resource policies that are environmentally, socially, and economically sustainable." Its executive director is Elizabeth Brubaker.

Fraser Institute
1770 Burrard Street, 4th Floor
Vancouver, British Columbia V6J 3G7
Tel: (604) 688-0221
www.fraserinstitute.ca

The granddaddy of Canadian public policy think-tanks, the Fraser Institute champions free-market solutions in all areas of public policy, including taxation, health care, education, child care and the environment. It was founded in 1974 by a group of concerned citizens, including Michael Walker, who served as its executive director until 2005. Its executive director is now Mark Mullins.

Frontier Centre for Public Policy
Suite 25 Lombard Concourse, One Lombard Place
Winnipeg, Manitoba R3B 0X3
Tel: (204) 957-1567
www.fcpp.org

The Frontier Centre for Public Policy, founded in 1999, is a think-tank that focuses on issues including rent control, aboriginal policy renewal, equalization dependency and rural policies. It concentrates primarily on issues affecting Manitoba. Its president is Peter Holle.

Mackenzie Institute
P.O. Box 338, Adelaide Station
Toronto, Ontario M5C 2J4
Tel: (416) 686-4063
www.mackenzieinstitute.com

The Mackenzie Institute works to raise awareness about issues such as political instability and terrorism. It is headed by John Thompson.

Manning Centre for Building Democracy
P.O. Box 1988, Station M
Calgary, Alberta T2P 2M2
Tel: (403) 255-8100
www.manningcentre.ca

The Manning Centre for Building Democracy is a new, non-profit foundation that is committed to achieving a democratic society guided by conservative principles, and it will support research, education and communication initiatives directed to that end. It is headed by former Reform Party leader Preston Manning.

Montreal Economic Institute
6708 St. Hubert Street
Montreal, Quebec H2S 2M6
Tel: (514) 273-0969
www.iedm.org

Founded in 1999, the Montreal Economic Institute is Quebec's leading voice in promoting free markets and sound economics. Its president is Michel Kelly-Gagnon.

National Citizens' Coalition
27 Queen Street East, Suite 501
Toronto, Ontario M5C 2M6
Tel: (416) 869-3838
www.morefreedom.org

Aside from having the coolest URL on the Internet, the National Citizens' Coalition (NCC) promotes free enterprise, individual freedom and personal responsibility under limited government. Founded in 1967, it is run by vice president Gerry Nicholls.

Organization for Quality Education
160 Columbia Street West
Waterloo, Ontario N2L 3E3
Tel: (905) 763-5611
www.oqe.org

The Organization for Quality Education promotes issues such as higher education standards, open reporting of school performance and charter schools. Its president is Nancy Wagner.

Society for Academic Freedom and Scholarship (SAFS)
1673 Richmond Street, Suite 344
London, Ontario N6G 2N3
www.safs.ca

SAFS was founded in 1992 to maintain freedom in teaching, research and scholarship, and to uphold standards of excellence in academic decisions about students and faculty. Its president is Clive Seligman.

Work Research Foundation
45 Frid Street, Suite 9
Hamilton, Ontario L8P 4M3
Tel: 1-888-339-8866 / (905) 528-8866
www.wrf.ca

The Work Research Foundation thrives in helping restructure public life within the framework of "sphere sovereignty" and to allow revitalization of civil society in North America.

ACKNOWLEDGEMENTS

This project began when two long-time friends realized they were thinking the same thing without the other's knowledge. In December 2003, Tasha Kheiriddin started work on a book proposal about the future of the right in Canada. Six months later, Adam Daifallah published an article in the *National Post* entitled "Building a conservative Canada—from the ground up," calling for the creation of a conservative infrastructure. Tasha immediately contacted Adam, and over drinks the blueprint for *Rescuing Canada's Right* was born.

Heartfelt thanks go to our literary agent, Sam Hiyate, principal of The Rights Factory. Sam initially approached Tasha to write a book. He guided us through the process and persevered to get us a book deal with John Wiley & Sons Canada.

Special thanks also to Mark Steyn for contributing the foreword. His style and substance are second to none, and he serves as an inspiration to conservative writers everywhere.

Ezra Levant and Kevin Libin of the *Western Standard* magazine deserve our gratitude for giving *Rescuing Canada's Right* its first promotional break—and the idea for its title. They published an essay that lays out this book's main ideas in the magazine's November 8, 2004, issue.

Adam would also like to thank the Jeanne Sauvé Foundation in Montreal for awarding him a fellowship for the 2004–05 academic year, which he used to research and write this book. Also to his girlfriend Emmanuelle, whose constant encouragement and support (despite her opposition to our ideas) made life much easier. Tasha would like to thank her parents, Fareez and Rita Kheiriddin, for their love and support in all her endeavours, and in this last year especially.

Tasha would also like to thank her colleagues at the Canadian Taxpayers Federation (CTF), especially John Williamson, who diligently reviewed our manuscript and offered constructive criticism and editing, and Bridget Gajardar, for her research and analysis work. Adam is especially grateful to Peter White for his help with this book and his friendship over many years.

The following people also deserve recognition for their contributions, which took the form of ideas, interviews, words of wisdom, and/or personal support: Sonia Arrison, Ken Azzopardi, Charlotte Bell, Conrad Black, Michael Bliss, Peter Brimelow, Link Byfield, Alister Campbell, John Carpay, John Crosbie, Chantal DaSilva, Tanis Fiss, David Frum, Linda Frum, Allan Gotlieb, David Gratzer, Lorne Gunter, Rohit Gupta, Megan Harris, Mike Harris, Gordon Harvey, Duncan Jackman, Michel Kelly-Gagnon, Karl Kierstead, James Lee, Sylvia LeRoy, Dan Mader, Susan MacArthur, Preston Manning, Marla McAlpine, Helen McLean, Alim Merali, Laurent Moss, John Mykytyshyn, Zoltan Nagy, Véronique Nasser, Gerry Nicholls, Rick Petersen, Naresh Raghubeer, Brian Rogers, Shawn Saulnier, John Spence, Michael Taube, Michael Walker, John Weston and Nigel Wright.

At Wiley, we would like to thank our editor, Don Loney, who believed in this project right from the beginning. His enthusiasm, encouragement and constant support have been very helpful. We are also grateful to the whole Wiley team, in particular Lucas Wilk, Meghan Brousseau, Sarah Trimble and Liz McCurdy, as well as everyone else involved in copy editing, cover design and, of course, marketing.

And, finally, we'd like to thank the conservatives of Canada who inspired us to write *Rescuing Canada's Right* and whom we hope will benefit from its proposals.

— Tasha and Adam

INDEX

ABOUT THE AUTHORS

Tasha Kheiriddin (Toronto, ON) is an award-winning journalist, lawyer, and political activist. She served as president of the Progressive Conservative Youth Federation of Canada from 1995 to 1998, after which she worked for CBC Newsworld and CPAC, the Cable Public Affairs Channel. Tasha is currently the Ontario director of the Canadian Taxpayers Federation, a non-profit, non-partisan organization that advocates for lower taxes, less waste and accountable government.

Adam Daifallah (Quebec City, QC) is a former member of the *National Post* editorial board and Washington correspondent for *The New York Sun*. He was president of the Ontario Progressive Conservative Campus Association from 2001 to 2002. In 2001, he co-authored the book *Gritlock: Are the Liberals in Forever?* Adam is currently studying law at Laval University.